A New Strategy
for Complex Warfare

A New Strategy for Complex Warfare

Combined Effects in East Asia

Thomas A. Drohan

Rapid Communications in Conflict and Security Series
General Editor: Geoffrey R.H. Burn

CAMBRIA
PRESS

Amherst, New York

Requests for permission should be directed to:
permissions@cambriapress.com, or mailed to:
Cambria Press
University Corporate Centre, 100 Corporate Parkway, Suite 128
Amherst, New York 14226, U.S.A.

Cover Image: SOUTH CHINA SEA: Amphibious assault vehicles exit the well deck
of the forward-deployed amphibious dock landing ship USS Tortuga (LSD 46) for
a joint amphibious assault exercise with the royal Malaysian navy as a part of the
exercise Cooperation Afloat Readiness and Training (CARAT) Malaysia 2013. U.S.
Navy photo by Mass Communication Specialist 3rd Class Amanda S. Kitchner.

Library of Congress Cataloging-in-Publication Data

Names: Drohan, Thomas Alan.
Title: A new strategy for complex warfare : combined effects in East Asia /
Thomas A. Drohan.
Other titles: Combined effects in East Asia
Description: New York: Cambria Press, [2016] |
Series: Cambria rapid communications in conflict and security series |
Includes bibliographical references and index.

Identifiers: LCCN 2015045383 |

ISBN 9781604979206 (alk. paper)

Subjects: LCSH: Security, International--East Asia. |
East Asia--Strategic aspects. | National security--East Asia. |
East Asia--Military policy.

Classification: LCC UA830 .D76 2016 |
DDC 355/.03355--dc23
LC record available at http://lccn.loc.gov/2015045383

TABLE OF CONTENTS

List of Figures

ACKNOWLEDGEMENTS

This book is the product of two worlds, one professional and one academic. Military academies blend both and at the US Air Force Academy, the military and strategic studies department focuses on contemporary strategy, military doctrine, and joint operations. Roaming across academic disciplines, we integrate the context, theory, and application of military and strategic power.

I am grateful for the perspectives and insights of our military and civilian faculty and staff, past and present. Clay Chun, Charles Krupnick, Dorri Karolick, Jim Titus, John Blumentritt, Ed Westermann, Dan Yinger, Rick Walker, Brent Talbot, John Farquhar, Don Smith, Judy Saunders, Glenna Linton, Jim Schlagheck, Mike Veneri, Patrick Donley, Steve Pomeroy, Terry Pierce, Mike Fowler, Jasin Cooley, Tom Swaim, and many others have developed cadets into the future airpower and joint force leaders our nation needs.

I benefited from numerous mentors as well. The intellectual impact of Paul Viotti, Doug Murray, Bill Berry, Kent Calder, Aaron Friedberg, Jim Smith, Tom Keaney, John Lewis, Dave Deptula, Charlie Dunlap, and Erv Rokke is reflected throughout this project. The Council on Foreign Relations in Japan program and Carl Green, and the Reischauer

Center under the directorship of Kent Calder were also instrumental in generating valuable experiences that have informed this study. At Cambria Press, Geoffrey Burn provided outstanding advice from the beginning, continuous support, and constructive critiques; and Toni Tan's welcoming style and detailed attention brought the book to completion with amazing efficiency.

Finally, my family's unwavering personal support through deployments and other challenges enabled the research and writing of this book.

PREFACE

The pursuit of security and conduct of warfare are dynamic and diverse activities. With the advent of the information revolution, this competition has intensified. Technological innovations generate unprecedented capabilities such as virtual recruitment, distributed operations, and zero-day attacks.[1] Mobile weapons, remote sensors, and mass media empower more individuals with skills and access. Advanced analytics craft intelligence from amorphous data and uncertain information. Web-based social networks magnify all of this, and tactics yield strategic effects instantly. So what makes for superior strategy in this environment? We begin with two propositions.

First, defeating complex threats requires more effective power than combined-arms warfare.[2] Combat capability concentrates on military units; precision engagement employs high-tech systems in kill-chains;[3] preemptive strike targets armed or identifiable combatants. Even doctrine for hybrid warfare focuses on forces in armed conflict.[4] Adaptive enemies exploit this myopia with asymmetric wit and severity.[5] In a predictable reaction, the United States Congress authorized the president "to use all necessary and appropriate force against those nations, organizations, or persons he determines planned, authorized, committed, or aided the terrorist attacks that occurred on September 11, 2001, or harbored such organizations or persons, in order to prevent any future acts of international terrorism against the United States by such nations, organizations or persons."[6] The massive effort includes extensive combined-arms campaigns that are neither sufficient nor sustainable.[7] Long-term success means out-thinking proactive opponents who expediently blend cooperation with confrontation.

Second, excellence in strategy requires a multicultural understanding of security. Why? Presuming common values is dangerous conceit. Cultures can regard ethics and interests in different ways that confound insular thinking. Ignoring nuances promotes poor threat assessment, with lost opportunities to deter conflict and to persuade cooperation.[8] This guarantees strategic surprises: the fall of the Berlin Wall (1989); Iraq's invasion of Kuwait (1990); the dissolution of the Soviet Union (1991); nuclear detonations (India in 1974 and 1998, Pakistan in 1998, North Korea in 2006); Al Qaeda attacks on American targets (1992, 1998, 2000, and 2001); Russian invasions of Georgia (2008) and Ukraine (2014); and the rise of Daesh in Syria (2011) and Iraq (2014), and attacks in France (2015). How can we anticipate and prepare for these anomalies?

Superior strategy calls for broad concepts and adjustable operations informed by effects-oriented thinking and cultural perspectives on security. The United States has to up its game. To do this, we don't necessarily need more resources. We need better ideas.

THE ARGUMENT

American exceptionalism[9] and combined-arms doctrine[10] inhibit our ability to make effective strategy. This culture and practice proscribe an approach inferior to rival strategies. The narrow logic of US security relies on radical technologies. This makes historical sense based on lessons from 1941 to 1942 when US aircraft and tanks were outmatched by the best of Germany and Japan. Our commitment to greater firepower finds confidence in the synergy that can be achieved on a battlefield when applying combat forces simultaneously, rather than separately. Today's battlespace is an expansive contest to possess terrain, control sea lanes, command the air, access space, and exploit cyberspace. Despite new complexities in the natural and cyber domains, we still organize for security in terms of functions more than performance. The basic form of America's defense remains sculpted by the National Security Act of 1947. Given the diffusion of information, autonomous actors, and weapons technology, the consequences of oversimple assumptions loom ever larger.

Recent Defense Strategic Guidance,[11] for instance, confidently projects changes in the global security environment, announces a "rebalance toward the Asia Pacific region," and exhorts the nation to deter and defeat aggression "by conducting a combined-arms campaign across all domains—land, maritime, air, space, and cyberspace." Its fixation on forces dominating domains is crippling when we really need better combined effects. That is, what to deter and defeat, and how? To be sure, we need to find, fix, and destroy enemy forces—and reactively so, because the policy also predicts that wars are ending and calls for an international order of universal individual rights. The National Security Policy expresses the optimism in even grander terms. This becomes problematic when we attribute these values to friends and define potential foes accordingly. The triple flaw is that US leaders are more likely to misjudge intentions and actions, organize for types of operations more than types of effects, and narrow the range of considered solutions. How long can any government afford to make such amateurish mistakes?

Combined arms are comfortably intact within the US military. The combined-arms method refers to how joint forces—elements from two or more military services under one commander—ought to operate. Technical experience and expertise are needed and prized. The overriding role of each service is to provide competent forces to the joint force commander. Strategy becomes the exercise of existing doctrine, tools, and methods applied to problems within an organization's jurisdiction. Outside an operator's lane of well-trained capabilities, security and strategy are supposed to be someone else's job. Accordingly the military is optimized to excel in high-end warfighting functions, rather than contribute to broader effects. Senior military leaders recognize their responsibilities to provide a range of military options, but they regard combined arms as core functions to protect. Constitutional authorities that push military roles away from political decisions reinforce this priority. As a result, exercises that role-play innovative threats challenge our joint forces to muster the diverse capabilities needed to execute a superior strategy.

The problem with an approach rooted in exceptionalism is that situational strategy matters. Competitors have proven adept in hybrid and asymmetric techniques that circumvent supposedly superior forces.[12] The profession of arms needs to become a profession of effects. This requires overcoming three weaknesses. First, weapons-centric identities that dominate military culture inhibit flexibility needed to address complex problems. The mastery of maneuvering and firing weapons does not include how these operations affect other diplomatic, informational, military, economic, and social effects. Unless weapons qualification courses and advanced schools teach how operational effects interact in various contexts, operations will be more standardized and less relevant to adaptive threats. Second, an ingrained belief in enduring lessons kills thinking about new solutions. For example, the very idea of effects-based operations, an objective approach that threatened existing mission sets, was banned outright in Joint Forces Command (now defunct) to oblige "time-honored principles and terminology."[13] Third, the projection of our own cultural expectations onto other societies creates bogus common standards. Stove-piped planning exacerbates the misunderstanding when we expect others to conform to our expectations. All of this limits envisioning new combinations of effects.

It should be obvious that improving how to think about strategy is fundamental to effective operations. Nevertheless, mental rigidity clouds our ability to anticipate an adversary's actions. Consider the following events paired with erroneous attributions of intent (which are noted in parentheses): North Korea's seizure of the *USS Pueblo* in 1968 (communism is monolithic so this must be a Soviet-related conspiracy), the outbreak of the Iranian Revolution in 1979 (authoritarian states such as the Shah's are strong), Iraq's nuclear bluff in the 1990s (Arab terrorists such as Saddam Hussein and Osama bin Laden must be allied), the Arab Spring in 2011 (democracy like ours is universally valued), and the rapid expansion of Daesh in 2014 (splinter groups of Al Qaeda are small threats with local goals).

These episodes of stagnant thinking seize initiative during budget reductions as risk-averse managers cling to traditions.[14] Short-term leaders emphasize the need to fill immediate requirements. Strategy becomes planning for current events rather than shaping the future.

This book therefore advances a complement to the combined-arms construct: combined effects. Drawing from theory, doctrine, and policy across historical circumstances, the model is more inclusive than the combined-arms tradition employed in the West. By comparison, East Asian strategists have adopted holistic approaches to countering threats for over two thousand years. Confrontation and cooperation in China, the Koreas, and Japan coexist as a way of warfare—such as coercion *and* persuasion. In today's globalized security environment where weapons of influence are diverse and accessible, strategists need to consider more than precision-guided lethality.

Anyone can learn to think more strategically with a Janus-like outlook. One face safeguards the values and interests of properly constituted authority. The other face looks beyond familiar conventions to envision unfamiliar effects and prepare for them.

Notes

1. Zero day refers to the day that a vulnerability becomes widely known. A zero-day attack occurs before a software patch can be distributed to mitigate the vulnerability.
2. For distinctions between combined-arms warfare and combined-effects power, see Ervin J. Rokke, Thomas A. Drohan, and Terry C. Pierce, "Combined Effects Power," *Joint Force Quarterly* 73 (2014): 26–31.
3. The "kill-chain" sequence used in the US Air Force is "find, fix, track, target, attack and assess."
4. See Tim McCulloh and Rick Johnson, *Hybrid Warfare*, JSOU Report 13-4 (McDill Air Force Base: The Joint Special Operations University Press, 2013); and eds. Williamson Murray and Peter R. Mansoor, *Hybrid Warfare: Fighting Complex Opponents from the Ancient World to the Present* (Cambridge: Cambridge University Press, 2012).
5. US joint military doctrine defines asymmetric as "the application of dissimilar strategies, tactics, capabilities and methods to circumvent or negate an opponent's strengths while exploiting his weaknesses." http://www.dtic.mil/doctrine/new_pubs/jp1_02.pdf (accessed September 15, 2015).
6. http://www.gpo.gov/fdsys/pkg/PLAW-107publ40/html/PLAW-107publ40.htm (accessed May 12, 2015).
7. "We are not going to buy our way out of this challenge. We're not going to blast our way out of this problem with overwhelming force. We're going to have to think our way out of this problem." Lt Gen David A. Deptula, "Pacific Air Forces Conference Keynote Speech," Honolulu, Hawaii, September 14, 2012.
8. On perspective-taking, see Sam Wineburg, *Historical Thinking and Other Unnatural Acts: Charting the Future of Teaching the Past* (Philadelphia: Temple University Press, 2001).
9. On American exceptionalism, see Walter A. McDougall, *Promised Land, Crusader State* (NY: Houghton Mifflin, 1997), 18.
10. "Combined arms" is the full integration and application of two or more arms or elements of one military service into an operation.
11. *Sustaining Global Leadership: Priorities for 21st Century Defense.* http://www.defense.gov/news/Defense_Strategic_Guidance.pdf (accessed August 3, 2015).

12. See Arthur N. Tulak, *Hybrid Warfare and New Challenges in the Information Environment.* http://www.crows.org/images/stories/conferences/2015PACOM/Tulak_Hybrid_Warfare_Paper.pdf (accessed September 2, 1015).

13. United States Joint Forces Command was founded as an innovative force-provider. For a directive against effects-based thinking, see: "Commander's Guidance for Effects-Based Operations." http://www.carlisle.army.mil/usawc/parameters/Articles/08autumn/mattis.pdf .

14. See Terry Pierce, *Warfighting and Disruptive Technologies: Disguising Innovation* (London: Routledge, 2005).

A New Strategy
for Complex Warfare

CHAPTER 1

SECURITY AND STRATEGY

To begin, we first develop a framework for complex warfare through a discussion of security and strategy. Much of the literature about security strategy is concerned with structures and dynamics of the global system. What are the principles that govern relations among various actors? What is the emerging distribution of power? When do shifts in influence occur, and what are the consequences of such changes?

While these exercises are important, practitioners wrestle with problems of how to pursue security. What are the best strategies under actual conditions? What tools are most effective in a given situation? These concerns are shaped by assumptions about the operating environment. Therefore strategists need broad concepts and practical starting points to envision, plan, and adaptively execute operations.

Where should one look to find frameworks to inform the application of strategy? Ideological approaches to international security may be appealing, but these tend to seduce practitioners away from details that matter. Strategic studies below the level of policy are rare.[1] Enter military doctrine, a hands-on genre neglected by security theorists. Filled with principles and procedures derived from historical experience, doctrine deals with variables and constants in warfare. Doctrine tends to be conceptual yet instrumental, a guideline for developing operations that support broader outcomes. Relevant doctrine must allow for integration with other instruments of power and be adaptable to different contexts. This suggests we need to broaden military doctrine from combined arms toward more inclusive methods.

Our exploration of how strategy operates begins with international relations theory, military strategy, and doctrine. Then a framework for strategists and operators is introduced. The threads of this review weave a normative theory about how to achieve combined effects in any context. Next, three cases test the framework in high-stakes crises along the East Asian littoral, a region of vital importance to global peace and prosperity.

Broad Concepts, Precise Questions

Theorists and practitioners often talk past one another, clinging to different views of what makes good theory, strategy, and doctrine. Imprecision aggravates the miscommunication. This tendency is evident in the first thread of our discussion—the dominant theories of international security: liberalism, realism, neoliberalism, and neorealism.

Liberalism is an optimistic outlook that values international interdependence, open markets with modest governmental intervention, and democratic governance. States ought to embrace transnational networks, and their leaders should cooperate on the basis of universal principles, common values, and human rights. Realism is a pessimistic perspective that sees independent sovereign states competing to advance their own interests. States ought to be self-help oriented and accountable to their citizens. Neoliberalism and neorealism imply a modern outlook, their assumptions applied to international organizations. Whereas neoliberalism favors regulating cooperation and competition through institutional agreements, neorealism asserts the right of states to cooperate or compete as they see fit.

Despite these differences, security theorists ask the same central questions—what is the structure of the international system and why is it so? What is the nature of power, influence, and wealth among states and influential nonstate actors? Why does conflict reoccur and how can we prevent it? Answers vary. Liberals see a globalizing system that confounds state power and influence. They prefer regimes such as the United Nations (UN) and World Trade Organization (WTO) to bring justice and order to the system.[2] Realists see a system of self-interested states constrained by countervailing interests. Whereas liberals view the strengthening of regimes as the best way to secure conflict, realists focus on states as the ultimate defense against it.[3] The role of theory for international security is to explain these fundamental questions of structure, power, conflict, and cooperation.

Strategists and operators may be interested in such big theories but routinely confront dilemmas of how to, rather than why, pursue values and interests. To be sure, the "why" of security and strategy can shape the "how" through unexamined assumptions. But the bottom line is about implementation. How can deterrence and defense be achieved and maintained? What constitutes credible deterrence? Under what conditions do compellence and coercion work? What force structures and presentations afford such flexible strategic options? Several theorists offer insights on strategic choice,[4] grand strategy,[5] and strategic culture,[6] which are useful to those charged with developing courses of action, integrating instruments of power, and attributing intent. A persistent challenge for practitioners is to recognize flawed arguments, develop knowledge from uncertain information, and make sound decisions. In urgent operations, critical thinking can fade fast. This is when a better strategy can dominate.

Given the variety of cultures and the challenge of discerning intent, the strategist might turn to military thought about methods and capabilities. This is the second thread, needed to translate generalities of grand strategy into actions that we can plan and execute. An application-minded strategist needs to construct a causal logic of desired effects. In contrast to the first thread of international security, military theories tend to make assumptions about the origins of conflict and consider how to conduct warfare. Ideas from Sun Zi and Carl von Clausewitz continue to be relevant because they deal with human aspects of war, such as deception and uncertainty.[7] Their classic questions still inform strategy today. Sun Zi posed the following questions:

> How can I probe my opponent's disposition?
> How can I shape my opponent's perceptions?
> How can I attack my opponent's plans?
> How can I disrupt my opponent's alliances?
> How can I attack my opponent's forces?
> How can I combine direct and indirect methods against weakness?

Carl von Clausewitz asked:

> What is the unchanging nature of the conflict?
> How can I prepare an active defense and transition to offense?
> How can I arrange battles to achieve my objectives?
> What are my opponent's vital centers of movement and strength?
> How can I exploit military victory for political success?
> When will my attack or that of my opponent's culminate?

In contrast to these broad considerations, modern military theorists incline toward ground, maritime, air, space, and cyber strategies that assert the primacy of favored domains.[8] This tendency is not unique. The absence of grand strategy in Western military thought in between the time of Sun Zi and Niccolò Machiavelli (a strategy of politics)[9] is also striking. A thousand-year-long stream of writings from commanders and rulers focused on tactics, stratagems, and operations.[10] Eastern strategists did not leave much in the way of written works that survived China's dynastic warfare, occupations, and purges.

The third thread is military doctrine, which draws from historical events and traditions. These are often clumped together as experience, implying that judgment is being mentored and that lessons are actually learned. The strands of doctrine are arranged into three levels, whether for an individual armed service or for multiservice ("joint") doctrine. Basic doctrine lays out principles to provide guidance for planning, resourcing, and employing military forces. Operational-level doctrine is about how to organize for types of operations: offensive, defensive, stability, irregular, counterinsurgency, air warfare, and maritime. The tactical level comprises tactics, techniques, and procedures for missions and capabilities (e.g., reconnaissance, counter-air, and maritime-interdiction operations). Joint doctrine can help practitioners integrate different capabilities for common purposes and use operational concepts to gain advantages over threats. Principles of war are applied through these concepts, such as gaining the initiative with better tempo, momentum, position, maneuver, decisions, and knowledge. Joint operation planning is particularly relevant to developing an approach to achieving combined effects because the doctrine includes designing operations and other efforts for an interagency, intergovernmental, and multinational environment.[11] To discuss security strategy that includes nonmilitary methods and goals, we need to return to theorists and historians concerned more with why, rather than how to, employ force.

These bits of theory and doctrine can help us to imagine strategic possibilities if we rearrange them and are attentive to the advantages of different approaches. Along the way, we need to clarify what are the goals of strategy. The essence of theory consists of testable propositions, while doctrine is grounded in historical inferences that inform the conduct of military operations. International security and military theories use multiple levels of analysis to construct alternative explanations of past, present, or future phenomena. Doctrine looks backward in time to prescribe desired arms and capabilities. Strikingly, there is no strategic US doctrine that integrates desired effects.

Instead, each national strategy interprets what US national security interests are by referring to the National Security Strategy and deriving strategic objectives in its own realm. The National Military Strategy, for instance, provides supporting military objectives and states them clearly: (1) deter, deny, and defeat state adversaries; (2) disrupt, degrade, and defeat violent extremist organizations; and strengthen our global network of allies and partners. From these objectives, military priorities are drawn: deter attack, stop aggression, and defeat adversaries.[12] The reduction of objectives into supporting actions continues into specifying required forces and weapons. This fragmented process is tempered by the pragmatic trade-offs of operating and maintaining current inventory while researching and developing future capabilities. Unfortunately, the tools of strategy are described as strategic, operational, or tactical based on capabilities such as range or yield, rather than potential contributions to objectives. The approach lacks synergy.

Gathering our relevant theoretical and doctrinal strands, we seek an approach to strategy that includes rational and intuitive thinking. From a perspective of making strategy, the environment is rich with competitors who blend high-/low-tech, direct/indirect ways and means in attempts to achieve desired ends. Actors generally pursue physical and psychological gains consistent with their values and interests.[13] Rationality is relative, in the same sense that Clausewitz described war as having its own grammar, but not its own logic.[14] Distinct cultures can exhibit different preference structures. Asserting group identity, for instance, may be a valued existential end, whether its instrumental means and ways are based on reason or faith.[15] War is seen as a violent, chance-prone instrument of policy, not as an end in itself, in an attempt to link desired ends, ways, and means. Intelligence is constructed from incomplete, often inaccurate, information, so we have to make assumptions and use structured analyses.[16] Fundamental questions of strategy concern what to accept as a given nature, and what to treat as a changing characteristic.

The theory threads of our discussion speak to rationality, but what about intuitive thinking? The holistic is not entirely perceptible. We need intuition to pierce through and appreciate the whole. David Bohm's concept of implicate order describes universal reality as consisting of both explicit order and intricate order that connect space, time, matter, and consciousness.[17] Intuitive responses explain abstract feelings such as emotion and inspiration. Werner Heisenberg's uncertainty principle accounts for the physical limitation that not all properties of an object can be measured accurately. Daniel Kahneman's work on fast and slow thinking contrasts the roles of intuitive and rational processes.[18] We can reasonably assume that culture influences intuition. Strategists who acquire a deep level of understanding may feel an idea that rational approaches either ignore, treat as uncertainty, or selectively quantify as risk factors.

The range is wide when considering the assorted threads which relate to strategy. The international security theory thread can help clarify assumptions about why and how the international system works—how much trust do we place in international organizations and national governments to deter, defeat, compel, and coerce threats to security? Which values do we assume as common? And which do we expect to vary according to local conditions or systemic disruptions? When will people pursue self-interests and shared interests? Unless we consider the answers to these questions, our strategy is not likely to be effective. The military theory thread is useful in ensuring that grandly strategic thinking does not overlook questions about how to achieve outcomes by affecting will or capability. These are fundamentals about what to assess, how to set priorities, types of conflict to expect, what is static, and what will change. Doctrine has been a thin thread that details how to employ service-specific and joint capabilities at tactical, operational, and strategic levels of interaction; this is the essence of combined-arms thinking. The conflation of combined operations with the whole of strategy is unfortunate.

In principle, all three threads when combined help compensate for weaknesses in each. After all, limitations can emerge from philosophical convictions (realism, idealism), preferred methods (indirect, direct), doctrinal assumptions (domain superiority), and rational (group-think) and intuition-driven (emotions) behavior. Strategic rigidity also arises from preferred warfighting identities or domains. We can break free from these restraints by establishing broad parameters with precise terms.

STRATEGIC DESIGN

This section brings the international security, military theory, and military doctrine threads together into a practical framework of complex effects. These are subject to the influence of multiple factors. Strategists need to account for them to make decisions that frame courses of action. To develop executable options in different contexts, a realist definition of security and an operational definition of strategy are adopted. First, security is recognized as a symbolic concept that justifies actions against perceived threats to acquired values.[19] If we accept this comparative perspective, we see that security is defined in several ways: communal stability and societal mobility, group identity and individual freedom, traditional entitlements, and new ways of life. Effective strategy needs to recognize diverse values emerging from cultural, economic, political, and historical factors. However, it is also true that each actor pursues power, motivated by interests. For states, these include political survival, national sovereignty, economic development, and military capability, the priority of which may reinforce or weaken societal values. Security, then, is also a competitive process of achieving leverage over threats to vital interests. Generically speaking, "strategy" is how an actor applies ways and means to achieve ends. These working definitions of security and strategy apply to any environment.

Because of the impact of culture on values, interests, and operational options, security culture is treated as factor that influences decision making. Culture changes slowly; hence its long-term importance. We use Alastair Johnston's model of cultural realism because it focuses on conflict, threats, and applied strategy.[20] With respect to values and interests, Johnston questions assumptions made about (1) the role of war in human affairs, (2) the nature of the adversary as a zero-sum or variable-sum threat, and (3) the efficacy of the use of force against threats. For each these three questions, we include cooperation *and* conflict. Our questions now become:

1. What is the moral thinking about confrontation and cooperation in matters of security?
2. What are the political authorities' prevailing judgments about variable- or zero-sum threats, breadth of threats, and probability of success?
3. How effective is force against threats, and how are the latter distinguished?

We expanded the concept of warfare in two ways. First, we include the use of force, threatened use of force, and the use of cooperation. This integrates a broader variety of ways and means found in threads of international security, military theory, and military doctrine. Second, to the zero-sum and variable-sum description of threats, we add diplomatic, informational, military, economic, and social context. With these modifications, we understand security culture in terms of confrontational and cooperative strategies in diverse contexts.

Equipped with the vocabulary of academic and military theory, strategists might artfully coordinate various instruments of power in support of goals. But how might such grand notions get implemented during times of crisis? The following process shows how effective strategy might work in confrontational and *cooperative* interactions (the latter are *italicized* for ease of reference).

In confrontational interactions, combined effects comprise two spectra of preventative and causative effects. First, there is the spectrum of Deterrence--Compellence, which describes psychological states of mind. This represents factors that primarily affect will—such as motives and determination—and then affect capability. A second spectrum is framed by the effects of Defense–Coercion, which describes physical states of condition. This spectrum works primarily on influencing capability—

such as material resources—and then works on will. So the use or threat of force may operate both psychologically and physically to prevent or cause behaviors and attitudes. That is, force may be used or threatened to: (a) establish a state of mind that Deters and/or Compels, and (b) change a physical condition that Defends and/or Coerces. Combined-arms thinking does not begin to account for this real-world complexity.

In cooperative interactions, the framework's spectra of effects consist of *Dissuasion--Persuasion*--psychological states of mind and *Security--Induce-ment*--physical states of condition. The difference with respect to confrontational interactions is that in these interactions, force is not actually applied. We need this distinction because we use cooperative terms for allies, partners, and friends. The framework does not presume that common goals preclude confrontation. Cooperation and confronta-tion can coexist. Force may operate in the background as well. This begs the question, is a relationship cooperative, or is it confrontational? The answer often is, *yes*-yes, which leads to another realistic distinction.

Cooperative and confrontational effects may be planned via symmetric or asymmetric ends with respect to the tools used. This is an expansion of the combined-arms definition of *asymmetric*. Symmetrically speaking, psychological conditions result from the application of psychological tools, and physical conditions result from the application of physical tools. Asymmetrically, however, psychological conditions result from the use of physical tools, and physical conditions result from psychological tools. All of this may be done simultaneously or sequentially.

We distinguish between symmetrical and asymmetrical, as well as psychological and physical, because these differences can create advan-tages. Organizational routines and dominant subcultures, however, perpetuate a bias for the symmetrical and the physical. Moreover, new ideas are placed into familiar categories based on individuals' experi-ences. This retards creative strategy. Therefore, the combined-effects framework defines each desired effect as an ideal-type endpoint along a spectrum of possibilities. This helps clarify a key question that often gets lost in complex contexts: *What is the desired effect anyway?* The construct of a spectrum is also useful for combining opposite or similar effects.

In any operational environment, cause-and-effect relationships are not so simple to discern because they are linkages embedded in networks. Therefore, we need to distinguish between outcomes and effects. Outcomes are the result of combinations of effects. Uncertainty ensures that unintended consequences will occur; hence the need to anticipate multiple possibilities of cascading effects. The more complex the system, the less likely we are able to predict effects or outcomes. Most of the time, the best we can do is to anticipate likely and less-likely results. The combined-effects-strategy framework accounts for a basic level of complexity. Strategists, planners, and operators will need to map or assume further detail among effects, perhaps as tiered tactical, operational, and strategic levels of analysis. For our purposes, the most important aspect of the combined-effects approach is the attention given to effects and the matching of tools on targets to bring about such effects.

The creative result is a network of ends, ways, and means that translates strategic interactions into three tasks of mastering strategy: (1) developing combinations of Effects that prevent or cause behaviors and attitudes; (2) evaluating and selecting Targets to influence will and capability in ways that bring about desired effects; and (3) choosing appropriate Tools for particular targets. While we describe these components sequentially, strategists may begin the process with any component.

Figure 1. Confrontational *[Cooperative]*

EFFECTS	TARGETS	TOOLS
Psychological		
Deterrence--Compellence *[Dissuasion--Persuasion]*	Will	Intimidate *[Assure]*
	Capability	Neutralize *[Enhance]*
Physical		
Defense--Coercion *[Security--Inducement]*	Will	Punish *[Demonstrate]*
	Capability	Deny *[Exercise]*

EFFECTS

This concept is from our thread of international security theory and portrays four spectra of effects that change conditions in some respect. A strategist seeks these effects by influencing a target's will or capability using psychological and physical tools. The interplay of effects may set up derivative nth-order effects, and support broader outcomes. Targets may be individuals, groups, networks, or systems. The desired effects are expressed as precisely as possible: to prevent or cause certain behaviors or attitudes. Relative to attitudes, behaviors are easier to observe and assess, but this does not mean they are more important. Indeed, strategy often is driven by irrelevant data that effortlessly yields attractive metrics.

The framework treats any agent of strategy as an analytical equal. Agents of strategy may be actors or systemic conditions (such as natural disasters), but our focus is on actors with human intent. This approach is unconcerned about whether an actor is regarded as strong or weak; it is the strategy that matters. Among actors, confrontational interactions are paired in terms of opposite effects: Deterrence (D_t)--Compellence (C_p), and Defense (D_f)--Coercion (C_r). Cooperative relations are also framed in terms of opposite effects: *Dissuasion (D_s)--Persuasion (P)* and *Security (S)--Inducement (I)*. Again, each of these eight ideal effects marks an endpoint along a spectral blend of opposites. This use of the dialectic helps frame and craft various combinations. At the same time, we can use these distinctions to clarify strategy by asking the essential question: *what is an actor trying to prevent, and what is an actor attempting to cause?*

Answering these questions requires us to concentrate on the purposes of strategy. This is not easy. Given the hold of combined-arms identities on strategic thinking, several text boxes throughout the book are provided to stay oriented on types of combined effects. For readers with a knowledge of Chinese characters, our use of abbreviations to represent holistic effects is similar—simple characters can be combined to create a compound with a new meaning.

In order to view complex warfare in terms as combinations of psychological and physical effects, we highlight the types of effects in the three crisis chapters and the concluding chapter with the following convention:

1. Each Effect will be capitalized in full or abbreviated form.
2. Cooperative Effects will be italicized—psychological *Dissuasion (D)* and *Persuasion (P)*; physical *Security(S)* and *Inducement (I)*.
3. Confrontational Effects will be in plain font—psychological Deterrence (D_t) and Compellence (C_p); physical Defense (D_f) and Coercion (C_r).

By highlighting these distinctions in the narratives, we can better track intended and unintended effects. Recall that the two psychological spectra of effects are Deterrence D_t--Compellence C_p and *Dissuasion D_s--Persuasion P.* The two physical spectra of effects are Defense D_f--Coercion C_r and *Security S--Inducement I.*

Being attentive to preventive/causative effects is essential to balancing and countering multiple effects. This competency must be actively cultivated and protected. Why? Organizational and personal biases run deep. Dominant subcultures overvalue traditional arms, prestigious identities, and popular methods irrespective of their effects. If the effects are compound or asymmetric, they are valued even less by organizations that want to "keep the main thing the main thing." Indeed, the essence of the US Army, Navy, Marine Corps, and Air Force service roles is influenced by bedrock beliefs in their respective primacies: boots on the ground, sea control, semper fi, and air superiority respectively.[21] So, to counteract undue impact that loyalties toward particular arms have on strategy, consider four propositions about dual effects, each of which will play out in our featured East Asian crises:

1. China is credibly Deterred by the US from attacking Taiwan with nuclear weapons while at the same time somewhat Compelled to conduct an intimidating missile launch toward Taiwan.

2. Taiwan and US military forces can conditionally Defend Taiwan against a Chinese invasion, but Taiwan is utterly Coerced by the financial impact of unarmed Chinese missiles landing in nearby international waters.

3. North Korea is inconsistently *Dissuaded* by foreign powers to not withdraw from the nuclear Non-Proliferation Treaty, yet is consistently *Persuaded* to maintain the appearance of violating the Treaty's provisions.

4. Japan is ambivalently *Secure* due to US exercises of military capability even as it is persistently *Induced* by the US to increase host nation support payments.

For these situations, strategy making requires an awareness of combined effects beyond the purview of combined-arms responsibilities. In each case of crisis, at least one of the desired effects becomes the basis upon which to achieve a new desired effect. That is, ends can become ways and means to achieving other ends.[22] So when we consider a range of combined effects and variety of potential tools to apply on targets, we also need to recognize conditions in which Deterrence and Compellence can work together to create a combined effect.

With these distinctions among effects, operational planning can begin to identify linkages among outcomes and effects. The key question in this first step is *what are the desired effects and outcomes in terms of confrontational and cooperative behaviors and attitudes?* Given that effects and outcomes can be causes of new effects and outcomes, we need to consider condition setting that sets up multiple-order effects. This mental preparation can develop judgment about costs and benefits, the desirability of alternative goals, and the need to plan for them.

TARGETS

This component of the combined-effects framework draws from our thread of military theory and from security culture, to influence will and capability for desired effects. Linkages are complex, so threats are advisedly approached in direct and indirect ways. Targets may be agents such as an individual or groups, or conditions such as the environment. Targeting seeks to affect attitudes and behaviors by exploiting vulnerabilities. Willpower is assumed to be separate from cognitive capability. The cultural questions we will use to inform our understanding of targets are:

1. What is the role of confrontation and cooperation in matters of security?
   a. Is the use of force considered to be an aberration or inevitable?
   b. What is the thinking about just cause, timing and relative injustices?

2. What is the nature and assessment of the threat?
    a. Are the conditions narrow or broad, zero sum or variable sum?
    b. What are political authorities' assessments of success?
3. Is confrontation effective in achieving outcomes and eliminating threats?
    a. What are the confrontation/cooperation options?
    b. Are threats distinguished in terms of types of people or conditions?

Answers to these questions can provide insight into threat perceptions, values, and interests. Preventing undesirable effects by removing a capability may not be feasible, so methods to affect will need to be considered. Causing desirable effects by affecting an actor's will requires developing intelligence about values, incentives, and interests, and this involves risky decisions about uncertain relationships.

The key question in the second step is *what are the vulnerabilities and strengths of will and capability we can influence?* To answer this, we need to develop data into information, intelligence, and knowledge through advanced analysis. Informed by cultural insights, an agent or condition may be understood from different points of view. The target may be a system of interdependent parts, aggregates of related linkages, loosely connected networks, or isolated cells. Rational approaches may be used to attribute incentives, opportunity costs, and preference structures. Intuition-derived hypotheses about will and capability may be tested against observations and modified as appropriate.

TOOLS

This portion of the framework is informed by all three threads, and it involves selecting kinetic and non-kinetic instruments to affect actor will and/or capability, depending on the influence needed to achieve the desired outcome. Tools are expressed as verbs so that they can extend beyond combined arms. Tools may be used as a psychological operation to intimidate or assure will, and neutralize or enhance capability. Tools also may be used as a physical operation to punish or demonstrate will, or to deny or exercise capability. Consider the targeting of capability. Information may be used psychologically to enhance or neutralize an individual's capability to make decisions, or physically to deny or exercise the capability of a software program to process reliable data. As mentioned in the first step, strategy is designed as psychological or physical operations of tools on targets to: Deter or Compel, and Defend or Coerce, in confrontational interactions; and to *Dissuade* or *Persuade*, and *Secure* or *Induce*, in cooperative interactions. The key question in step three is *what assets are best suited to influence will or capability?*

The logic of strategy creates lines of effect that connect means and ways to ends. This concept subsumes the lines of operations and lines of effort described in joint US military doctrine.[23] By using the term *effect*, we stretch and unify strategy to include the purposes of various operations and efforts. The idea is to select Tools on Targets to bring about Effects that change conditions in support of outcomes. A line of effect can include any type of activity and focuses attention on combinations of their purposes.

Visually, the strategist may draw lines of causality using the combined-effects strategy framework. Beginning with Tools, moving right to left: psychological Tools on will and capability Targets; and physical Tools on will and capability Targets.

This rendering of strategy produces sequences, each with its own logic. Designing combined effects in support of desired outcomes is an extension of this basic process. Each line of effect can be considered for bundling with other lines to design combinations such as dilemmas, resilience, and synergy. The compatibility and incompatibility of these lines need to be scrutinized with respect to attaining all desired effects, and with respect to avoiding undesirable effects. The emergent whole also should be related to supported outcomes. The more complex this becomes, the more challenging it is to achieve synergy in context, time, and space.

While this combined-effects framework can help design and assess a particular strategy, it is not sufficient for success. A strategist also needs to anticipate how each actor's strategy interacts with other strategies. Taking this further, a reasonable assumption is that contending strategies will operate as complex adaptations to each other, rather than preset sequences. We also need to consider how thoughtful opponents adjust their efforts. In order to represent a few of the possible interactions among combined-effects strategies, the cases contain four basic patterns. Each case illustrates strategies' lines of effect that intersect, collide, careen, or conjoin with one other.[24] These patterns are not all-inclusive or permanent. Other possibilities might converge or diverge without intersecting, and they may exhibit other forms under different conditions. The following four forms may be used to stir broader thinking about configurations of complex interactions:

Intersect: Each strategy proceeds along its own path, passing one another, seeding future outcomes that are not immediately apparent. This avoids assuming that all results are immediate.

Collide: Each strategy's desired effects are opposed to each other; their differences are not resolved by mutual agreement, and they clash in a zero-sum result.

Careen: Strategies interact, then alter their courses in different directions. Any or all of a strategy's effects, targets, or tools may change.

Conjoin: Strategies are resolved, whether they initially meet cooperatively or in a confrontational clash. They retain elements of each strategy in a new whole.

The combined-effects construct is intended to be a place from which to begin proficient strategy, not a doctrinaire application that halts critical thought. Even though the construct is broad compared to combined arms, its focus on strategy as a process of effects, targets, and tools should not be applied heedlessly. Context and contingency are always at play. By itself, the framework functions merely as a translator, not as an interpreter. Strategists will need to assume the risk of interpreting cultural meanings and intentions for better-informed decisions.

To help the reader translate the language of combined effects throughout the cases, the following reference aid portrays the basic elements and logic of strategy as lines of effect. This Lines-of-Effect Logic textbox also appears at the beginning and ending sections of chapters 3, 5 and 7. The entire book is written in a manner consistent with this fundamental logic:

Figure 2. Lines-of-Effect Logic.

Lines of Effect Logic	
Psychological:	intimidate will / neutralize capability to **Deter** D_t -- **Compel** C_p
	assure will / enhance capability to *Dissuade* D_s -- *Persuade* **P**
Physical:	punish will / deny capability to **Defend** D_f -- **Coerce** C_r
	demonstrate will / exercise capability to *Secure* **S** -- *Induce* **I**

Mere translation usually is not sufficient for success, so we have to interpret context. Given this, each of the three cases—China, the Koreas, and Japan—consists of two chapters. The first describes the dominant security culture according to our three questions about confrontation and cooperation, threats, and effectiveness. This backdrop informs the subsequent strategic analysis chapter. While book space does not permit including more security cultures, one can appreciate the importance of adopting a comparative, contextual perspective to the making of effective strategy.

The point of the historical review is not to become a country expert, but rather to show how beliefs affect decisions made about security strategy. Gaining this appreciation informs the second chapter of each case, which begins with how strategy actually operated in the crisis. Applying our framework, we see how ends, ways, and means interacted. Strategic concepts are illustrated by organizing complex history thematically, even though many components of strategy actually happen simultaneously. Each crisis ends with an analysis from a combined-effects perspective. This is followed by a chapter summary of the major actors' strategies and constituent lines of effects. The concluding chapter compares these analyses and draws conclusions across cultures and crises for the purpose of improving strategic and operational judgment.

NOTES

1. Two examples are John Baylis, James J. Wirtz, and Colin S. Gray, *Strategy in the Contemporary World* (Oxford: Oxford University Press, 2013); and Elinor C. Sloan, *Modern Military Strategy: An Introduction* (London: Routledge, 2012).

2. See Robert Keohane and Joseph S. Nye, *Power and Interdependence* (Boston: Little, Brown, 1977).

3. See Kenneth N. Waltz, *Theory of International Politics* (Reading: Addison-Wesley, 1979).

4. See Thomas C. Schelling, *Arms and Influence* (New Haven: Yale University Press, 1966); and Robert Pape, *Bombing to Win: Air Power and Coercion in War* (Ithaca: Cornell University Press, 1996).

5. See Edward Luttwak, *The Grand Strategy of the Byzantine Empire* (Boston: Belknap Press, 2011).

6. See Alastair Iain Johnston, *Cultural Realism: Strategic Culture and Grand Strategy in Chinese History* (Princeton: Princeton University Press, 1995).

7. Sun-Tzu, *The Art of Warfare*, ed. and trans. Roger Ames (New York: Ballantine Books, 1993); Carl von Clausewitz, *On War*, ed. and trans. Michael Howard and Peter Paret (Princeton: Princeton University Press, 1976); Niccolò Machiavelli, *The Prince* (New York: Penguin Classics, 2009).

8. For examples in each domain, see Halford J. MacKinder, "The Geographical Pivot of History," in *The Geographical Journal* (1904): 298–321; Alfred Thayer Mahan, *The Influence of Sea Power Upon History, 1660–1783* (Boston: Little, Brown, 1890); Giulio Douhet, *The Command of the Air*, trans. Dino Ferrari (Washington, DC: Air Force History and Museums Program, 1998); James Oberg, *Space Power Theory* (Washington, DC: U.S. Government Printing Office, 1999); and William D. Bryant, *International Conflict and Cyberspace Superiority: Theory and Practice* (London: Routledge, 2015).

9. Niccolò Machivelli, *The Prince* trans. Daniel Donno (New York: Bantam, 1966).

10. See Martin van Creveld, *The Art of War: War and Military Thought* (London: Cassell, 2000).

11. On strategic design of operations, see *Joint Publication 5-0, Joint Operation Planning* (Washington, DC: Joint Chiefs of Staff, 2011), III-1-III-46.

12. *The National Military Strategy of the United States of America 2015: The United States Military's Contribution to National Security* (Washington, DC: Joint Chiefs of Staff, 2015), 4.

13. See Thomas C. Schelling, *The Strategy of Conflict* (Cambridge, MA: Harvard University Press, 1980).

14. Clausewitz, *On War*, 605.

15. On existential and instrumental war, see Andreas Herberg-Rothe, *Clausewitz's Puzzle: The Political Theory of War* (Oxford: Oxford University Press, 2007), 17–21, 65–66. On contrasting reason and faith, see Soren Kierkegaard, *Fear and Trembling* (London: Penguin Classics, 1985).

16. For examples of structured analyses, see Wayne Hall and Gary Citrenbaum, *Intelligence Analysis: How to Think in Complex Environments* (Denver: Praeger Security International, 2010).

17. David Bohm, *Wholeness and the Intricate Order* (London: Routledge, 2000).

18. Daniel Kahneman, *Thinking, Fast and Slow* (NY: Farrar, Strauss and Giroux, 2011).

19. Wolfers, Arnold. "National Security as an Ambiguous Symbol," *Political Science Quarterly* 67 (December 1952): 481–502.

20. Alastair Iain Johnston, *Cultural Realism: Strategic Culture and Grand Strategy in Chinese History* (Princeton: Princeton University Press, 1995). Johnston examines commanders' accounts of Ming China's wars against the Mongols.

21. Note that the Marine Corps identity is expressed in terms of a value rather than performance in a particular domain. All services promote core values: Army—loyalty, duty, respect, selfless service, honor, integrity, personal courage; Coast Guard—honor, respect, devotion to duty; Navy and Marine Corps—honor, courage, commitment; Air Force —integrity, service, excellence.

22. Dissuasion by deterrence, and persuasion by compellence, may be found in Avery Goldstein, *Deterrence and Security in the 21st Century: China, Britain, France, and the Enduring Legacy of the Nuclear Revolution* (Stanford: Stanford University Press, 2000), 28–31.

23. "Line of operation" refers to the geographic orientation of a force in relation to an enemy or objective. "Line of effort" was developed to link military as well as nonmilitary activities toward desired conditions. *Joint Publication 5-0: Joint Operation Planning*, p. III-28. http://www.dtic.mil/doctrine/new_pubs/jp5_0.pdf (accessed July 30, 2015).

24. Wayne Hall, "Complex Adaptive Systems" (presentation at Advanced Analysis Course, Maxwell Air Force Base, Alabama, September 2010).

CHAPTER 2

CHINESE SECURITY CULTURE

Contested rule in China (*Zhongguo*; "middle kingdom")[1] spans well over two millennia. A Chinese civilization has existed for twice that long, from the Xia, Shang, and Zhou settlements in the Yellow River valley, through warring states and dynasties, territorial expansion and contraction, foreign invasions, nationalism and republicanism, communist rule and capitalist reforms.

Sovereignty in unified China has expressed itself in complex forms.[2] Most of China's experience has involved dynastic rule in which subjects and outsiders paid tribute to a celestial emperor. Resistant foreigners were deemed to be uncivilized—they were barbarians to be conquered and converted, divided, or kept away. The emperor's legitimacy rightly derived from a Mandate of Heaven (tianming 天命), a concept of sovereignty in between coercion and persuasion.[3] Signs of imperial weakness would lead rivals to demonstrate that they merited the mandate. This system of dynastic power eventually confronted European-style states,[4] which by the mid-nineteenth century had coerced and compelled relations according to their own rules.

Such was China's introduction to modern sovereignty, enforced through extraterritoriality. The last emperor abdicated in 1911; as the Great War distracted Western attention, the new Republic of China faced new aggression from Japan which was also besieged. The ensuing military occupation and World War I overlaid the ongoing internal conflict among China's warlords. Civil war resurfaced after Japan's defeat in 1945. The Communist Party's victory over the nationalists on the mainland produced dual claims of total sovereignty: one by the Peoples' Republic of China (PRC) and the other by the Republic of China on Taiwan.

Through all of this, beliefs in China's centrality have endured. The people who regard themselves as Chinese are overwhelmingly ethnic Han, a Confucian identity signifying the unification of warring states by Emperor Qin Shih Huang-di ("Qin, the first Emperor") in 221 BCE. Local orientations survive under this imposed overlay. Moreover, dozens of ethno-linguistically distinct minority groups populate inner pockets and border regions where identities and loyalties are decentralized.[5]

China's leaders consistently constructed threats through perspectives on moral order, central authority, and territorial integrity. Familial authority contends with state loyalties. Ordered relationships, rooted in Confucianism, Taoism, Buddhism, Legalism and other moral beliefs persist as nationalism, republicanism, communism, and capitalism added their contemporary rationales. Ancient philosophies and assorted hybrids can gird or undermine central authority. Ideology mobilizes allegiance to a sanctioned sovereign. Tensions among traditional and modern relations frustrate efforts at centralized control. The current regime's theme, national development, calls for a righteous return to historical borders for restoring the territorial integrity of China.

The continuity of a great Chinese civilization promotes its own expectation of permanency and righteous boundaries. Ethnic Han rulers expanded borders to engulf non-Han populations, while "foreign" rulers—the Mongols (Yuan dynasty, 1279–1368) and the Manchus (Qing dynasty, 1644–1912)—struggled to retain their ancestral identity as they became more "Chinese." We see this aspect of Chinese security culture today. The People's Republic of China's claims and seizures of disputed islands, islets, rocks, and reefs along its margins assert territorial control that exceeds that of any previous Chinese empire.

What is the Role of Confrontation and Cooperation in Security?

Chinese history is layered with struggles over identity and power, as well as confrontation ranging from veiled conciliation to open annihilation. Partial accounts date to the Spring and Autumn period (770–481 BCE) that reduced the Zhou dynasty's 148 states to a mere dozen. Monarchies thrived during the Warring States (481–221 BCE) period when Confucianism and Taoism developed their moral tenets.[6] Military expertise was at a premium; the earliest known strategies are attributed to General Sun Wu, who led Wu's undersized armies to victory against Chu (ca. 500 BCE). Three concepts from this formative period remain most relevant today: superior generalship, strategic advantage, and deception.

Sun Zi (Master Sun) advocated a way of warfare that conserved resources. The pinnacle of generalship, the "army attack plan" (*shang bing fa muo* 上兵伐謀), was breaking an opponent's will without fighting. Attacking the enemy's strategy was best; the next attack priority, alliances; then fielded armies; and walled cities as a last resort. These do not have to be carried out in a sequence; they can be applied simultaneously as multiple lines of effect with variable speed, direction, and duration.

Qin unified the Warring States by enveloping competitors' strategies, splitting rival alliances, and devastating armies and population centers. Reforms and campaigns strengthened Qin defenses as other states wrecked one another.[7] After a hundred years of confrontational and cooperative alliances that preserved peace, Qin unleashed "irrevocable expansion."[8] The new strategy targeted the full territory of each state, capability of its armies, and will of its people to resist.

Sun Zi also enjoined sovereigns to seek strategic advantage (*shi* 势) and adopt an inscrutable form (*xing* 形). Attaining *shi* entails recognizing what can and cannot be changed, as well as manipulating conditions to build strengths and exploit selected weaknesses. *Xing* is an observable position; the idea is to hide one's own form and compel, coerce, induce, or persuade an opponent to reveal his. The gist of Sun Zi's thirteen-chapter text is how to create such advantages. Deception is the key to success, a combination of the straightforward or direct (*zheng* 正) and the strange or indirect (*qi* 奇).

Psychological methods of persuasion and inducement, then, could produce the effect of cooperation. For instance the *ho-chin* (five baits)[9] attributed to the Han dynasty, Qin's successor, transformed the Xiongnu tribe from recalcitrant outer barbarians living beyond the Great Wall to compliant inner barbarians. The Han induced partial control of targeted tribes by coopting them as frontier guards and permitting them to retain their own culture.[10]

Physical *zheng-qi* effects were compellent and coercive, a point well illustrated by Sui dynasty General Wang Shicong.[11] In 618, Wang's soldiers infiltrated behind the lines established by rebel leader Li Min, then reappeared in plain sight in order to demonstrate their resolve. In response Li deployed his larger force to intimidate Wang, not knowing that Wang's cavalry hid nearby. Before dawn, Wang's infantry crossed hidden bridges to attack Li's soldiers. At the same time, Wang's cavalry burned Li's vacated camp, demoralizing the survivors. Wang claimed the Mandate of Heaven, only to surrender it later to the Tang army that established the next Chinese dynasty. The Tang's twist was to combine small *zheng* and large *qi*: lighter units raided and lured the enemy; a hidden main force annihilated them.

Through the next millennium, Chinese strategies sought various effects in nuanced ways. The Tang army bargained to persuade and induce pacification, using force to compel and coerce compliance.[12] A number of tribal federations coerced payments and sovereignty from the Tang army as well. Aided by better technology, the Northern and Southern Song dynasties restored central authority. Nomadic Jurchen tribes established the Jin dynasty, accommodating Han traditions to gain influence and maintain control. The Mongol's Yuan dynasty subjugated Koryŏ, tried to compel Japan's surrender, then coerced Korean support for the ultimately unsuccessful invasions of Japan.

Ming rebels used complex confrontation to restore Confucian order.[13] To the south, they maintained Annam as a tributary region to dissuade incursions. In the southwest, they annexed and populated Yunnan to secure its resources, assimilated Bozhou to coerce the resistant Miao, and occupied Tibet to secure trade and deter raids. In the west, they coerced other rebels and compelled Mongol and Turkic tributary relations. Ming forces neutralized the northern steppe by allying with Jurchens against Mongols. To the northeast, military expeditions attempted to annex the Korean kingdoms, yielding a restive tributary relationship. Farther east, the Ming army failed to persuade Japan into tributary status. Against pesky pirates, the Ming army defended strongholds, offered bribes, and conducted raids.

The multiple Manchu tribes defeated the overextended Ming to establish the Qing dynasty. They doubled China's territory by exploiting Han rivalries, wishfully sealing the coast with edicts that banned oceanic ships and trade. Wars, natural disasters, and rebellions hobbled Qing rule, which was characterized as a precarious balance among royalty, officials, and merchants.[14]

The Qing dynasty's attempts to cause confrontation among surrounding military powers eventually failed. British mediation helped recover territory lost to a Russian Turkistan invasion (1871), which the Qing troops annexed as Xinjiang Province.[15] When Japan conducted a punitive raid (1884) against Taiwanese Aborigines, then declared sovereignty over the Ryukyu Islands, the Qing finally declared Taiwan a province of theirs. The Qing navy, however, could not defend this upgrade. A subsequent Japanese expeditionary force in Chosŏn compelled a downgrade to coprotector status. Russia and Great Britain then seized their own ports.[16] Japan instigated the Sino-Japanese War (1894), routing Qing forces to establish Chosŏn and Taiwan as its exclusive protectorates. China's Liaodong Peninsula would have been occupied as well, had the Triple Intervention (Germany, Russia, and France) not compelled its retrocession. Afterwards, France invaded Qing-claimed Indochina and made it a protectorate.[17]

At this point the Qing dynasty faced a moral dilemma. Harmonious acquiescence to foreign influence perpetuated humiliation; righteous resistance was crushed. The court's exit strategy was a "self-strengthening movement" to acquire technology. Unfortunately, this empowered domestic rivals. Using the Open Door Policy and unequal treaties as a baseline of its diminished sovereignty, the Qing prolonged their relevance by balancing foreign interests. At the same time, students, intelligentsia, military, secret societies, and overseas Chinese congealed in the anti-Manchu Revolutionary Alliance.

As elites acted to strengthen central authority, they produced opposite effects. Nurturing new groups empowered a revolutionary network.[18] Foreign-financed nationalization of railways unified provincial rivals. The Revolutionary Alliance reorganized with the Chinese Nationalist Party (Kuomintang) in the lead.[19] In 1911, massive uprisings and regional declarations of independence spread. Province representatives appointed nationalist-democrat Sun Yat-sen as president of the Republic of China. Prime Minister Yuan Shih-kai, former commander of the Beiyang (Northern Ocean) Army negotiated the emperor's abdication in return for supplanting Sun with himself. As the incumbent in an election that enfranchised only five percent, Yuan became the first nonprovisional president of the Republic of China.[20]

Yuan centralized his authority at the expense of China's territorial integrity. He dissolved the national parliament and parties, attacked provincial forces, and bribed political opponents with funds from foreign banks.[21] Pressed by Japan to accept its Twenty-One Demands, he assented.

This compliance accommodated Japan's control of Shandong Province and ceded South Manchuria and Eastern Inner Mongolia. China's loss was reaffirmed at the Paris Peace Conference (1919), where Japan also snatched Germany's possessions in the northern Pacific.[22]

China's national resistance fragmented as warlords bankrupted provinces and great powers funded their favorites.[23] The Chinese Nationalist Party and the Communist Party of China (Gongchandang) became an anti-imperialist so-called "united front," actually riven by distrust.[24] Chiang Kai-shek, whom Sun Yat-sen had appointed commandant of Whampoa Military Academy, garnered Russian aid and seized cities and warlord strongholds. Chiang's victories also earned British backing to instill order. The Gongchandang infiltrated the Kuomintang and agitated local grievances. Mao Zedong headed the peasant committee; they won rural allegiances as the communists lost battles to the nationalists.

The rivals employed different strategies. The Gongchandang adapted Marxism-Leninism into its moral order. Revolutionaries fought to replace Confucianism and foreign occupation with peasant-based communism. Favored by the Western powers as "Free China," the Kuomintang failed to resolve rural grievances—so as Mao Zedong and other Gongchandang cadre preserved forces through guerrilla warfare, Chiang Kai-shek wasted many in a war of attrition and fixed positions.

The prize was postwar rule. Both parties established base areas, resolved leadership issues, and separately engaged Japanese forces. While nationalists benefited from foreign military support, communists stressed righteous self-reliance and political struggle. Meanwhile major Allied campaigns took aim at Japan, not China. Per the Yalta Agreement of February 1945, the Soviet Union entered the war on August 9, 1945, right after the United States dropped its second atomic bomb in Japan. As Emperor Hirohito surrendered, Soviet troops poured into Manchuria.

Nationalists planned a combined-arms campaign to capture population centers and control communications routes and then deal with the political problem.[25] But they faced a radical, peasant-rooted Gongchandang that already operated as a network—a political, military, and social movement. Mao Zedong's People's War strategy integrated land reforms, indoctrination, and recruitment. In October of 1949, Mao Zedong proclaimed the Peoples' Republic of China. By December, Chiang Kai-shek and remnants of the Kuomintang had escaped to Taiwan to establish his Republic of China.

Chiang's command of island affairs and obstinate plans to invade the mainland delayed Taiwan's political and economic development. Martial law ruled the predominantly Taiwanese population. In the 1950s, the Kuomintang began to permit local elections and governance, and enacted market reforms. State investments incentivized agricultural productivity and generated capital for industrialization. Manufacturing and exports sparked further growth. Diversification into technology-intensive services enabled Taiwan to adapt to dynamic economic challenges.

By the end of the 1960s, opposition movements and independent candidates compelled national elections. Martial law persisted for two more decades, by which time Chiang Kai-shek and his son Chiang Ching-kuo had ruled for six consecutive terms. In the 1990s, legalized opposition parties and multiparty elections for the National Assembly led to a democratic presidential election. This brought Taiwan-born Lee Teng-hui into office, which ignited debates over sovereignty. In 2000 and 2004, the Taiwan people elected the first non-Kuomintang president, pro-independence Chen Shui-bian from the Democratic Progressive Party. In 2008 and 2012, Taiwan voters swung back toward the Kuomintang, electing moderate President Ma Ying-jeou. In 2016 the electorate reversed course again, voting for Democratic Progressive Party candidate Tsai Ing-wen who became Taiwan's first female president.

In the People's Republic, Chairman of the Communist Party Mao Zedong manufactured confrontation to transform society. Relentless "anti-whatever" campaigns and purges induced class struggle to unify the party and incite revolution. Initially dependent on Soviet aid, Mao led China on a socialist path that empowered the party and inspired anticolonialism, but inhibited modernization. The Great Leap Forward (1958–1960) and Great Proletarian Cultural Revolution (1966–1976) mobilized the masses, but caused mass deaths and economic distortions. Ideological differences ruptured Sino-Soviet relations and estranged China for two decades. Mao proclaimed war as inevitable, first with the Soviet Union and later with the United States.

The Sino-Soviet split (1969) complicated China's support of North Korea and Southeast Asian insurgencies. Beijing needed both to retain influence in Pyongyang and improve relations with Washington. Also with the Soviets in mind, President Richard Nixon resolved to end US intervention in Vietnam. The 1972 Sino-American rapprochement overlooked domestic differences to counter Soviet expansionism. For China, it also led to another problematic self-strengthening effort. Authoritarian Beijing would not interfere in other states' affairs yet sought to modernize by integrating itself into a globalizing economy.

After Mao's death in 1976, Deng Xiaoping's "Reform and Opening" (*Gaige Kaifang* 改革开放) policy boosted Chinese competitiveness.[26] Since 1978, Four Modernizations (agriculture, industry, technology, and military) have driven China's rise. The Chinese Communist Party's revolutionary identity gave way to a nationalism that promoted the very capitalism which Mao would have crushed. Instigation of communism overseas evaporated into a fog of neutrality.

China's unfinished business is to reclaim lost territory and sovereignty. The domestic political-economic component of this goal challenges the Chinese Communist Party's hold on government and society. Leadership succession has become less lethal, but a nationalist-prone middle class is weighing in on a number of previously hidden or centralized processes. The Communist Party of China (CPC), loathe to rush democratic change, intends to retain order, authority, and control. Consistent with dynastic forebears, China's leaders use diverse forms of confrontation and cooperation to gain advantages over threats.

What is the Nature and Assessment of the Threat?

Predynastic warring states threatened one another to perpetuate their sovereign rule. In this sense, threats were zero sum as one state seized another state's territory and replaced the defeated regime. The Qin dynasty changed the rules from limited territorial conquests to unification of all states under one ruler. As Chinese power and population radiated outward from its Han cradle, threats were handled in more variable-sum ways. Through a variety of tributary arrangements and security bargains, a defeated state or tribe could retain partial sovereignty over its territory and garner economic benefits in return for loyalty and service to the empire.

If a potential threat accepted unequal status, it gained the privilege of trading with the empire. Even barbarians could retain cultural practices and local rule. Tribes on the northern and western frontiers exploited this opportunity. Mongol warriors used superior mobility and swarm tactics to conquer a China fractured into Song and Chin empires. Unified Manchus overwhelmed the overstretched Ming dynasty. In both cases, foreign rulers seized the throne and became Sinicized, duly recorded as emperors of China. The continuity of a recognized ruler perpetuated a belief that threats were permanent—as was the enduring concept of a unified Chinese civilization.

Territorial competitors were ever-present. When Russians massed in Manchu homelands, the Qing granted equal sovereignty. This was China's first treaty (Nerchinsk, 1689), which traded away western territory for eastern Manchuria. When the Jesuits arrived, the Qing initially tolerated them as interpreters of science but later banned all missionaries.[27] European naval power followed, enforcing their rights through southern ports. The first Opium War (1839–1842) began China's "century of humiliation" as victorious powers coerced forty "treaty ports" to open. A second Opium War (1856–1860) bore more concessions that exposed interior China and displaced traditional jobs, brewing rebellion in all quadrants.

Foreign powers became existential threats by coercing access—spheres of influence. Germans occupied the Shandong Peninsula, Russians the Liaodong Peninsula; Hong Kong and Weihai were leased to Great Britain, whose sphere penetrated into the Yangtze River valley; Japan's was opposite Taiwan, France's extended northward from Indochina. In 1899 the United States proposed an Open Door of mutual access and respect, through which Western powers and Japan readily marched. Japan allied with Great Britain to secure its holdings.[28] The Boxer Rebellion of 1900 triggered a multinational expedition that occupied Beijing. Russian troops moved into Manchuria, coercing railway and mining rights. In 1905, Japan attacked Port Arthur and destroyed the Russian Baltic Fleet in the Tsushima Strait, gaining control of oceanic approaches to Beijing.

The danger posed by Western states and Japan was cultural and high tech. They challenged the Chinese moral order, coerced trade, occupied ports, and enforced extraterritoriality. Russian designs were on peripheral regions and ports. Imperial Japan posed a particular peril, a military occupier whose bushidō (way of the warrior) code commanded social obeisance. [29] Where tributary sovereignty was vague, China lost ground. Some Qing reformists recognized that failure to adapt was a threat, but so was foreign occupation. Racism magnified the threat. Chinese widely regarded the Paris Peace Conference's treaty terms (1919) as outsiders ganging up on China. Demonstrations ignited the May Fourth Movement, marking Japan as a permanent threat.

World War II clarified the risks to China of entering into alliances. The Molotov-Ribbentrop Pact of 1939 led to Germany's invasion of Poland. Russia advanced in Manchuria against Japan. Japanese forces invaded southward. In 1940, Germany and Japan closed the French Indochina and British Burma roads, sealing China's wartime capital Chongqing from overland resupply. After joining the Tripartite Pact with Germany and Italy, Japanese air forces intensified their bombing of Chinese cities. In 1941, the Soviet Union and Japan signed a neutrality pact, unlimbering each for expansion. When Germany abandoned its pact with the Soviet Union to march on Moscow, it siphoned Soviet aid from China. Japan's expansion into Indochina, attack on Pearl Harbor, and invasion of Southeast Asia brought US, European, and Australian forces to China, but not in great force. A Europe-first strategy limited the allies to defending the Chinese nationalist government and coercing the surrender of Japan.

China's war was between the Kuomintang and Gongchandang, as well as against Japan. Allied intervention in China to defeat Japan rebooted the civil war. The Chinese nationalists had modern weaponry, training, and logistics, but they had misjudged their opponents' strategy. Even when they defeated enemy forces in battle, the nationalists lacked the support of the population. The communists would concede the ground and return later. Gongchandang assessed the threat in political, economic, social, military, and moral terms. Targeting the will and local grievances of rural peasants, its cadre invoked Marxist-Leninist justice, coerced rent reductions and land redistributions, and induced recruitment.

In Mao's China, the most urgent threat was opposition to communist rule. Party themes sketched enemies of the state through media control that shaped ideas and channeled activities. The Politburo Standing Committee directed networks and mobilized movements via doctrinal guidance. The Central Committee recruited elites and enforced the party line, vilifying external threats with selective history and a People's War ethos. Territorial menaces were all around—Taiwan independence, British Hong Kong, US alliances, the Soviet border to the north, the Indian border in the west, Association of Southeast Asian Nations (ASEAN) claims in the South China Sea, and Japanese control in the East China Sea.

Deng Xiaoping redefined the long-term threat as uncompetitive economic growth. Without it, the party's domestic influence and the modernization of the People's Liberation Army of China (PLA) would weaken. China's strength grew under a low profile that conceals capability (*taoguang yanghui* 掏光楊輝). The end of overt confrontation with the United States expanded China's market, gained membership in the World Trade Organization, and globalized China's economy. This also opened new political fissures and more disagreement about what constituted threats to China.

Dissidents grew emboldened and threat perceptions more diverse. When student demonstrators tested the limits of freedom at Tiananmen Square in 1989, obedient PLA soldiers killed hundreds of them. Netizens face a Great Firewall of China that filters content and suppresses government criticism. Party cadres disagree over whether authoritarianism or democracy poses a greater threat.[30] Similar differences exist over Chinese autonomy and interdependence.[31] The CPC's official line in any venue is that opposing it threatens stability. As elite domestic and international threat perceptions change, there is a consensus on the need for economic growth and access to energy resources.

In Taiwan, threats developed in ideological and territorial terms. The Korean War delayed Mao's plans to invade Taiwan and increased US aid in East Asia. As a result, in his first decade of rule Chiang Kai-shek built a 600,000-strong modern military that depended on US support. This worked both ways. American military presence and assistance demonstrated commitment to Taiwan's defense while moderating Chiang's own plans to retake the mainland. The Mutual Defense Treaty between the United States and the Republic of China restricted American aid to resisting armed attack and subversion.[32]

Taiwan's incremental democratization and derecognition by the United States in 1979 polarized attitudes in Taiwan toward China; these sentiments formed a domestic tension that became a new normal. Henceforth, an ambiguous and conditional US security commitment deters aggression from China and independence by Taiwan.

Thus, the nature of the threat on both sides of the Taiwan Strait became assessed as zero sum, in contrast to past tributary arrangements of de facto sovereignty. Did the remnants of communist ideology and single-party control replace Confucian orthodoxy as a confrontational moral order? Will China become more tolerant? The answers to these questions partly depend on whether confrontation is thought to work.

Is Confrontation Effective in Achieving Outcomes and Eliminating Threats?

Chinese leaders have used confrontation to forge collective identity and promote other effects, rather than eliminate threats outright. Warfare and stratagems operated as instruments to create outcomes that were existential, diplomatic, informational, military, economic, and social. Cycles of success and failure were regarded as natural, the way (*dao* 道). Powerful states and better strategies could eliminate certain rivals through warfare, but the respite from threat conditions was temporary. Confrontation with cooperation was more sustainable than continuous warfare. Broad strategies shaped receptive threats during times of nego-tiated sovereignty and heavenly mandates. As an outcome, security is recognized as an ongoing dynamic, not an end state.

The effectiveness of confrontation varied as courts framed threats and adapted to them—or not. Consider the last two dynasties. Ming reexpansion of a Chinese dynasty compelled and coerced peripheral peoples, establishing defensible borders. Yet, expeditions sent to subdue a unified Korea weakened China's centralized rule and hastened the last Han dynasty's collapse. The Ming's Manchu replacements also stretched China's territory; they neutralized and punished local threats. The Qing were slow to adapt to high-tech intruders streaming through open ports. Unable to deter or defeat them, China ceded territory and sovereignty. The court was able to survive by accommodating and balancing foreign powers, which lost moral authority over the population.

During the first years of the Republic and the Pacific War, revolution-aries transformed Chinese society, resisted military occupation, and vied for power. Allied attacks against Japan's home islands ended the external war. Chiang Kai-shek's military campaigns and Mao's protracted political-military social operations shaped the contours of the civil war. The communists' ability to organize and engage the nationalists with indirect and direct actions was decisive.

In the early years of the People's Republic, Mao's fight against "Soviet revisionism," "US imperialism," and support for communist movements created a compelling party image. The calamitous Cultural Revolution purged domestic rivals. Border conflicts with India, the Soviet Union, and Taiwan—coupled with Soviet and American nuclear threats—enhanced China's role as an independent power. They also served to spin failures as successes: the Great Leap Forward, "re-revolution" of the military,[33] and the "Sixteen Point Decision."[34] Reams of ruinous party missives forged a socio-political identity under the useful shadow of foreign threats. China's support of Maoist insurgencies were portrayed as righteous rejections of power politics, in contrast to illegitimate capitalist interventions.

Communist China's attempts to balance Soviet and American power failed. The Sino-Soviet Treaty of 1950 was a negotiation to deter Japan and the United States, as well as to persuade Russian troops to leave China. The unequal relationship helped Joseph Stalin manipulate Mao into consenting to Kim Il-sung's invasion of South Korea. As Mao entered the war and Stalin backed out, Sino-Soviet partnership disintegrated.[35] The United States deployed air and sea power to the Taiwan Strait. The PLA's surprise offensive in North Korea knocked back US forces there, but generated a US embargo, ensuring both Sino-American distrust and the existence of the U.S.–Republic of China alliance. Stalin had succeeded in fostering conflict between China and the U.S. China's attacks in the Taiwan Strait were countered by US logistics and nuclear threats, as well as the establishment of the Southeast Asia Treaty Organization (SEATO).[36] As the United States ratcheted up assistance to South Vietnam, the Sino-Soviet split destroyed what domino theory adherents feared would be a coordinated Red-communist campaign in support of North Vietnam.[37] Beijing's ire over Moscow's reluctance to confront the United States in Vietnam revealed larger rivalries. After a decade of backing

North Vietnam's war of unification, China waged a costly campaign against Hanoi for overthrowing China's client regime in Cambodia.[38]

Toward Taiwan, Beijing's superficial shift from conflict to cooperation encountered short-term resistance. Three months after China established formal relations with the U.S., President Jimmy Carter signed the Taiwan Relations Act (1979) which continued a U.S.-Taiwan relationship. Beijing faced US policy that predicated Sino-American relations on resolving Taiwan sovereignty through peaceful means. The act also resolved to "resist any resort to force or other forms of coercion that would jeopardize the security, or the social or economic system, of the people on Taiwan," and included providing Taiwan with "arms of a defensive character."[39]

As China changed the way it confronted Taiwan politics and US military power, external alliances were not an option. References to past wars (e.g., the Agrarian Revolutionary War, the War of Resistance Against Japan, the War of Liberation, the War to Resist U.S. Aggression and Aid Korea, the War to Aid Vietnam and Resist U.S. Aggression) instilled an independent, collective identity. Maoist propaganda[40] and post-Mao marketing both bore directly on exclusive national claims.[41] With similar self-assertion, Deng's drive toward a modern China assumed future conflicts would be limited. Wrapped in heroic themes and propelled by advances in infrastructure and technology, the PLA's new doctrine is about expanding sovereignty.

Party elites filtered how the effectiveness of confrontation was assessed. One theme was that peaceful development promotes party control: a stable environment sustains economic growth for single-party rule. Another belief was that calibrated confrontation can maintain the party's legitimacy: recovery of lost territory sustains the moral order. To prepare for conflict, the PLA implemented "military transformation with Chinese characteristics."[42] Military doctrine established principles and concepts for operational victories that support political, economic, and foreign policy goals; international circumstances; national sovereignty; and territorial integrity. A stated intent was to secure development:

In a future war, the PLA will implement and execute the Military Strategic Concept of the New Era, undertaking the historical mission of safeguarding national sovereignty, realizing the general objective of national development and providing a secure and reliable environment.[43]

Citing these goals, the PLA offered new tools. As we turn to a current crisis of unsettled sovereignty, we see the three major characteristics of Chinese security culture coincide. Moral justification is strong, central authority is at risk, and territorial integrity is very much at stake.

Notes

1. The characters for *Zhonguo* 中国 depict "center" and "kingdom." This originally referred to principalities closest to the capital of the eastern Zhou dynasty (770–221 BCE), then to other states in the Yellow River basin.

2. See Jane Burbank and Frederick Cooper, *Empires in World History: Power and the Politics of Difference* (Princeton: Princeton University Press, 2010).

3. See William Theodore de Bary and Irene Bloom, "The Imperial Order and Han Syntheses," in *Sources of Chinese Tradition Volume I: From Earliest Times to 1600* (NY: Columbia University Press, 1999), 283–352.

4. Philip J. Stern. *The Company-State: Corporate Sovereignty and the Early Modern Foundations of the British Empire in India* (NY: Oxford University Press, 2011).

5. China recognizes fifty-five nationalities. See Colin MacKerras, *Ethnic Minorities in Modern China* (NY: Routledge, 2011).

6. Laozi (ca. 400 BCE) and Huangzi (c. 369–286 BCE) developed Taoism, "The Way" of living in harmony with nature. Confucianism developed under Mengzi (372–289 BCE) and Xunzi (310–215 BCE), promoting order, social roles and benevolent power.

7. Mark Edward Lewis, "Warring States Political History," in *The Cambridge History of China: From the Origins of Civilization to 221 B.C.*, eds. Michael Loewe and Edward L. Shaughnessy (Cambridge: Cambridge University Press, 1999), 613–615.

8. Lewis, "Warring States Political History," 639.

9. The five baits corrupted the eyes, mouths, ears, stomachs and minds by "using the superior material culture as well as the luxurious way of life of Han China to paralyze the barbarous Hsiung-nu." See Yingshi Yu, *Trade and Expansion in Han China: A Study in the Structure of Sino-Barbarian Economic Relations* (Berkeley: University of California Press, 1967), 37.

10. Yu, *Trade and Expansion in Han China,* 65–89.

11. David A. Graf, *Medieval Chinese Warfare, 300-900* (NY: Routledge, 2002), 163–168.

12. See examples in: Howard J. Wechsler, "The founding of the T'ang dynasty: Kao-tsu (reign 618–26)", in *The Cambridge History of China: Sui*

and T'ang China, 589–906, Part I, ed. Denis Twitchett (Cambridge: Cambridge University Press, 1979), 160–168.

13. See John W. Dardess, *Ming China, 1368–1644: A Concise History of a Resilient Empire* (NY: Rowland and Littlefield Publishers, 2012), 3–23.

14. Examples may be found in Alexander Woodside, "The Chi'en-Lung Reign," in *The Cambridge History of China: The Ch'ing Empire to 1800*, ed. Willard J. Peterson (Cambridge: Cambridge University Press, 2002), 239–243.

15. Immanuel C. Y. Hsu, "Late Ch'ing foreign relations, 1866–1905," in *The Cambridge History of China, Volume 11: Late Ch'ing, 1800–1911, part 2*, eds. John K. Fairbank and Kwang-Ching Liu (Cambridge: Cambridge University Press, 1980), 93-6.

16. On occupied Korea at this time, see Immanuel C. Y. Hsu, "Late Ch'ing foreign relations, 1866–1905," in *The Cambridge History of China, Volume 11*, 104–108.

17. Hsu, "Late Ch'ing foreign relations, 1866–1905," 97.

18. Michael Gasster, "The Republican Revolutionary Movement," *The Cambridge History of China, Volume 11*, 507–515.

19. "Guo-min-dang" 国民党 consists of country, people, and party.

20. Ernest P. Young, "Politics in the Aftermath of Revolution: the Era of Yuan Shih-k'ai, 1912–16," in *The Cambridge History of China, Volume 12: Republican China 1912–1949, Part 1*, eds. John K. Fairbank and Kwang-Ching Liu (Cambridge: Cambridge University Press, 1983), 222–223.

21. Young, *Politics in the Aftermath of Revolution: the Era of Yuan Shih-k'ai, 1912–16*, 232, 235.

22. On Japan's motives in entering the Great War, see Margaret MacMillan, *Paris 1919: Six Months That Changed the World* (NY: Random House, 2001), 312–313.

23. James Sheridan, "The Warlord Era: Politics and Militarism under the Peking Government, 1916–1928," *The Cambridge History of China, Volume 12*, 296–302.

24. Gong chan dang 共产党 consists of altogether, production, and party.

25. Suzanne Pepper, "The KMT-CCP Conflict 1945–1949," *The Cambridge History of China, Volume 12*, 758.

26. Cheng Li, ed., *China's Changing Political Landscape: Prospects for Democracy* (Washington, DC: Brookings Institution Press, 2008), 1.

27. Jonathan D. Spence, "The K'ang-hsi Reign," in *The Cambridge History of China, Vol 10: The Ch'ing Empire to 1800*, ed. Willard J. Peterson (Cambridge: Cambridge University Press, 2002), 123.

28. See Philips Payson O'Brien, ed., *The Anglo-Japanese Alliance, 1902–1922* (NY: RoutledgeCurzon, 2004).

29. See Inazo Nitobe, *Bushido: The Soul of Japan* (New York: The Knickerbocker Press, 1906).

30. A political analysis of the Party's role may be found in Kjeld Erik Brodsgaard, "China's Communist Party and the Evolving Political Order," in David Shambaugh, *Charting China's Future: Domestic and International Changes*, (Oxon: Routledge, 2011), 26–33, 18.

31. See David Shambaugh, *China Goes Global: The Partial Power* (Oxford: Oxford University Press), 26–43.

32. The following excerpt from the Treaty's Article 2 supports this: In order more effectively to achieve the objective of this Treaty, the Parties separately and jointly by self-help and mutual aid will maintain and develop their individual and collective capacity to resist armed attack and communist subversive activities directed from without against their territorial integrity and political stability.

33. This refers to the revision of doctrine empower commissars, such as abolishing rank.

34. The Central Committee Plenum in 1965 laid out goals of 16 points, promoting massive disorder that threatened the Party and had to be suppressed itself. Harry Harding, "The Chinese State in Crisis," 107–217, in *The Cambridge History of China, Volume 15: The People's Republic Part 2, Revolutions Within the Chinese Revolution 1966–1982*, eds. Roderick MacFarquhar and John K. Fairbank (Cambridge University Press, 1991), 107–217.

35. Sergei N. Goncharov, John W. Lewis, and Xue Litai, *The Decision for War in Korea, Uncertain Partners: Stalin, Mao and the Korean War* (Stanford: Stanford University Press, 1993), 130–167, 218.

36. SEATO (1954–1977) was a US-led, anti-communist coalition headquartered in Bangkok that consisted of the United States, France, Great Britain, New Zealand, Australia, the Philippines, Thailand and Pakistan.

37. The Domino Theory posited that non-communist states would fall to contiguous communist regimes. See Frank Ninkovitch, *Modernity and Power: A History of the Domino Theory* (Chicago: University of Chicago Press, 1994).

38. For a study of "Deng Xiaoping's War" in the context of China's foreign policy, see King C. Chen, *China's War with Vietnam, 1979: Issues, Decisions, and Implications* (Stanford: Hoover Institution Press, 1987).

39. Taiwan Relations Act, United States Code Title 22 Chapter 48 Sections 3301–3316, Enacted 10 April 1979. www.taiwandocuments.org/tra01.htm (accessed July 7, 2015).

40. The Shanghai Propaganda Poster Art Center is an example of a surviving collection. http://www.shanghaipropagandaart.com/home (accessed April 15, 2015).

41. On the Party's Central Propaganda Department's guiding role, see Ann-Marie Brady, *Marketing Dictatorship: Propaganda and Thought Work in Contemporary China* (Plymouth, UK: Rowman and Littlefield, 2009), 9–18.

42. David Lai, "Introduction," in *The PLA at Home and Abroad: Assessing the Operational Capabilities of China's Military*, eds. Roy Kamphausen, David Lai and Andrew Scobell (Carlisle, PA: Strategic Studies Institute, 2010), Kindle location 250 of 12080.

43. Zhang Xuliang, ed., *The Science of Campaigns* (Beijing: National Defense University Press, 2006), 89.

CHAPTER 3

CHINA'S UNSETTLED SOVEREIGNTY

The broad features of Chinese security culture can help us understand sovereignty issues, particularly in the Taiwan Strait. To be sure, we have to be careful about overstating the impact of legacies and traditions throughout any society. In most of China however, the pull of a common identity remains strong. The dominant security culture is one that claims moral order to legitimate central authoritarian rule, which protects territorial integrity. As other cultures and forms of sovereignty clashed with China's states and dynasties, Beijing emerged as a moralistic, centralized authority hypersensitive to territorial boundaries. A post-dynastic Chinese civilization has endured—but in conflicted forms that reflect uneasiness over how to deal with newly acquired values.

In the People's Republic, Taiwan remains the main unfinished business of China's liberation from foreign occupation and influence. American support of the Republic of China, triggered by Kim Il-Sung's sudden invasion of South Korea, prevented Mao Zedong from achieving that goal. Maoism transformed mainland China's politics and economics through the ideological filter of communism. Underneath, nationalism provides a strong undercurrent regardless of the themes which party cadres wave about on the surface. Deng's hard turn toward modernization transformed economic relations and official doctrine, but in ways that reinforce China's mission to reclaim Taiwan.

As Taiwan absorbed the initial influx of Kuomintang fleeing Gongchandang rule, its political economics and social identity also changed. Chiang Kai-shek's martial law gave way to democracy as economic then political controls loosened. The Han Chinese shared power with the Taiwanese, splitting and merging with the rise of multiparty politics and representative institutions. Chiang's ambitions of a republic, one that wielded sovereignty over all of China, faded into reconciling its offshore identity with the need to globalize and counter mainland influence. In a growing northeast Asian economy dominated by mainland manufactures and markets, the people of Taiwan enjoy freedoms which mainlanders disdain and envy. Similarly, Beijing's growing economic and political leverage is both loathed and embraced by Taipei's government and business leaders caught in complex linkages. Beijing's sizable shadow shapes Taiwan perceptions of itself and the world.

The thickening of cross-Strait ties complicates the warfare of sovereignty. Beijing's tendency has been to emphasize its inevitable military-economic superiority with a common Chinese identity. Taipei has had to deal with a substantial non-Han minority and a home-grown Taiwan identity, both of which are sensitive to mainland assertions of cultural superiority. As we shall see, China's embrace of cooperation with Taiwan is founded upon a strategy of confrontation that seeks to impose a grand dilemma on its renegade province. Taiwan's response is colored by the polarizing issue of independence from and unification with the mainland.

CRISIS

Figure 3. Lines of Effect Logic.

Lines of Effect Logic	
Psychological:	intimidate will / neutralize capability to **Deter D$_t$ -- Compel C$_p$**
	assure will / enhance capability to ***Dissuade D$_s$ -- Persuade P***
Physical:	punish will / deny capability to **Defend D$_f$ -- Coerce C$_r$**
	demonstrate will / exercise capability to ***Secure S -- Induce I***

Littoral Strategies

On both sides of the Taiwan Strait, post-Mao and post-Chiang leaders sought to transform bilateral relations. By 1981, Deng Xiaoping's "one country, two systems" framework had become "peaceful offense."[1] The party endorsed economic catch-up, and the National People's Congress proposed expanding ties. The stated purpose was to reduce distrust and promote understanding. In terms of overall combined effect, Beijing induced a dilemma. The strategy consisted of *Persuasion*, Deterrence, and *Inducement* ($P D_t I$), depicted here in terms of its indirect *qi* and direct *zheng* elements:

> (*qi*) PD_t - *Persuade* unification and Deter independence by assuring Taiwan of inevitable unification, enhancing trade and investment, and promoting a common cultural identity
>
> (*zheng*) *I* - *Induce* a reversal of proindependence policies by demonstrating China's will and capability to exercise force

China's goal remained unification; the new emphasis was on *Persuasion* and *Inducement*, relative to Coercion. Force still played an instrumental role. As Beijing built economic-military capability, leaders expected to elicit unification from Taipei. This could happen when the strategic advantage was favorable—such as a pliable government in Taipei and a disengaged one in Washington. Deception was integral to Beijing's strategy. Assurance cloaked intimidation to conceal Deterrence as more acceptable *Dissuasion*. These reformed tools and effects were subject to judgments about how to bring about unification.

In Taiwan, government and business leaders overcame restrictions on contact with the mainland. Coalitions formed, cross-Strait forums organized, and public discourse spread. Options ranged from Kuomintang consensus on eventual unification to Democratic Progressive Party calls for independence now. In terms of desired effects, Taipei's strategy tried to block Beijing control. The combined effect sought sovereign independence through *Induced* relations and *Secured* Defense. The elements consisted of Deterrence, *Dissuasion, Inducement, Security*, and Defense ($D_t D_s I S D_f$):

> (*qi*) $D_t D_s I$ - Deter attack, *Dissuade* forced unification, and *Induce* acceptance of sovereignty by respectively: intimidating China's will to use force and neutralizing China's military-economic capabilities; assuring China of Taiwan's will and economic benefits of sovereign unification; and demonstrating and exercising sovereignty.

> (*zheng*) $S D_f$ - *Secure* and Defend against attack, and Defend against economic control by respectively: demonstrating and exercising the will and capability to limit damage and inflict losses; denying China the capability to degrade key industries.

Taipei's goal was to coexist as a sovereign democratic-capitalist state. Deterrence, *Security*, and Defense depended upon a US promise to protect Taiwan from Coercion. Compared to the Sino-American Mutual Defense Treaty (formally known as the Mutual Defense Treaty between the United States of America and the Republic of China) of 1954, this was a weak US commitment against a narrow threat.[2] Taipei's indirect obtainment of Deterrence is why we include that as a *qi* element of strategy, relative to *Secure* and Defend which is straightforward *zheng*. The other desired effects were *Dissuasion* and *Inducement*. Mainstream parties favored *Dissuading* forced unification until terms could be negotiated with a trustworthy China. There were sharp divisions over *Inducing* mainland acceptance of Taiwan sovereignty. The Kuomintang supported sovereignty with unification, while the Democratic Progressive Party advocated sovereignty as an independent state.

To anticipate how China and Taiwan strategies interacted, we examine the logic of the two strategies and then derive key linkages going into the 1995 crisis.

Beijing fashioned a dilemma of *Persuasion* and Deterrence, aggravated by *Inducement*. China *Persuaded* unification through assurances of economic benefits, while Deterring independence with intimidating costs. If Taiwan sovereignty leaned toward declaring independence, a demonstration of force sought to *Induce* the dilemma. Beijing had to sustain this effect to integrate Taiwan into China economically. In a stable cross-Strait environment, this could elicit cultural and, subsequently, political acknowledgement of China's exclusive sovereignty. The *dao* was to leverage trade, capital and financial linkages, and cultural exchanges to influence political change. Ensuring Taiwan's economic dependence on China was critical, requiring China to sustain economic growth and expand Taiwan's access to its market. Later, a unified China could enact a Compellent or Coercive takeover of assets as conditions permitted.

Taipei's strategy was highly conditional. First, Deterrence relied on strong US relations. US security policy itself was a balancing act to Deter both China Coercion and Taiwan independence. The United States was less committed to preventing Taiwan's *Inducement* of its de facto sovereignty. Taiwan cultivated US will and the capability to Deter China, but Taiwan could not expect US support of outright independence. Second, *Dissuading* China from forcing unification required two lines of effect: (a) assuring China of Taiwan's will to unify, and (b) enhancing Taiwan's capability to do so with sovereignty intact. Third, *Inducing* China to accept de facto sovereignty meant showing that Taiwan was already sovereign. Yet, social discourse in Taiwan over sovereignty, unification, and independence projected lack of resolve to authoritarian Beijing. Finally, the resumption of cross-Strait ties held the hope of instilling in China tolerance of political freedom to yield compatible unification terms.

China's key linkages to bring about its *Induced* dilemma were twofold. First, demonstrations of force had to connect with indications of Taiwan independence. Until China could prevail against American military power, this was required to Deter US intervention. Second, sustained economic growth needed to propel and deepen cross-Strait economic ties.

Taiwan's linkages for its problematic preservation of sovereignty needed to connect domestic politics to external security and economic ties. Ironically, Taiwan's elected leaders had to restrain social movements that advocated independence. This might maintain the ambiguous security "guarantee" from the US and reap benefits from a global economic network that included China. As we shall see, many preferred linkages are not automatic.

Shaping Lines of Effect
Cross-Strait ties provided new opportunities as China and Taiwan sought the other's compromise over what sovereignty meant. First, how did China shape a durable *Induced* dilemma?

China
Beijing fashioned three main lines of effect: diplomatic isolation, economic-moral suasion, and demonstration of force. Diplomatic isolation sought to marginalize Taiwan with the tools of "One China" and "peace with Taiwan." Desired effects were simple: Deter independence and *Persuade* unification. Compellence replaced *Persuasion* when promises became warnings. Party propaganda claimed Taiwan as part of China under a principle that prohibited independence. Deng Xiaoping's 1983 proposal of "one country, two systems" proposed Taiwan as a special

region that was free to administer its own domestic affairs. The agreement would be between two parties—not governments—and implied unification.[3] Beijing's lead refrain was a peace accord predicated on One-China. By 1992, this peace accord had produced results through semiofficial meetings that Beijing claimed as a summit. China's Association for Relations Across the Taiwan Strait (ARATS) chairman Wang Daohan and Taiwan's Strait Exchange Foundation (SEF) chairman Koo Chen-fu reached an ambiguous consensus. They agreed to agree in writing on "One-China" (*yige Zhongguo*) while voicing "different interpretations" (*gezi biaoshu*). Hence, Beijing dismissed as irrelevant the Kuomintang politicians' "multi-system" options for a One-China confederation.[4]

When Chinese officials referred to peaceful reunification, they inferred war. Mainland media hyped images of a motherland seething against Taiwan independence. US derecognition of Taiwan and promise to reduce arms sales boosted Beijing's *Persuasion*-Deterrence $P\,D_t$ effect. Beijing remained confrontational about US support of separatism. In 1991, in response to US ambassador James Lilley's comment that the "One Country, Two Systems" formula would not work to reunify China,[5] President Yang Shangkun threatened force. A Democratic Progressive Party proposal to establish a Republic of Taiwan provoked scathing mainland editorials.[6] President George H. Bush's 1992 decision sell F-16 aircraft to Taiwan rekindled Beijing's fears of a permanently dismembered China. Similarly, the Bill Clinton administration's upgrading of protocols for Taiwan's unofficial diplomats signaled a proindependence US policy.

China stayed on message, rejecting Lee Teng-hui's idea for a "form of two Chinas" (*jieduanxing liangge zhongguo*) on the way to One-China. Beijing also blocked Taipei from international events.[7] Particularly annoying to China, however, were overseas visits made by the Taiwan president and premier. By 1994, agitated PLA leaders called for Foreign Minister Qian Qichen's resignation, blaming Taiwan's arrogance on a foreign policy that permitted US interference.[8] In synch, the party's information campaign assured neighbors that China's foreign policy would never become imperialistic.[9]

China's second line was a softer effect of economic-moral suasion.[10] In the way of a ho-chin stratagem, more trade and cultural attraction could Deter Taiwan independence, and *Persuade* or intimidate unification. Timing was auspicious. China's Gross Domestic Product (GDP) was six times that of Taiwan and growing twice as fast. Taiwan's per-capita GDP, however, was ten times that of China, so islanders were content with the status quo.[11] Beijing kept painting its picture of the future—small, rich Taiwan depends on large, rising China. From 1994 to 1996, Taiwan enjoyed a 15% increase in its trade surplus with China, driven by a 22% increase in exports. However, a 66% increase in imports portended dependence on mainland-manufactured goods.[12] Beijing advocates of strategic patience anticipated China's capital, financial, and political influence to follow. Characterizing a tenfold increase in bilateral trade as a trend, Beijing emphasized the benefits of trade, relaxed restrictions in Taiwan, and more business opportunities on the mainland.

When international sovereignty threatened to become policy in Taiwan, Beijing's assurances became intimidations. General Secretary Jiang Zemin's 1992 report before the National Party Congress addressed separatism as peaceful reunification. In March 1994, China Premier Li Peng distinguished between a peaceful path of administering Taiwan and the warpath that was implied if Taiwan were to become independent. Vice Chairman of the Central Military Commission (CMC) Liu Huaqing urged preparing for war. Remarkably, he cited Taiwan's vote for Australia to host the 2000 Olympics as evidence of "anti-China, anti-Communist" activities.[13] Party spokespersons warned that independence was a dual threat to reunification of the motherland and to Taiwan's economic well-being.

Beijing's common culture argument faced demographic and democratic challenges in Taiwan. Island-born Taiwanese and Aborigines comprised three-quarters of the population, a distinction sharpened by the surge of Chinese immigrants in 1949. Kuomintang control ensured that Han homogeneity was presented as Chinese culture, showcased in national museums. Beijing sought to use this claim of heritage to its advantage. However, by 1995, high birthrates and an immigration ban meant that an overwhelming proportion of the populace was born in Taiwan. There was now a generation of islanders who regarded themselves as different from mainlanders. This became a sovereignty issue in elections as President Lee Teng-hui courted non-Han voters. He asserted Taiwan's cultural sovereignty by advocating a new Taiwanese identity to prepare for closer relations with the mainland.[14] The Democratic Progressive Party (DPP) took another direction, rejecting unification as incompatible with Taiwan sovereignty. In a 1993 survey, 41% of all voters favored independence.[15]

If the DPP enacted such a "splittist" policy, Beijing's third line of effect acted to reverse it. A demonstration of force could clarify Taipei's choice: reap the economic and cultural benefits of correct political relations, or risk costly war. Given Taiwan's dependence on external resources and trade, a display of Chinese will and capability to employ force could destabilize financial markets and *Induce* panic.

For other rough effects, such as disrupting communications and disabling combatants, PLA concepts were ahead of its capabilities. Still, the military's role in contingency planning had increased during preparations to Defend China's periphery.[16] To be credible, the PLA needed survivable forces with reliable command and control, as well as weapons capable of escalation dominance. China also needed to win engagements to avoid loss of face. Factoring in US capabilities and adequate will, PLA military capabilities would have been insufficient. The PLA lacked nuclear or conventional capability to neutralize or deny intervention, and it was barely into its high-tech limited warfare doctrine. Even for high-priority strategic systems, the disruptions of the Sino-Soviet split, Great Leap Forward, and Cultural Revolution were still being felt. Although the PLA was prepared to demonstrate China's will to use force, they were not ready for a contested military campaign.

What China's army did have, besides minimal nuclear forces, were battalions of conventional warhead missiles on mobile launchers. If deployed to Fujian Province across from Taiwan, short-range missiles could threaten shipping routes and island targets. From a combined-effects perspective, this capability could play a synergistic, more-than-military role.

Overall, China's lines of effect *Persuaded,* Deterred and *Induced* Taiwan with diplomatic isolation and economic-moral suasion, a tension aggravated through demonstration of force. Against Beijing's comprehensive campaign to reduce its will, Taipei managed a three-line response.

Taiwan

Taiwan's lines of effect—guarded globalization, trilateral assurance, and military *Security*—were complicated and difficult to integrate. The Kuomintang came to recognize globalization as a trend to exploit. Taiwan's technocrats first focused on market incentives in agriculture, aquaculture, and industry. Import substitution in the 1950s built up the manufacturing industry before shifting to export-led growth. This reduced dependence on US aid and expanded access to international markets. Pragmatism ruled ideology.

Flexible planning sustained high growth with labor-intensive exports in the 1960s, and later through electronics in the 1970s and 1980s. Regional ventures and direct investments made Taiwan a hub of "internationalizing subcontractors."[17] Small firms nurtured skilled industries sensitive to changes in demand. Export-oriented incentives and financial liberalization diversified Taiwan's market and increased capital outflow.[18] By carving out niches in global supply chains, Taiwan created comparative advantages. How did Taiwan position this potential leverage to help *Dissuade* forced unification and *Induce* acceptance of sovereignty?

First, global engagement skirted China's diplomatic blockade, expanding Taiwan's space. In 1986, Beijing agreed to "Taipei, China" participating in the Asian Development Bank. In 1991, Taipei joined the Asia-Pacific Economic Cooperation (APEC) as an economic entity. The next year, Taipei had wooed recognition from eight African and Caribbean states. By 1996, Taiwan provided over $600m in disaster relief, mostly to these eight African and Caribbean states.[19] Constrained as a state, Taiwan's citizens networked through various associations and produced leaders in engineering, medicine, law, economics, and human rights. President Lee's vacation diplomacy expanded influence and irritated Beijing. All of this bought time for political accommodation with China, but it also threatened to edge Taiwan toward independence.

Taiwan's move toward globalization included guarding against the loss of economic sovereignty. This meant protecting energy and industrial sectors from the influx of Chinese capital while expanding cross-Strait trade. Taipei retained its ban on direct trade and restricted cross-Strait investment. Beijing countered by offering investment zones and legislative protection.[20] To hedge against overintegration, Taiwan's Economic Ministry sought domestic development and non-China foreign technology and investment. Local producers in Taiwan, however, lobbied for commodity protection and sourced low-cost labor from the mainland. By 1995, cross-Strait economic integration was still uncertain. Bilateral trade increased fivefold in five years and both side's money supply rose, though stock markets and interest rates were not yet linked.[21]

Taiwan's leaders also juggled three key relationships. This trilateral assurance line of effect tried to convince its own electorate, US elites, and anyone in China of Taiwan's commitment to democracy and peaceful unification.

Internally, Taipei needed to assure Taiwan citizens that democracy was *Secure* from China's single-party rule. Public opinion revealed a need for confidence in order to enter into negotiations with China. Unification might be acceptable if China became a prosperous democracy, but not if China used force against Taiwan. It was unclear whether an authoritarian China with a higher standard of living would change these views. Domestic assurance that Taipei would safeguard its democracy was necessary to *Dissuade* Beijing from forcing unification before Taiwan was ready. Behind these considerations was an assumption that a divisible form of sovereignty might be acceptable in a unified China.

Such optimism was not unfounded. The rise of democracy created a separate identity from the mainland, as reflected in the policies of President Lee Teng-hui. Vice president under Chiang Ching-kuo, Lee became president when Chiang died in office (1988). Chiang's Three-No's Policy toward China had mandated "no contact, no compromise, no negotiation" with the mainland. Lee replaced this with a One-China policy, establishing a National Unification Council (1990) and Guidelines for National Unification (1991). The guidelines declared Taiwan and the mainland as Chinese and called for democracy, participation in international organizations, and discussions on a constitution.[22] However, by 1992, Lee was advocating his "Two Chinas" form of unification, which many equated with separatism.[23] President Lee explained his position in terms of Taiwan's need for an identity and international status before unification. As he pursued populism at home and engagement abroad, Beijing regarded Lee as a threat.

The China-directed side of trilateral assurance was a compromise of assumed effects. The idea was to facilitate access to China and marginalize advocates of forced unification and independence. Within this rationale, the Asia Pacific blueprint by the Council for Economic Planning and Development's reflected Taipei's guarded approach to economic engagement. The business hub plan envisioned Taiwan as a center for media, transportation, finance, telecommunication, and manufacturing. The Guidelines for National Unification, however, prohibited mainland capital. As cross-Strait postal and communications links started, the same incentives that eroded Taiwan protectionism were at play. Businesses were drawn to China's inexpensive labor and market potential.

The United States–directed side of trilateral assurance was needed to retain credible Deterrence. All Taipei had to do was avoid a policy of independence and have an acceptable human rights record. China's oppression of dissidents provided a convenient contrast to recent Kuomintang rule. Two processes at work in the United States created a favorable profile of Taiwan democracy: US policy toward East Asia and Taiwan, and the strength of the Taiwan lobby.

Wrapped in democratic values and moral obligations, US policy opposed the dominance of East Asia by any resident power. Forced unification by China would be regarded as communist suppression of democracy. US opposition to Chinese dominance manifested itself firmly via human rights complaints, and tenuously by the withholding of Most-Favored Nation status. When the Clinton administration finally granted this status to China (1994), Taipei redoubled its efforts to highlight its democratic identity and solidarity with Washington.

The Taiwan lobby was organized and effective. The Formosan Association for Public Affairs had dozens of chapters advocating Taiwan independence.[24] The Democratic Progressive Party opened a mission in Washington, DC, to influence Congress, think tanks, and the media. The World United Formosans for Independence promoted self-determination and human rights, and it was particularly critical of the Kuomintang's early record.[25] The Taipei Economic and Cultural Representative Office functioned as an embassy with political, congressional, and defense liaison; consular; press; cultural; economic; and science and technology sections.[26] It had hired the American firm which lobbied Congress to grant President Lee a visa for the visit which triggered Peoples' Liberation Army outrage. By comparison, groups lobbying on behalf of China were, like the PLA, only on the cusp of expanding.[27]

Taiwan's military *Security* line of effect was razor thin. Taiwan's military Defended against China military operations with a combined-arms approach in a patchy national security process that inhibited interagency cooperation.[28] A declining defense budget raised the risks of self-reliance during a time ripe for new operational concepts. The old guard stuck to tradition. A split between the Chief of the General Staff and the Ministry of National Defense, and a rift with the Ministry of Foreign Affairs, did not help matters. Military leaders, however, did enjoy a direct chain of command to the president, separate from the administrative line to the national defense minister. Not until 1998 could the national Legislative Yuan summon a Chief of the General Staff to a committee hearing.[29] Military *Security* was a constricted effort of air superiority, sea control, and defensive land operations.

Taiwan's force structure provided niche capabilities to limit damage and inflict losses on an attacker. Most major weapons were interoperable with US forces. The benefits of diversification, however, were undermined by high-maintenance platforms and corruption.[30] Training exercises practiced denying PLA objectives in anticipation of US support, which constrained missions and tied them to American-provided Command, Control, Intelligence, Surveillance and Reconnaissance (C²ISR). There was no intergovernmental reassessment of capabilities beyond those needed in conventional scenarios—blockade, attack, and invasion. Taipei had outsourced Deterrence to hoped-for US intervention. Other military relationships were negated by China's *Dissuasion* of Taiwan's potential allies. Taiwan's focus on *Securing* and Defending against orthodox threats limited its strategy as both China and Taiwan set favorable conditions.

Setting Conditions

Since its inception, China has been reorganizing its littoral map with new *xing* that creates *shi* for opportunities to facilitate diplomatic, economic-moral, and military lines of effect. Following the failed assault on Quemoy in 1949, Beijing prepared to seize other Kuomintang-held islands with an indirect approach that produced larger effects. In 1954, Beijing Radio announced its shelling of Quemoy and Matsu as a preinvasion opportunity to surrender. The bombardments Coerced the United States to *Persuade* Chiang Kai-shek to withdraw, which he refused.[31] The absence of a specific US response conveyed uncertain commitment. Exploiting this in January 1955, China assault forces overwhelmed the defenders of Yijiangshan Island (north of Quemoy and Matsu), Compelled the US to evacuate survivors, and seized the rest of the Tachen Islands unopposed. The operation set conditions for unification: Deter and Defend against Taiwan provocations; *Induce* social tensions in Taiwan; *Persuade* mainlanders to support the Party; Compel Taiwan and the United States to react; and Deter US allies from aiding Taiwan.

The US Congress responded with the Formosa Resolution and more military assistance. Shaming President Dwight Eisenhower and his doctrine of massive retaliation, China resumed routine bombardment of Quemoy (1958), calling for its surrender and liberation of Taiwan. As Beijing talked of surviving a nuclear war, Washington invoked the Formosa Resolution then proposed a ceasefire and no-force policy. Dreading a "chain of disaster" in East Asia, President Eisenhower sent a warning of US action through Soviet chairman Nikita Khrushchev and considered using small-yield atomic weapons.[32] Faced with this possibility, Premier Zhou Enlai accepted a ceasefire. Regular shelling of Quemoy resumed in the form of propaganda leaflets.

China continued its multiple-effect campaign via domestic legal reforms that framed territorial seizures as rightful reclamations. In the Taiwan Strait, Beijing's goal was to increase coastal claims from three to twelve miles to encompass most offshore islands. China launched the international effort in 1971 as it displaced Taiwan in the United Nations. Using the United Nations Convention on the Law of the Sea (UNCLOS) as a venue against superpower hegemony and extraterritoriality, Chinese representatives advocated extending maritime states' national sovereignty limits, establishing exclusive economic zones, and rejecting the right of innocent passage.

In the South China Sea, the American withdrawal from South Vietnam led to two opportunities for China. First, South Vietnam annexed the Spratlys, portions of which were claimed by four other states, including China. Second, United Nations debates over seabed rights presaged overlapping claims by states around the South China Sea. In both circumstances, Beijing seized the initiative.

In 1974 China preempted Vietnamese control of the Paracels by dispatching fishermen to occupy them.[33] The PLA Navy defeated arriving South Vietnamese naval forces, establishing administrative control. Against Hanoi's claim in the Spratlys, China followed its punitive invasion of Vietnam (1979) with drilling operations contracted through international energy corporations. Through the United Nations Educational, Scientific and Cultural Organization (UNESCO), Beijing established a survey outpost in 1987. This drew Vietnamese countersurveys and more naval engagements. The PLA Navy won its Coercive presence. The fall of the Soviet Union and rise of Sino-Vietnamese relations ended the matter on Chinese terms.

Two domestic legal actions reinforced Beijing's claims: (1) designating Hainan as a province encapsulating the Nansha Qundao (the Spratlys), Zhongsha Qundao (Macclesfield Bank), and Xisha Qundao (the Paracels) to inscribe a "south-middle-west" arc; and (2) passing the Law on the Territorial Sea and the Contiguous Zone to claim all of the South China Sea against claimants Vietnam, Malaysia, Taiwan, and the Philippines.

China's southern maneuvers create a sphere of activity to control access to resources and trade routes, including the Taiwan Strait. The first island chain of defense extends from the Malacca, Lombok, and Sunda straits through the South China Sea and the Philippines, to the east of Taiwan, and just west of Okinawa to the main islands of Japan. Chinese strategists view this archipelago as a barrier and the South China Sea as a gateway connecting the Indian Ocean to the Western Pacific. The second island chain is displaced to the east abutting Guam, the Federated States of Micronesia, and Northern Marianas Islands. Increased Chinese maritime activity promotes perceptions of Chinese military and economic momentum. Beijing also set diplomatic conditions for success in its relations with the United States.

Several U.S.-China communiqués, the U.S.-Taiwan Relations Act, and US assurances to Taiwan created new circumstances for cross-Strait relations.[34] The 1972 Shanghai Communiqué stated principles to broaden contacts and promote trade for normalized relations. The U.S. acceded to One-China which included Taiwan, affirmed US interest in a peaceful settlement, and agreed to remove US forces from Taiwan. The 1978 Normalization Communiqué added US intent to maintain unofficial relations with the people of Taiwan and to normalize U.S.-China relations the following year. The 1979 Recognition Communiqué reaffirmed previous points and opened diplomatic relations. Noted areas of disagreement included ideological and social values, as well as US arms sales to Taiwan.

Three arms sales-related agreements soon followed. The Taiwan Relations Act (1979) announced a six-point US policy:[35]

1. promote relations with the people of Taiwan, China, and the Western Pacific
2. declare peace and stability as US and international interests
3. clarify that US relations with China depends upon a peaceful Taiwan resolution
4. consider non-peaceful action against Taiwan as a threat
5. provide Taiwan with defensive arms
6. maintain US capacity to resist coercion against Taiwan

The Arms Sales Communiqué (1982) reaffirmed previous agreements and highlighted the disagreement over Taiwan. China reasserted Taiwan as an internal matter, while the United States assured China that its arms sales to Taiwan would not exceed recent levels and gradually be reduced.[36] At the same time, the United States provided Taiwan the following Six Assurances:[37]

1. no US termination date for arms sales to Taiwan
2. no US change in the terms of the Taiwan Relations Act
3. no US prior consultation with China about arms sales to Taiwan
4. no US mediation between Taiwan and China
5. no US change in its position about the sovereignty of Taiwan

6. no formal US recognition of Chinese sovereignty over Taiwan

In January 1995, an impatient General Secretary Jiang responded with Eight Points for peaceful reunification. In April, President Lee countered with Six Points:

Figure 4. Jiang – Lee Points.

	Jiang Zemin: 8 Points	Lee Teng-hui: 6 Points
1	No Taiwan independence	Taiwan: independently governed
2	Non-governmental ties permitted	Chinese culture: basis for tolerance
3	One-China: precondition for talks	No direct transportation/trade yet
4	No promise to not use force	Leaders meet as international equals
5	Direct transportation/trade links	Renounce the use of force
6	Chinese culture: basis of reunification	Taiwan is sovereign nation
7	Visit China for reunification	
8	Reunification is irreversible	

Jiang's 8-course arrangement of China's elegant $P\,D_t\,I$ effect was served as follows.[38]

Invoking a need for undivided sovereign territory, he opposed Taiwan independence and international space, but accepted nongovernmental international relations as "Chinese Taipei" (Points 1 and 2, to Deter independence and *Persuade* unification). He called for equal negotiations with Taiwan authorities, but the precondition was acceptance of One-China (Point 3, to *Persuade* talks for unification). Jiang warned that there would be no promise to avoid force, but he assured that it would be used only against intervening foreign forces, not Taiwan's (Point 4, to *Induce* Taiwan's dilemma). He insisted that political disagreements not impede economic cooperation; he encouraged investment and direct communications, and he offered incentives (Point 5, to *Persuade* economic unification). Referring to Chinese culture as a basis for peaceful reunification, Jiang claimed all Taiwan people were Chinese (Point 6, to *Persuade* unification and Deter independence). He enjoined all Chinese to respect the wishes of Taiwan while "welcoming" total support of reunification (Point 7, to *Persuade* reunification). The leaders of Taiwan were also invited, "in their proper status." Jiang ended with assurances of the Communist Party rule, the irreversibility of reunification, and China's imminent resumption of sovereignty over Hong Kong and Macao (Point 8, to *Persuade* unification).

In contrast, Lee's 6 counterpoints provided a partial setting to achieve Taiwan's combined effects. He presented conditions to Deter, *Dissuade*, and *Induce* China, but did not mention *Securing* and Defending Taiwan:[39]

Lee portrayed Taiwan's equal jurisdiction as a fact for national reunification and consensus building (Point 1, to *Induce* acceptance of sovereignty). He claimed that Taiwan advocated Chinese culture to promote nationalistic sentiment, brotherliness, and mutual prosperity. (Point 2, to *Dissuade* forced unification). Lee offered to help the mainland develop its economy and upgrade its living standards while rejecting direct transportation and trade links (Point 3, to *Dissuade* forced unification). He urged meeting as equals in international settings to foster relations and peaceful unification (Point 4, to *Induce* acceptance of sovereignty). He also called on Beijing to renounce the threat or use of force to pave the way for negotiating an end to hostilities. (Point 5, to *Deter* attack). Lee concluded by referring to Hong Kong and Macau as parts of the Chinese nation with which the Republic of China would maintain normal contact (Point 6, to *Induce* acceptance of sovereignty).

Then President Lee toured the Middle East, his fourth overseas campaign to raise both Taiwan's profile and his own. In the run-up to Taiwan's first free presidential elections (March 1996), he ran on a Kuomintang platform of democratic reform and economic development.

When invited by Cornell University to speak at his alumni reunion, Lee applied for a visa.

The visa issue challenged Beijing to *Induce* Taiwan's dilemma of being *Persuaded* and Deterred without provoking US military action. Secretary of State Warren Christopher assured Foreign Minister Qian Qichen that a US visa for President Lee would be inconsistent with Taiwan's status. That was the Clinton administration's position until May, when the Senate voted 97-1 and the House of Representatives 360-0 in support of a visa, duly issued by the Department of State the same month. As Beijing railed against independence, Lee pressed forward. He delivered a speech whose theme was multiparty democracy and economic development. Mainland media roundly criticized Lee's references to Taiwan as "the Republic of China, my country, my nation, our two nations...among the family of nations, and popular sovereignty" as expressions of independence.

PLA leaders insisted on a forceful response. Between January and May, the PLA and Philippine Navy encounters near Mischief Reef, as well as other incidents involving China, Taiwan, Indonesia, and Vietnam in the Spratlys, heightened regional tensions.[40] China's frustration over American policy and the proindependence movement in Taiwan culminated in June. At an emergency meeting of the Taiwan Affairs Leading Small Group, the two vice chairmen of the Central Military Commission and the deputy chief of the general staff confronted General Secretary Jiang and Foreign Minister Qian and demanded stronger action.[41] The Association for Relations Across the Taiwan Strait notified the Strait Exchange Foundation that it was postponing talks. As China's media increased personalized criticism of President Lee, the media and military leaders of Taiwan cautioned against overreacting.

Strait Confrontation
China responded militarily from July 1995 to March 1996. The military expanded annual exercises and, for the first time, launched missiles (unarmed) that landed progressively closer to Taiwan. The missile tests

were new, but the maneuvers were the fifth iteration of the Donghai ("East Sea") exercises that assaulted and occupied Dongshan Island, which simulated Taiwan.[42] As three US-leased frigates left California for Taiwan, the Taiwan Defense Ministry assured the public that the PLA was conducting annual training of its Nanjing Military Region forces. President Lee pressed Beijing to assure peace and Taiwan's international sovereignty for future development and unification. Unimpressed, China deployed mobile DF-15 missiles from northern Jiangxi to Fujian Province.[43] On July 21, 22, and 23 during Donghai 5, the conventional short-range missiles impacted ninety miles from Taiwan.[44]

Taipei continued to send mixed messages. In August, a Democratic Progressive Party representative called for nuclear weapons to Deter Beijing. President Lee proposed further study but then rejected the option while claiming Taiwan had the technological capability.[45] He later warned that it was impossible to permit Kinmen and Matsu islands to live under communist rule. Then he repeated demands for China to renounce use of force before unification talks would continue.

Bejing answered with another ten-day live-fire exercise in waters off of Fujian province. The Taiwan Ministry of National Defense declared it was restraining combat readiness, while the Ministry of Foreign Affairs criticized the missile launches as intimidation. Meanwhile economic statistics hinted at a future of Taiwan dependence on China. The first half of 1995 showed that cross-Strait investment volume had increased by one-quarter over the previous year, while Taiwan's overall outbound investments had dropped by one-fifth.[46]

Political-military confrontation and economic cooperation continued through the rest of the year. As President Bill Clinton met with General Secretary Jiang at the United Nations, Taiwan forces practiced artillery attacks and touted the benefits of the Patriot anti-missile system. The PLA conducted more air and sea maneuvers south of Taiwan in November. In December, President Lee acknowledged their psychological impact on Taiwan residents and negative effect on cross-Strait relationships.[47] The same day, the Taiwan Aviation Transportation Association announced a five-year agreement, which included Hong Kong-based Cathay Pacific Airlines, that would permit direct flights to and from Macao. The China representative on the Joint Liaison Group claimed that this infringed upon China's sovereignty because the agreement extended beyond Hong Kong's reversion date (1997) to China. On December 19, the *USS Nimitz* aircraft carrier passed through the Strait, acknowledged by Beijing as legally permissible but noted with concern. This prompted a third series of missile tests the following year.

Beijing's announcement of exercises from March 12–25, 1996, began an information campaign leading up to the main event. Residents of Quemoy and Matsu stockpiled rice and gold, fishermen avoided PLA maneuver zones, and Lee Teng-hui's domestic popularity rose. The Taiwan National Defense Ministry still downplayed the significance of PLA maneuvers. Intelligence sources interpreted China's two-fleet blockade exercise, Haijing ("Sea Whale"), as Jiang Zemin's appeasement of the hardline PLA.[48] The Taiwan Ministry of Defense announced improvements in its Tien Kung ("Sky Bow") surface-to-air missile. Mainland media disseminated themes of peaceful economic growth while heaping verbal abuse upon Lee Teng-hui, pro-independence candidates, and the Clinton administration. China's Civil Aviation Administration pressed for direct air linkages while the Minister of Foreign Trade and Economic Cooperation pushed for more exports to Taiwan. The Taiwan Board of Foreign Trade reported a record $24b surplus with mainland China. Days before the first missile launches, SEF Chairman Koo called for alignment with the One-China policy.[49]

Beijing seeded future compliance with more missile launches in March. Official media announced splash zones within fifteen miles of the northern tip of Taiwan, to be followed by amphibious landing and air attack exercises. Chinese and American counterparts exchanged information about the number of missiles that would be fired, and what the US response likely would be.[50] The stage set for no operational surprises, on

March 8 and 13, three and five DF-15 missiles impacted less than fifty miles from Taiwan and very close to ocean transit routes. The Taiwan Ministry of Foreign Affairs approvingly noted that the *USS Independence* aircraft carrier was monitoring the activity. During the exercises, the Taiwan National Ministry of Defense avoided provocations and reported no increase in its combat readiness posture.

Before the exercise ended, Beijing was lauding its success and Taipei was calling for resumed cross-Strait dialogue. PLA spokesmen claimed a "relentless expansion of Army power" that would reunify the country.[51] The DPP vowed to increase its efforts for independence while the New Party (NP) called for immediate unification. A roundtable of academics predicted that Beijing would press for a unification timetable, but they disagreed on whether the tactics would be threats or concessions.[52] The Taiwan Ministry of Economic Affairs released a survey indicating over 80 percent of export businesses were not affected by the missile crisis. Transshipments through Hong Kong however, fell over 8% in February, causing concern about the future.[53]

Business interests and civil society reestablished Taiwan's ties with the mainland. Taiwan's shift to information technology and electronics sought mainland labor, driving suppliers to coastal provinces. Political dialogue haltingly resumed. In response to DPP and NP attempts to abolish the Guidelines for National Unification, Taiwan Mainland Affairs Council Chairman Chang King-yu urged that Beijing acknowledge sovereign Taiwan as the basis for cross-Strait talks. Beijing just kept reiterating Jiang's 8-Point conditions. Soon the SEF was in contact with ARATS requesting a resumption of ties. Premier Lien Chan also called for talks and a peace agreement. Academic ties blossomed in June at a judicial assistance seminar in Taiwan. As cross-Strait trade ballooned to over $20 billion, SEF Chairman Koo visited the mainland in 1998, where he was praised by Chairman Jiang.

ARATS Chairman Wang's return visit the following year was cancelled after President Lee referred to China-Taiwan ties as "special state-to-state."[54] Beijing replied with increased fighter aircraft patrols, matched by Taiwan's air force. Tensions were high, but restrained by worries about miscalculation. As the next presidential election in Taiwan approached, China's premier Zhu Rongji warned that China would not tolerate separatism. Vice-Chairman of China's Central Military Commission Zhang Wannian went further to state, "Taiwan's independence means war."[55]

Regional Reverberations

China invested in power projection, propelled by annual defense spending increases of 11% in real terms.[56] Rapid modernization of missiles, aircraft, and ships created new capabilities and ambitions. Military documents and publications indicate China's desires for a global military role.[57] Comparisons of China and Taiwan forces in conflict scenarios point to the growing importance of airpower.[58]

Defense industrial reforms support this trend.[59] Beijing decentralized its state shipbuilding corporation, outstripping Japan and South Korea to become the world's largest commercial shipbuilder. Amphibious assault ships, littoral frigates, and super-quiet submarines followed. China's restructured ordnance industries became leading suppliers of small arms and artillery. Recentralization efforts include integrating civilian research and military C^4ISR production, ministerial consolidation of science, technology and industrial procurement, party control of military armament decisions, and civil-military aviation projects. In 2012, China's aerospace industry produced a long-range fifth-generation fighter with Russian-built engines. Indigenous jet engine development is a top priority. Despite bureaucratic inefficiencies in China's state-owned enterprises, growth in supply chain and financial networks and sporadic market reforms help sustain strategic effects on Taiwan.

Taiwan military modernization has sought pockets of qualitative advantages. In 2012, real defense spending decreased by percent, even though GDP increased 10.8% over the previous year. Since 2006, Taipei has requested newer F-16C/D models that Washington refuses to sell. US-approved upgrades and sales of fighter and early warning aircraft, air defense systems, helicopters, frigates, and antiship missiles to Taiwan became miniscule compared to what China was accumulating. European suppliers provided Taipei unweaponized platforms. Indigenous weapons include the Ching Kuo fighter aircraft and Hsiung feng-series cruise missile. Future plans include antiradiation and remotely piloted weapons, graphite bombs, electromagnetic pulse emitters, a hypersonic vehicle facility, stealth materials, and a catamaran-hulled ship. New ideas indicate emerging operational concepts with uncertain funding.

Multiparty politics heavily influence Taipei's complicated blocking scheme of Deterring China and Securing Taiwan against attack, Dissuading forced unification, Inducing China's acceptance of Taiwan's sovereignty, and Defending against China's economic control. President Lee's "no use of force" prerequisite for resuming formal cross-Strait talks after the Strait Crisis attempted to Dissuade and Induce Beijing. This split domestic conservatives. In the 2000 presidential election, cleavages among the Kuomintang, Independent, and New Party enabled Democratic Progressive Party candidate Chen Shui-bian to win with 40 percent of the vote. President Chen's accommodating inaugural speech included a qualified promise—he would abandon independence as long as Beijing renounced the use of force.[60] Beijing refuted all points and insisted on its own interpretation of One-China. This demand violated the 1992 semi-Summit's Consensus. Taiwan's combined effect weakened when the three major opposition parties refused to participate in Chen's task force for mainland policy.[61] Then in 2001 former President Lee established the proindependence Taiwan Solidarity Union. Beijing kept its vise tight.

Beijing's strategy weathered both terms of the Chen presidency. In 2001, the DPP garnered more seats in the Legislative Yuan. In 2003, President Chen pushed referenda on domestic issues and Taiwan's international status, short of independence. This reversed his abandonment of the 1999 DPP platform and retained his core constituency for the 2004 election.

Chen advocated economic and cultural ties as the path toward unification, but with words that indicated Taiwan sovereignty.[62] To Beijing, this signaled independence.

President Chen's narrow reelection in 2004 led to a bolder second term. A referendum that sought United Nations membership as "Taiwan" failed to receive the requisite majority of the popular vote. China increased the tension of the PD_t dilemma on Taiwan with commercial incentives and a sweeter-carrot/harder-stick Anti-Secession Law.[63] President George W. Bush gave the vise a turn by opposing "any referenda that would change Taiwan's status or move towards independence." Other developments bode ill for the Democratic Progressives: declining household incomes while the mainland's economy boomed, deteriorating U.S.-Taiwan relations, corruption in the Chen family, and a doubling of Kuomintang seats in the January 2008 parliamentary elections.

Beijing's refusal to consider international sovereignty for Taiwan paid a big dividend in March. Kuomintang candidate Ma Ying-jeou was elected by an 8-percent margin on a platform of "three yes's" and "three no's"—"yes" improve economic performance; "yes" increase cooperation with China; "yes" reduce tensions in Taiwan-U.S. relations, "no" negotiations on unification with China, "no" de jure independence; "no" use of force by China or Taiwan. In his inauguration speech, Ma proclaimed, "Taiwan is the sole ethnic Chinese society to complete a second democratic turnover of power." At the time, ethnic Chinese comprised 14% of Taiwan's population and Taiwanese 84%.

Ma's triple "yes-no" formula undercut Deterrence and *Inducement* of China. This left Taiwan's complicated $D_t D_s I S D_f$ strategy as a simpler mainland-friendly combination of *Dissuasion, Security* and Defense. *Dissuasion* took the lead in a visible, unprecedented expansion of trade and investment. The emphasis on peaceful cross-Strait economic development mollified Beijing and gained domestic support—as long as China was nonthreatening. The deal for Ma's Kuomintang included not criticizing China's territorial claims in the South China Sea. President Ma's restart of SEF and ARATS negotiations yielded the Economic Cooperation Framework Agreement (ECFA). Its multiple rounds spawned agreements on tourism, nuclear power, aviation, cultural exchanges, investment protection, arbitration, and customs procedures. General Secretary Hu Jintao of China offered to discuss confidence-building measures and how to meet Taiwan's desires for international space.

This suits PLA ideas for economic development and territorial control. Naval strategists advocate *haiyang quanyi* (maritime rights and interests), asserting the right to transit, exploit, and protect resources throughout all claimed territories. Taiwan is a key link in the first island chain, connecting the East China Sea with the South China Sea, thereby complicating China's territorial defense and outward access. PLA Navy concepts for maritime sovereignty and national development are expansive.[64] China's need for energy imports led to combined fleet operations and an international presence from the Gulf of Aden to the Sea of Japan. The New Silk Road initiative includes a China- Pakistan Economic Corridor to transport oil from Gwadar Port to western China.[65] Control over energy and resource flows will influence energy dependent states such as Taiwan and Japan. Naval deployments provide presence to promote China's own sovereignty claims and coastal buffer zones, rather than common goods such as freedom of navigation.

Internal PLA competition incentivizes Chinese expansion. Joint campaign documents indicate that the air force seeks to become a campaign-leading service. This is resisted by army and navy concepts that tie airpower and ISR to surface operations.[66] It's all about more sovereign space. In 2012, China Compelled Cambodia, host of the Association of South East Asian Nations (ASEAN) Foreign Ministers' Meeting that year, to omit any mention of the Philippines-China territorial dispute in the South China Sea. This prevented a joint communiqué for the first time in the summit's forty-five-year history.[67] In 2013, SinoMaps Press released a map that depicted for the first time 130 disputed islets claimed by China. The same year, the Ministry of National Defense announced an East

China Sea Air Defense Identification Zone in international space that was also claimed by Japan, South Korea, and Taiwan. However, criticism from Taiwan has been restrained.

China's strategy against Taiwan independence continues to shape regional conditions for national development. For Taiwan, General Secretary of the Communist Party and President of the People's Republic of China and Chairman of the Central Military Commission Xi Jinping's ambitious "Chinese dream" is a widening form of *Persuasion* and Compellence, couched in global terms.[68] In a specific effort to counter American and European financial influence in the World Bank and International Monetary Fund, and Japanese financial leadership of the Asian Development Bank, Beijing announced in 2014 the creation of the Asian Infrastructure Investment Bank. There is little doubt about what China expects: "ASEAN member nations will have to readjust their policies to reflect those [China's] interests in a realistic manner."[69]

In 2015, a militarily confident China began constructing and militarizing islands in the South China Sea, a new reality with which prospective borrowers can align. Across the Strait, China's broadened bullying polarized politics in Taiwan again, increasing support for the Democratic Progressive Party now led by Tsai Ing-wen. Like her predecessors who opposed Kuomintang coziness with authoritarian China, she is proindependent democracy and pro-cross-Strait status quo. Internally, Beijing suppresses, distracts, and subsidizes restive separatists, students, and entrepreneurs. Taipei's strategy under President Ma complemented Beijing's settlement of sovereignty issues. The culmination of Ma's relations with China came about in November 2015 when they met in Singapore; this was an historic meeting between the leaders of China and Taiwan. Said Xi, before the meeting, "Today we are sitting together so as to not replay the tragedies of history."[70] Like the construction of islets or islands (the bigger the better) in disputed territory, this strategy *Induces* Taiwan toward unification in ways that preclude outside intervention. Without an independent commitment to military *Security* and Defense,

Taiwan's globalization and trilateral assurance seem to be all that is left to counter Beijing's strategy.[71]

COMBINED-EFFECTS ANALYSIS

Figure 5. Lines of Effect Logic.

Lines of Effect Logic	
Psychological:	intimidate will / neutralize capability to **Deter** D_t -- **Compel** C_p
	assure will / enhance capability to *Dissuade* D_s -- *Persuade* *P*
Physical:	punish will / deny capability to **Defend** D_f -- **Coerce** C_r
	demonstrate will / exercise capability to *Secure* *S* -- *Induce* *I*

Chinese security culture is holistic. Its operational hallmark is combining physical and psychological effects by influencing the will and capability of rivals. In the decade leading up to the Taiwan Strait Crisis of 1995–1996, Beijing leaders formulated a strategy of *Persuasion*, Deterrence, and *Inducement*. In terms of combined effects, assurance to *Persuade* was employed with intimidation to Deter, and demonstration of force to *Induce*. Assurance worked through quasiformal relationships, such as the pivotal interactions between the Association for Relations Across the Taiwan Strait and the Strait Exchange Foundation. The 1992 Consensus established a One-China position that Beijing used to insulate economic relations from proindependence politics in Taiwan. Beijing adjusted its rhetoric to fit the situation, ranging from "peaceful unification" to "independence means war." Beijing messengers and missives reminded Taipei of the economic and cultural benefits in a unified China. Together, assurance, intimidation, and demonstrations of force created more tension than if they were separately pursued. China's economic performance sweetened the lure of closer relations. Domestic legislation, United Nations Convention on the Law of the Sea ratification, and seizures in the South China Sea improved the credibility of PLA intervention—which *Induced* the *Persuasion*-Deterrence dilemma on Taiwan. The four China-U.S. communiqués diluted US meddling and concentrated the $P D_t I$ effect on Taiwan against countervailing spurts of implied American intervention: the U.S.-Taiwan Relations Act, 6-Point Policy, Six Assurances, and rebalancing toward Asia.

Taiwan's strategic efforts were a labored orchestration of complexity. Multiple actors cobbled together elements of Deterrence, *Dissuasion*, *Inducement*, *Security*, and Defense. Harnessing globalization was an ambitious task, requiring a fusion of intelligence across a variety of complex activities: industrial, trade, energy, and financial policy; information technology, security, and services; defense policy, military operations, and diplomacy. Global engagement was regarded as compatible with Taiwan's assurances to China of economic ties to Deter forced unification. Taipei's guarded globalization expanded linkages in all directions while intending to access China's market. At the same time it was hoped that Taiwan's de facto sovereignty would *Induce* political acceptance. Meanwhile, Taiwan tried to Defend key industries through protectionism while also assuring China of eventual reunification. Tools of trilateral assurance—the domestic politics of democracy and sovereignty and identity, cross-Strait diplomacy, and the Taiwan lobby in the U.S.—were meant to *Dissuade* forced unification. Their success, however, depended upon variables outside Taipei's interagency processes. Added to this challenge were Taiwan's military tools, narrowly focused on PLA operations against Taiwan territory. Domestically stove-piped and dependent upon American capabilities for Deterrence and Defense, Taiwan's military provided only a sense of *Security*.

How did these lines of effect interact? To envision strategic possibilities, we compare the lines of effect as they were intended to relate to each other and consider interactions that collided, intersected, conjoined, and careened.

Our first comparison is China's diplomatic isolation of Taiwan and Taiwan's guarded globalization to break free from it. The US government's derecognition of Taiwan facilitated Beijing's isolation of Taipei from international forums. As long as China used non-Coercive means to *Persuade* and Deter Taiwan, the Taiwan Relations Act did not apply. This condition limited US influence. Taipei's political-economic networking worked against such containment. However, Taiwan's economic growth occurred in the shadow of China's opening to global organizations, trade, and finance. As Beijing tried to isolate Taipei, acknowledging disagreement over sovereignty risked collision. The fundamental differences papered over in the 1992 ARATS-SEF meeting were "One China" with "different interpretations." These positions reflected China's diplomatic isolation line, and Taiwan's globalization line that tried to circumvent it. The two lines of effect veered toward collision when President Lee visited Cornell University and asserted his interpretation of Taiwan's sovereignty; Beijing heard, "two Chinas." This angered key PLA leaders, who advocated for the missile launches.

President Lee reset the collision course in July 1995 weeks before the first missile launches when he clarified that cross-Strait development and unification required Beijing to assure Taipei of peaceful international sovereignty. What would have happened if Lee had renounced de jure independence, as Ma did years later? The exercises probably would have gone as scheduled, given the humiliation of cancellation. However, the missile shots were an add-on to routine exercises, a preplanned collision that etched a red line for the future. The missiles could have been readied, then stood down on permanent alert. Instead, after the first missile firings, President Lee's verbal misfire about a Taiwan nuclear option sustained the collision until March 1996.

Now we compare China's economic-moral suasion to Taiwan's trilateral assurance. China's suasion sought to *Persuade* unification and Deter independence, while Taiwan's assurances sought to *Dissuade* forced unification and *Induce* international sovereignty. If we break this inter-action down into each side's opposed desired effects, there are two related questions we need to answer. How did China's *Persuasion* of unification compare to Taiwan's *Dissuasion* of forced unification? How did China's Deterrence of independence relate to Taiwan's *Inducement* of sovereignty? China's unification offer of local sovereignty conflicts with Taiwan's insistence on international sovereignty, which China equates to independence. Taiwan investment in China and deepening cultural ties can break through this impasse if China is patient enough to withhold overt threats. How?

During the Lee and Chen administrations, Taiwan's domestic *Persuasion* of its sovereign identity and China's cultural *Persuasion* that Taiwan was Chinese passed each other by. Beijing was not interested in exploring Taiwan's identity due to fears that this would promote independence. Likewise, Taiwan pushed back on Beijing's version of Han culture as a unifying bond because of Beijing's threats to use force. Until the presidency of Ma Ying-jeou, Taipei and Beijing alternately restricted contact even though Beijing's incentives for Taiwanese investment were in harmony with Taipei's cross-Strait assurances. President Ma's promotion of "Chinese culture with Taiwan characteristics," and of Taiwan as a region of China have led to greater mainland interest in Taiwan's social systems.[72] Intellectuals in China debate different models of political and economic development, and foreign policy.[73] With moderate leadership on both sides of the Strait and sustained mutual economic growth, the international-local sovereignty distinction could disappear into complexity. This is not yet a fait accompli, as China's creation of occupied territory in the disputed South China Sea undercut Kuomintang support in democratic Taiwan and contributed to the election of Tsai Ing-wen.

Our final pair of opposed lines of effect are China's demonstration of force and Taiwan's military *Security*. China signaled its exercises and missile launches in advance to dramatize the *Persuasive* and Deterrent effects of its dilemma. In response, consistent with its desired effects, Taiwan restrained its military reaction. The balancing role played by the United States buffered interaction between the two sides. Under these conditions all Taiwan's military could do was monitor the situation, avoid overreacting, and assure the public to stay calm. In case of an actual missile attack, Taiwan had no credible Defense against a determined effort. In addition, inflicting losses on dispersed mobile launchers protected by air defenses would be a risky operation. As an orchestrated exercise unopposed by Taiwan or the U.S., these two lines of effect intersected. After the crisis, they diverged. How?

Chinese force careened in a different direction, while Taiwanese security continued on its previous course. Each side still sought to counter the other in traditional combat scenarios, and China flexed its dilemma again in 1999 and 2003–2004 against Presidents Lee and Chen. China vied for more advantages than just improving military operations to *Coerce* Taiwan. Beijing seeks to contain Taiwan through regional control. Improved Chinese air and sea power demonstrated China's claims in combination with exclusive economic and air defense zones, as well as the continental shelf. The PLA developed a *yuanyang lanshu* (blue-water navy), and asserted *daguo* (big country) entitlement throughout the South China Sea, Taiwan Strait, and East China Sea. PLA Navy exercises displayed military power to *Induce* caution in rival claimants. Across from Taiwan, the PLA based over a thousand ballistic and cruise missiles on hundreds of mobile launchers and 500 PLA Air Force aircraft within striking distance. The PLA knows that in order to Deter Taiwan independence, it must Deter US intervention. In contrast, Taiwan military enhancements focused narrowly on how better to Defend against PLA operations.

Now that we have compared lines of effect, let's consider combinations of effects. Do the tools in each line of effect help bring about the other desired effects? The evidence reveals synergistic effects.

With regard to China's *Induced* dilemma on Taiwan, Beijing's refusal to consider international sovereignty for Taiwan in a unified China ensured that the tools used to isolate Taiwan and the tools used to offer benefits worked together. Both types *Persuaded* and Deterred, rather than canceling each other out. In theory, Taipei could not have sovereignty with economic benefits. A demonstration of force by Beijing could *Induce* this dilemma because the military action exaggerated both *Persuasion* and Deterrence. At an individual level, the combined effect ranges from annoyance to disorientation, hopelessness, and depression. At a systemic level, politics becomes unstable and economics volatile.

Three related political swings and economic shifts indicate that China's induced dilemma has been effective for Beijing. During the crisis, there was a patriotic resistance to China's demonstration against Taiwan. Then an anti-Kuomintang backlash led to the election of Democratic Progressive Party President Chen Shui-bian—an unintended consequence of China's *Inducement* operation. After two terms of Chen being shunned by Beijing, Taiwan voters elected pragmatic Kuomintang candidate Ma Ying-jeou. Investment during the crisis fell with stock prices, followed by a respectable 5 percent annual economic growth under President Chen until the global financial crisis (2007–2010). This, however, was half of China's total growth rate. With the reestablishment of cross-Strait political ties and acceleration of trade, exports to China helped fuel double-digit economic growth in Taiwan, which also became more dependent on the mainland market. It remains to be seen whether politics will follow economics to unification, or if Taipei's own combined effect will promote multiparty democracy on the mainland.

What about the tools that helped bring about each of Taiwan's intended $D_t\, D_s\, I\, S\, D_f$ effects? We consider each in turn.

Deterring China from attacking Taiwan depended upon one vital line of effect—assuring US policymakers to gain their support of Taiwan. This was an unofficial diplomatic, informational, economic, and social lobbying tool that advocated Taiwan democracy. It worked to *Persuade* targeted clients to maintain the US Deterrent against China Coercion.

Dissuading China from forcing unification on Taiwan was a product of two lines of effect—guarded globalization, as well as cross-Strait and domestic assurance. Globalization diversified economic growth and expanded political contacts, bypassing Beijing's diplomatic blockade. Broad engagement enabled Taiwan leaders to assert economic and political sovereignty. To satisfy Beijing's pressing interest in economic ties, Taipei tried to assure and regulate cross-Strait engagement. Assuring this required domestic support in Taiwan which was related to confidence in democracy. Taiwan's presidents also pushed a sovereign democratic Taiwan identity to strengthen domestic support against premature unification. Business owners just needed to know their investments would be safe, and they found ways to avoid cross-Strait restrictions. Separately, these lines of effect lacked what they provided when combined, and what the power of *Dissuasion* needed: international support, domestic confidence, and credible cross-Strait engagement.

Inducing China, like Deterring it, had only one supporting line of effect. The tool of Taiwan's identity, which had to be forged, also served as a moral basis from which to *Induce* China's acceptance of Taiwan's sovereignty. All of Taiwan's presidents have made the case for greater-than-local sovereignty; they just employed different words.

Securing Taiwan against threats was supported by two lines. Drills, sorties, and maneuvers demonstrated will and exercised capability to confront PLA operations directed at Taiwanese territory. Given Taiwan's dicey qualitative edge over China's numerous forces, providing such *Security* to citizens was limited to small-scale or short-lived crises and peacetime. In the absence of a sustained offensive capability to hold mainland targets at risk, US Deterrence was the only realistic provider of *Security*. *Securing* that effect for Taiwan was the job of the Taiwan lobby which would utilize its tools of assurance.

Defending against attack and economic control relied on two lines of effect. Military Defense required operations that could punish China's will to attack or deny its capability to inflict damage. As in the *Security* line of effect, Taiwan's tools for Defense were limited in terms of quantity and logistics, and relied on maintaining air, maritime, and ISR superiority. Achieving superiority against numerically superior PLA forces is no small task, requiring resilient integration of Taiwan's air, naval and ISR capabilities. With military expenditures comprising only 3 percent of GDP, Taiwan's military tools were restrained by political choice, not economic necessity. That left globalization to Defend against economic dependence on China, and the fear that China's mounting capital would devour key Taiwan industries. The Asian business hub plan, a tool to *Dissuade* China from forcing unification, was also supposed to Defend against China's economic largesse. It did not go as planned. Regulations protected inefficient industries and shunted capital to China. The Central Bank restricted currency flows into Taiwan to forestall inflation, but corporate and personal tax rates remained high. Defending against overintegration with China required an ability to compete with China. Taiwan needed to open its own market to attract and expand business.

What does our analysis of China's *Induced* dilemma (P D_t I) and Taiwan's *Induced* relations and *Secured* Defense (D_t Ds I S D_f) tell us about combined-effects strategy in general? We see that China's strategy included only three desired effects, supported by five lines of effect and five types of tools. All of the tools could generate all of the desired effects; they reinforced each other. Thus China's strategy was a resilient synthesis of power. In contrast, Taiwan's strategy of five desired effects supported by seven lines of effect used two multitask tools. Globalization served to *Dissuade* and Defend; and trilateral assurance meant to Deter, *Dissuade*, and *Induce*. These tools could not generate all of the desired effects. Taiwan's strategy combined more effects than China's, but it operated as a highly conditional strategy with little apparent synergy. To the extent domestic politics polarize as China territorializes around

Taiwan, in the aftermath of a first-ever China-Taiwan summit, Taiwan's dilemma is vulnerable to another *Inducement.*

This observation suggests that creating a competitive strategy is not a simply matter of adding more of the same types of tools in the way of combined-arms warfare. For China, the desired effects of *Persuasion* and Deterrence are brought about with tools which are less confrontational than diplomatic isolation, and less presumptuous than moral suasion. This also helps stay below the threshold of US intervention, in which case economic *Inducement* and United Nations activities are likely to be productive. For Taiwan, extended Deterrence via a lobbied US partnership can be made stronger with high-tech capabilities that both partners need. Instead of *Dissuasion* through separate lines of economic, political, and military engagement, an interagency process needs to combine Deterrence with *Dissuasion, Security,* and Defense. This requires using tools that reinforce one another and exploit Beijing intimidation, such as integrated missile defense that can be tested and improved during China's demonstrations of force. In addition, rather than trying to *Induce* acceptance of sovereignty with gestures toward independence, Taipei should practice independence through networks of international, domestic and cross-Strait relationships.

In this case of unsettled sovereignty, three theoretical implications of combined-effects strategy are apparent. First, synergistic effects can be constructed by selecting different tools for the same desired effects. Second, combinations of opposite effects can work well together, created by tools on targets in operations separate from combined arms. Third, combined effects can be varied by running lines of effect at different times and places. Sun Zi said as much 2,500 years ago in a reference to *shi, qi,* and *zheng:*

> There are no more than five cardinal notes, yet in combination, they produce more sounds than could possibly be heard; there are no more than five cardinal colors, yet in combination, they produce more shades and hues than could possibly be seen; there are no

more than five cardinal tastes, yet in combination, they produce more flavors than could possibly be tasted. For gaining strategic advantage (*shi*) in battle, there are no more than 'surprise' and 'straightforward' operations, yet in combination, they produce inexhaustible possibilities. 'Surprise' and 'straightforward' operations give rise to each other endlessly just as a ring is without a beginning and an end.[74]

Figure 6. Combined Effects Summary of *China's Unsettled Sovereignty*.

Combined Effects Summary of *China's Unsettled Sovereignty*

China

> **Strategy**   *P* D$_t$ *I*   Induced Dilemma
> (***Persuasion*-Deterrence-*Inducement***)
>
> **Lines of Effect**   Diplomatic Isolation to **Deter** Taiwan independence and ***Persuade*** unification
>
> Economic-Moral Suasion to **Deter** Taiwan independence and ***Persuade*** unification
>
> Demonstration of Force to ***Induce*** Taiwan's dilemma of responding to ***Persuasion-Deterrence***

Taiwan

> **Strategy**   D$_t$ *D$_s$ I S* D$_f$ Induced Relations and Secured Defense
> (Deterrence-***Dissuasion-Inducement-Security***-Defense)
>
> **Lines of Effect**   Guarded Globalization to **Deter** China diplomatic blockade, ***Induce*** other economic relationships and **Defend** Taiwan economic sovereignty
>
> Trilateral Assurance to ***Secure*** citizens' and US support for democracy, ***Dissuade*** China forced unification and retain US **Deterrence**
>
> Military Security to **Defend** against China operations

Notes

1. Suisheng Zhao, "Changing Leadership Perceptions," in *Across the Tai-wan Strait: Mainland China, Taiwan, and the 1995–1996 Crisis*, ed. Suisheng Zhao (NY: Routledge, 1999), 99–126, 100.

2. See www.taiwandocuments.org/mutual01.htm (accessed April 15, 2015).

3. Deng Xiaoping, "An Idea for the Peaceful Reunification of the Mainland and Taiwan" (26 June 1983) and "One Country, Two Systems" (22 June 1984) in *Selected Works of Deng Xiaoping*, Vol. 3, 1994, 27–28; 44–48. http://archive.org/stream/SelectedWorksOfDengXiaopingVol.3 (accessed April 15, 2015).

4. An idea proposed by KMT member Wei Yung in early 1995 was that Taiwan declare itself part of China in historical, cultural, economic, and geographic terms, but preserve its political independence internationally. "Confederation Predicted for Future PRC Ties," *Taipei Central News Agency*, 17 Jan 1995. http://infoweb.newsbank.com (accessed March 25, 2013).

5. "Former US Ambassador to Peking Decries 'Two-Systems' Formula," *Taiwan aujourd ' hui*, 26 June 1991. http://taiwanauj.nat.gov.tw/ct.asp?xItem=12451&CtNode=103 (accessed 7 November 2015).

6. Examples are "Taiwan Independence Activists Are Playing with Fire," 15 October 1991; "Plot to Split the Country and the Nation Will Never be Tolerated," 17 October 1991; "Farce Staged by Taiwan Independence Federation is Doomed to Tragic End," 21 October 1991; *Renmin Ribao Overseas Edition*. http://infoweb.newsbank.com (accessed March 22, 2013).

7. See Chien-min Chao and Chih-chia Hsu, "China Isolates Taiwan," in *China's Rise, Taiwan's Dilemma and International Peace*, ed. Edward Friedman (NY: Routledge, 2006), 41–67.

8. "CPC Military Attacks Foreign Affairs," *Cheng Ming* 1 July 1994. http://infoweb.newsbank.com (accessed March 25, 2013). The PLA was agitated over the US Navy's detainment of the Chinese freighter *Yinhae* in the Persian Gulf in September 1993.

9. See Fei-Ling Wang, "Self-Image and Strategic Intentions: National Con-fidence and Political Insecurity," in *In the Eyes of the Dragon: China Views the World*, eds. Yong-Deng and Fei-Ling Wang (Boulder, CO: Rowman & Littlefield, 1999), 21–45, 27.

10. "Suasion" conveys that assurance and intimidation are used to persuade and compel, respectively.

11. Ren Ruoen and Chen Kai, "China's GDP in U.S. Dollars Based on Purchasing Parity," Policy Research Working Paper 1415, The World Bank International Economics Department (January 1995), 2; *CIA World Fact Book*, 02771527 (1997), Johns Hopkins Libraries, EBSCO Host (accessed March 18, 2013).

12. Data from 1994-96. "Increased Trade Surplus with Mainland Cited," *Taipei Central News Agency*, 1 March 1996. http://infoweb.newsbank.com (accessed March 8, 2013).

13. "Column Views Use of Force Against Taiwan," *Hong Kong Hsin Pao*, 1 April 1994. http://infoweb.newsbank.com (accessed March 8, 2013).

14. Lee Teng-hui, *The Road to Democracy: Taiwan's Pursuit of Identity* (Tokyo: PHP Publishing Co,. 1999), 191–193, 125–127.

15. John Fuh-Sheng Hsieh and Emerson M. S. Niou, "Salient Issues in Taiwan's Electoral Politics," *Electoral Studies* 15 No. 2, (1996): 219–235, 222.

16. Paul H. B. Godwin, "Chinese Military Strategy Revised: Local and Limited War," in *Annals of the American Academy of Political and Social Science* 519 (January 1992): 191–201, 193.

17. Ichiro Numazaki, "The Export-Oriented Industrialization of Pacific Rim Nations and Their Presence in the Global Market," in *The Four Asian Tigers: Economic Development and the Global Economy*, ed. Eun Mee Kim (Bingley, UK: Emerald Group Publishing, 1998), 61–85, 82.

18. Murray A. Rubenstein, "Taiwan's Socioeconomic Modernization, 1971-1996," in *Taiwan: A New History*, ed. Murray A. Rubenstein (NY: M.E.Sharpe, 1999), 366–402, 375–376.

19. Ralph N. Clough, *Cooperation or Conflict in the Taiwan Strait?* (Oxford: Rowman & Littlefield, 1999), 70.

20. Richard C.K. Burdekin, YiJing Shen, and Hsin-Hui I.H. Whited, "Cross-strait linkage: historical perspective and empirical evidence," in *Economic Integration Across the Taiwan Strait: Global Perspectives*, ed. Peter C. Y. Chow (Northhampton, MS: Edward Elgar Publishing, 2013), 1–29.

21. Burdekin, Shen and Whited, "Cross-strait linkage," 9–19.

22. For the full text, see Wei Luo, "Internet Chinese Legal Research Center." http://law.wustl.edu/chinalaw/twguide.html (accessed March 4, 2013).

23. In 1991, the Democratic Progressive Party advocated a two-China model that included membership in the United Nations as a separate the Republic of China (1991).

24. See http://fapa.org/new/index (accessed March 19, 2013).

25. See http://www.wufi.org.tw/en/ (accessed March 19, 2013).

26. See http://www.taiwanembassy.org (accessed March 19, 2013).

27. Tsung Chi, "From the China Lobby to the Taiwan Lobby: Movers and Shakers in the U.S.-Taiwan-China Relationship," in *The Expanding Roles of Chinese-Americans in U.S.-China Relations: Trans-National Networks and Trans-Pacific Interactions*, eds. Peter H. Koehn and Xiao-Hung Yin (NY: M.E. Sharpe, 2002), 108–124.

28. See Michael D. Swaine, *Taiwan's National Security, Defense Policy, and Weapons Procurement Processes* (Santa Monica: RAND, 1999).

29. Arthur Shu-fan Ding and Alexander Chieh-Cheng Huang, "Taiwan's Military in the 21st Century: Redefinition and Reorganization," in *The Chinese Military in the 21st Century*, ed. Larry M. Wortzel (Carlisle, PA: Strategic Studies Institute, 1999), 253–288.

30. For examples see "The Looming Taiwan Fighter Gap," US-Taiwan Business Council paper, 2012). http://www.us taiwan.org/reports/2012_the_looming_taiwan_fighter_gap.pdf); http://www.defenseindustrydaily.com/full-steam-ahead-for-taiwan-frigate-corruption-investigation-01546/ (accessed February 20, 2013).

31. *The Papers of Dwight David Eisenhower, The Presidency: Keeping the Peace, Vol. 19, Part V: Forcing the President's Hand, June 1958–October 1958* (Washington, DC: The Johns Hopkins University Press, 2008), 1093.

32. *The Papers of Dwight David Eisenhower, The Presidency: Keeping the Peace Vol. 19, Part V*, 851; 1131; Dwight D. Eisenhower, *Waging Peace: 1956–1961* (NY: Doubleday & Co., 1965), 294–295.

33. Min Gyo Koo, *Island Disputes and Maritime Regime Building in East Asia: Between a Rock and a Hard Place* (NY: Springer, 2009), 140.

34. Text of the joint communiqués may be found on the Embassy of the People's Republic of China in the United States of America website: http://www.china-embassy.org/eng/ (accessed February 15, 2013).

35. "United States Code, Title 22, Foreign Relations and Intercourse, Chapter 48 – Taiwan," *Taiwan Documents Project*, http://www.taiwandocuments.org/tra01.htm (accessed February 15, 2013).

36. "Joint Communique of the United States of America and the People's Republic of China, August 17th, 1982," *Taiwan Documents Project.* http://www.taiwandocuments.org/communique03.htm (accessed February 15, 2013).

37. "The 'Six Assurances' to Taiwan, July 1982," *Taiwan Documents Project.* http://www.taiwandocuments.org/assurances.htm (accessed February 15, 2013).

38. Jiang Zemin, "Continuing to Strive for the Reunification of China," in *The People's Daily Online,* 26 September 2007. http://english.people.com. cn/90002/92080/92129/6271625.html (accessed February 12, 2013).

39. Taiwan President Lee Teng-hui's "Six Point" Response, April 8, 1995. http://csis.org/files/media/csis/programs/taiwan/timeline/sums/ timeline_docs/CSI_19950408.htm.

40. *The Military Balance* 94 Issue 1 (London: International Institute for Strategic Studies, 1994), 168.

41. Andrew Scobell, *China's Use of Military Force: Beyond the Great Wall and the Long March* (Cambridge: Cambridge University Press, 2003), Kindle e-book location 2433 of 4355; Michael D. Swaine, *The Role of the Chinese Military in National Security Policymaking* (Santa Monica: RAND, 1998), 15.

42. "Reportage Covers Mainland Military Exercise," *Hong Kong Lien Ho Pao,* 3 July 1995. http://infoweb.newsbank.com (accessed July 3, 2015).

43. John Wilson Lewis and Xue Litai, *Imagined Enemies: China Prepares for Uncertain War* (Stanford: Stanford University Press, 2006), 196.

44. See *Modernizing China's Military Progress, Problems, and Prospects* by David L. Shambaugh (Berkeley: University of California Press, 2002).

45. "Coverage of Li's Comments on Nuclear Program. Li Denies Development," *Taiwan Central News Agency,* 1 August 1995. http:// infoweb.newsbank.com (accessed July 3, 2015).

46. "Foreign Investment Tops $1.1b Jan-Jul, and Investment Abroad Declines Jan-Jul," *Taipei Central News Agency,* 9 August 1995. http://infoweb. newsbank.com (accessed July 3, 2015).

47. "Li: Wargames Having Impact on Residents," *Taiwan Central News Agency,* 1 December 1995. http:// infoweb.newsbank.com (accessed July 3, 2015).

48. "Beijing Said Planning Large Military Exercises," *Tzu-Li Wan Pao,* 5 January 1996. http://infoweb.newsbank.com (accessed July 3d, 2015).

49. "SEF Chairman Urges 'One-China' Policy Re-iteration, *Taipei Central News Agency,* 4 March 1996. http://infoweb.newsbank.com (accessed July 4, 2015).

50. Interview with former American official, July 2012.

51. "PRC: PLA 'Operational Plan' for Attack on Taiwan Highlighted, Expert Indicates that Taiwan Strait is not Impenetrable; PLA Strengthens

its Transport Capacity," *Wen Wei Po,* 20 March 1996. http://infoweb. newsbank.com (accessed July 4, 2015).

52. "Taiwan: Experts Urge Cross-Strait Dialogue after Elections," *Taipei Central News Agency,* 21 March 1996. http://infoweb.newsbank.com (accessed March 18, 2013).

53. "Beijing's War Games Cast Clouds on Export Prospects," *Taipei Central News Agency,* 20 March 1996. http://infoweb.newsbank.com (accessed March 18, 2013).

54. Shirley A. Kan, "China/Taiwan: Evolution of the 'One-China' Policy-Key Statements from Washington, Beijing, and Taipei," *CRS Report for Congress* RL 30341, 24 June 2011, 61.

55. Erik Eckholm, "China Army Reviews Threat Against Taiwan Separation," 7 March 200. *The New York Times.* http://www.nytimes.com/2000/03 /07/world/china-army-renews-threat-against-taiwan-separatism.html (accessed January 10, 2016).

56. *The Military Balance* 112 Issue 1 (London: International Institute for Strategic Studies, 2012), 210–216.

57. Lewis and Xue, *Imagined Enemies,* 212–213.

58. David Shambaugh, *Modernizing China's Military: Programs, Problems, and Prospects* (Berkeley: University of California Press, 2002), 311–327.

59. An overview may be found in Mikhail Barabanov, Vasiliy Kashin, and Konstantin Makienko, *Shooting Star: China's Military Machine in the 21st Century* (Minneapolis: East View Press, 2012), 1–48.

60. Chen's speech promised to not declare independence, not change the nation's title, not advocate that state-to-state be included in the Constitution, not promote a referendum regarding independence or unification, and not abolish the Guidelines for National Unification and the National Unification Council.

61. Richard C. Bush, *Untying the Knot: Making Peace in the Taiwan Strait* (Washington, DC: The Brookings Institution, 2005), 64.

62. Ibid., 69–71.

63. Weixing Hu, "Explaining Change and Stability in Cross-Strait Relations: a punctuated equilibrium model," in *Journal of Contemporary China* 21 Issue 78: 933–953, 944.

64. See Phillip C. Saunders, Christopher D. Yung, Michael Swaine, and Andrew Nien-Dzu Yang, eds., *The Chinese Navy: Expanding Capabilities, Evolving Roles* (Washington, DC: National University Press, 2011).

65. See Katharine Houreld, "China and Pakistan launch economic corridor plan worth $46 billion," *Reuters* 20 April 2015. http://www.reuters.

com/article/2015/04/20/us-pakistan-china-idUSKBN0NA12T20150420; and David Gosset, "China's Grand Strategy: The New Silk Road," *The World Post*, 8 January 2015. http://www.huffingtonpost.com/david-gosset/chinas-grand-strategy-the_b_6433434.html.

66. See Zhang Xuliang, ed., *The Science of Campaigns* (Beijing: National Defense University Press, 2006), 639, 642, 656.

67. Ernest C. Bower, "China Reveals its Hand on ASEAN in Phnom Penh," *Center for Strategic and International Studies*, 19 July 2012. http://csis.org/publication/china-reveals-its-hand-sean-phnom-penh.

68. Xi Jinping's "Chinese dream" calls for the revival of a Chinese nation as a world power. See "Full text: China's new party chief Xi Jinping's speech," *BBC*. http://www.bbc.com/news/world-asia-china-20338586 (accessed September 14, 2015).

69. Kung Phoak, "Why ASEAN should embrace Chinese initiatives," *East Asia Forum*. www.eastasiaforum.org/2015/10/01/why-asean-should-embrace-chinese-initiatives/.

70. Charles Hutzler and Jake Maxwell Watts, "China's Xi Jinping and Taiwan's Ma Ying-jeou Meet in Singapore," 8 November 2015, *The Wall Street Journal*. http://www.wsj.com/articles/china-s-xi-jinping-and-taiwan-s-ma-ying-jeou-meet-in-singapore-1446880724 (accessed November 15, 2015).

71. On Taiwan trade activism in Latin America, see Antoni Estevadeordal, Masahiro Kawai, and Ganeshan Wignaraja, *New Frontiers in Asia-Latin America Integration: Trade Facilitation, Production Networks, and FTAs* (London: Sage Publications, 2014). On DPP--KMT competition that moderates national identity, see Cal Clark, "Taiwan Enters Troubled Waters: The Elective Presidency of Lee Teng Hui and Chen Shui-bian," in *Taiwan: A New History*, ed. Murray A. Rubinstein (NY: M.E. Sharpe, 2007), 496–535.

72. Jens Damm, "Multiculturalism in Taiwan and the Influence of Europe," in *European Perspectives on Taiwan*, eds. Jens Damm and Paul Lim, (Weisbaden: Springer VS, 2012), 84–106, esp. 87.

73. See Leonard's review of the "New Left" and "New Right" among intellectual elites: Mark Leonard, *What does the new China think?* in China 3.0, ed., Mark Leonard (London: European Council on Foreign Relations Policy Report, November 2012), ecfr.eu, 9–24.

74. Sun-Tzu, *The Art of Warfare*, 119–120.

CHAPTER 4

KOREAN SECURITY CULTURE

For two thousand years, Koreans have dealt with prying neighbors through strategies of cooperation and confrontation. Predatory powers are fixtures in this security environment where peninsular alignment is pivotal to Pacific stability and the global balance of power. One might expect Korean security culture to reflect that of China, but there are key differences. There is scant self-regard for being the center of the civilized world. Korean civilization, rich in its own right, developed in between the vortices of expansionist empires and strong nation-states. Consequently, there is not a longstanding expectation of being the dominant power in the region. Instead, Korean rulers had to manage multiple centers of power to survive as sovereigns. Repeatedly, the locally woven fabric of Korean society was stretched, torn, and repaired in response to foreign occupiers. Depending on the situation, moral behavior involved pragmatic acquiescence, national negligence, fierce independence, or combinations thereof. As a result, the peninsula and outlying islands have proven to be contentious ground among the Koreas, China, Japan and western powers.

In describing the sensible practice of obliging a major power, the term *sadaejuui* (사대주의 in phonetic Korean, 事大主義 in ideographic Chinese) is popularly evoked, often derisively.[1] Its contemporary use usually portrays condescending foreign attitudes toward Koreans. Dating back to Korean kingdoms as tributaries to China, the connotation is that of being controlled, after giving in. In late-nineteenth-century Chosŏn, before Japan defeated China in the Sino-Japanese War, the Sadae ("main power") Party was pro-China, opposed by the reformist, pro-Japan Kaehwa ("enlightenment") Party. Successfully managing the influence of a foreign power meant aligning with the interests of another. This utilitarian ethic clashes with other societal beliefs, from neo-Confucianism and religious principles to community-based populism. Pride in national autonomy stirs intense debates. Which power ought to be confronted, and which accommodated? Which factions and individuals can be trusted, for how long, and under what conditions? How can independence be reconciled with resented external powers and alliance interests? Today, Korean *juche* (self-reliance) refracts through different political systems, north and south. In North Korea, the ideological term *juche* is mandated; in South Korea, *jagileul uijihaneun* (depending on oneself) and other freely constructed concepts of reliance are used. In both regimes, *sadaejuui* characterizes a fundamental practice of Korean security.

Not surprisingly, Korean cultural narratives emphasize virtues of loyalty, resolve, and just cause. Figurative analogies describe human surroundings as interrelated opposites, such as *um* ("light, hot"; yin in Chinese) and *yang* ("dark, cold"). Leaders are expected to accept the immutable but shape the changeable. Confrontation is taken to be natural, a complement to cooperation as a way to achieve harmony. That ideal has been a continuous struggle given the 900-odd invasions suffered by Koreans during their two-thousand-year history.[2] A cultivated heritage of having borne the brunt of injustices from outsiders reinforces a general societal awareness of vulnerability. Korean ancestry and *minjok* ("ethnic nation") identity are constructed from a strong and just legendary founder, King Tan'gun, mythical equivalent to China's Emperor Qin Shih Huang-di. *Minjung* ("the people") provides another image of populist struggles against oppression.[3] These traditions undergird remarkable social strength, common national identity, and endurance.

WHAT IS THE ROLE OF CONFRONTATION AND COOPERATION IN SECURITY?

Traditionally, Korean confrontation merged with cooperation to counter territorial and existential threats. To appreciate this pattern, we consider two formative experiences: China's imperial control and Japan's colonial occupation.

Chinese invasions date back to the Han dynasty in 109 BCE, a period of aggressive expansion following the Qin dynasty's unification of the Warring States (221 BCE).[4] By then, Korea was under the rule of Chinese commanderies (Lo-lang, Chen-fan, Lin-tun). Organized resistance led to the rise of confederated states and the Three Kingdoms—old Silla (57 BCE–668), Koguryo (37 BCE–668), and Paekche (18 BCE–660).[5] The peninsula's first unified dynasty took root in 676 when unified Silla, having cooperated with Tang China to eliminate rivals Koguryo and Paekche, defeated the Tang. This prevented outright annexation, as the Tang had turned on Silla to compel and coerce loyalty to China's "celestial army."[6]

As long as unified Silla (668–935) and successor dynasties recognized the Middle Kingdom's higher status and authority, Korean kings administered domestic affairs. The nobility embraced Chinese civilization for symbolic and practical reasons, including the enhancement of the royalty's moral authority. Buddhism added spiritual cohesion and state legitimacy. Confucianism constructed a social ethic and merit-based bureaucracy. The Chinese written language integrated recorded ideas (the indigenous Hangul alphabet was developed in 1446). As a result, China exerted indirect control, enhanced by cultural affinity.

Korean rulers prized independence, prestige, and wealth as they embraced the very culture and commerce that invited Chinese access. When China's authority weakened, Korean confrontation became more assertive—a Silla king who, during a time of disunity in China, dared to claim equal imperial status by entitling his own reign as an independent era.[7] On territorial issues, Koguryo and Silla confronted China directly, winning signal battlefield victories. But it was Sillan-Chinese cooperation that eliminated Koguryo and Paekche, but reduced China's presence. By comparison, Paekche ties with the Yamato kingdom (present-day Japan) were limited, gaining temporary military assistance to reduce Sillan influence along the coast. Silla's eventual defeat of China on the peninsula consolidated a Korean unification that remained subject to the influence of proximate powers.[8]

The Three Kingdoms period illustrates the ancient art of combining confrontation and cooperation to wage warfare against foreign intervention:[9] (1) the king of Silla resumes the dispatch of tribute missions to China's southern emperor, while ignoring the northern emperor, who supports rival Koguryo, in order to enhance his capability to attack Koguryo; (2) Koguryo defends against successive Chinese invasions by allying with Paekche against rising Silla, but fails to persuade nomadic tribes to weaken Silla-allied China; this enables Silla to conquer Paekche and Koguryo; (3) China's eastern Jin emperor confers the title of "Supreme Commander and King" upon the Paekche ruler, assuring the latter of military support against rival kingdoms, until a dynastic change realigns China's obligations; (4) the king of Paekche dispatches his son to Japan as a court hostage to persuade military aid against rival Korean kingdoms and China.

Successors to unified Silla—Koryŏ (935–1392) and Chosŏn (1392–1910) —also adopted aspects of Chinese culture, gaining legitimacy from Confucian and Buddhist obligations and loyalties. Sino-Korean trade and cultural ties increased during China's Northern and Southern Song dynasties (960–1279) and the nomadic Khitan's Liao dynasty (907–1125; its empire situated north of unified Korea). When Jurchen nomads conquered the Khitan in 1126, Koryŏ cut ties with the Song and paid off the nearby Jurchen Jin dynasty (1115–1234).

In 1231, the Mongol empire rode over Song and Jin into Koryŏ. Its Yuan dynasty (1279–1368) generated new extremes of confrontation and cooperation. Koryŏ's refusals to pay humiliating tribute triggered brutal punishments. Mongol conquerors permitted the Koryŏ court at Kaesong to rule, but coerced its subjects into invasions of Japan.[10] The Yuan also induced Koryŏ royalty and officials to live in Beijing— a method of cultural control. For Koryŏ, this provided opportunities to expand linkages with Chinese literati and acquire technology, including new methods of warfare.[11] The moral cost to Korean society was high. Marriage alliances enriched a few local elites while enslaving many more. Finally in 1356, the Koryŏ king was able to subvert Mongol control when a "fundamentalist Confucian moral-political revolution"[12] in China fragmented Yuan power. Before the Ming dynasty (1368–1910) could conquer Manchuria, the Koryŏ court commanded General Yi Song-gye to reclaim it. Instead, he marched on Kaesong to establish his own lineage in present-day Seoul. Thus began the Chosŏn dynasty (1368–1910).[13]

Chosŏn rulers leveraged their tributary status with the self-righteous Ming to challenge local tribes, warlords and pirates.[14] Domestic reforms that enforced Confucian morality also brought more trade. Against northern nomadic threats, Chosŏn kings colonized borders, launched punitive raids, and provided assurances of economic and military opportunities. From newly unified Japan, Chosŏn faced large, disciplined, and well-equipped armies. In 1592 and 1597, two massive invasions were eventually repulsed by a collection of Chosŏn troops, armored "turtle boats" (kobukson), monk and peasant-populated "righteous militias" (uibyong),[15] and hundreds of thousands of Confucian-obligated Ming soldiers.

Japan's invasions became a marker of Korean resilience—the willpower, adaptability, and persistence to overcome foreign threats. Bearing hardship became a symbol of cultural strength and national survival. The concept of Korean Han, for instance, describes a feeling of being oppressed, an injustice that inspires righteous reactions. A commonly recognized quotation is from Admiral Yi Sun-si, who outnumbered in 1597 by Japanese naval forces and ordered by King Seon-jo to disengage, declared:

"Your highness, I still have twelve battleships." Although Chosŏn had more advanced naval technology at the time compared to Japan's qualitative edge in ground forces, Korean narratives underscore the indomitable character of Korean will. Nearly ignored is the significant military support from China, the product of an unequal relationship.

After defending Chosŏn against Japan, Ming troops returned to China. Sino-Korean ties tightened, only to be disrupted by the next mainpower shift. Manchu attacks defeated the overextended Ming forces and advanced on Beijing. As Manchu victories mounted, the Ming court requested Chosŏn assistance in defending embattled garrisons on the Sino-Korean frontier. This presented an ethical choice that split the Korean court. Confucian loyalty to the Ming was so strong that King Gwanghaegun's reasonable order to surrender to Manchus who had overwhelmed Chinese defenses led to his overthrow.[16] The subsequent Manchu invasion of Korea coerced Chosŏn to submit to the new Qing dynasty (1644–1911).

The Koreans encountered indirect Chinese control based on their acceptance of China's cultural sovereignty. The insidious strategy produced dual effects of division and loyalty. Forward-deployed Chinese troops alternately threatened and protected Korean rivals, keeping the peninsula divided. Beijing also cultivated Korean compliance with its world order as a way to neutralize threats. The Confucian Ming could pull this off, but not the Manchu Qing, whom Korean elites agreed were uncivilized. When cultural submission was obtained, Chinese strategy formed a grand dilemma, welding Korean confrontation and cooperation into cooptation.

This military-cultural effect on Korean courts was evident during power surges and transitions in China. When anti-Buddhist Confucianism arose in China, the Korean ruling class either realigned its loyalties to the middle kingdom's new priorities, or lost out.[17] The rise of influential movements and shifts in Chinese court alliances did not need to be obvious because ambiguity levied conflicting demands on the Korean court. The core choice was clear: acknowledge China's supreme status, or be regarded as a threat. From the perspective of a fractious peninsula situated on the eastern edge of an aggressive empire, obeisance kept Chinese soldiers in their forts.

In the nineteenth century, the Yi dynasty balanced competing factions, confronting then-accommodating foreign powers. Fleeting aggregates of domestic resistance formed, the largest being the peasant-based Tonghak ("eastern learning") movement. Merchants, missionaries, and warships also appeared, igniting antiforeign sentiment. The murder of French missionaries led to a punitive French expedition in 1866 that was repulsed. The same year the merchant vessel *USS Sherman* was destroyed and its crew killed, triggering a punitive American expedition in 1871. By 1875, the Chosŏn court actively sought Chinese protection.[18] Japanese demands for open ports came next.

The Japan navy ship *Unyō* provoked and then counterattacked Ganghwa Island, coercing treaty terms. Chosŏn received nominal independence; Japan gained extraterritoriality along with commercial and trading rights.[19] Korean politics split between the Sadae and Kaehwa parties. Chinese troops crushed a pro-Japan coup attempt in 1884.[20] Ten years later with the Tonghak Rebellion in full swing, Seoul requested Chinese troops. Tokyo responded with its own expedition, beginning the Sino-Japanese War (1894–1895). Japan's prompt victory sent King Gojong to the Russian legation for refuge.

Seoul's sway toward Moscow was stopped by Japan's defeat of Russia (1904–1905). The Japanese Army occupied Seoul and advanced northward; the Japanese navy destroyed Russian seapower in the Korea Strait near Tsushima. US intervention against Japan was prevented by a secret agreement between Prime Minister Katsura Tarō and President William Howard Taft. Each tolerated the other's respective security interests in Chosŏn and the Philippines. Two months later, Chosŏn became a protectorate of Japan in the Treaty of Portsmouth (September 1905). King Gojong was forced to abdicate in 1907. Any independent status that remained was lost in 1910 when Japan annexed Chosŏn, thereby forcing King Sunjong's abdication.

Korean accommodation of and resistance to Japan were mixed. Korean "advisors" to the Japanese Governor-General's Central Council were selected by its Japanese president and councilors and were pressed to provide information about dissidents. Meanwhile "righteous armies" (*uigunbu*) attacked Japanese bases and authorities. Korean and Chinese guerrillas fought Japanese forces in Manchuria. Exiles in Shanghai, Manchuria, and the United States advocated self-determination, raised funds, and organized anti-Japanese demonstrations. As Chosŏn citizens were banned from speaking Korean, educators and agitators taught nationalism in private schools and study halls, openly so overseas. Overt resistance at home was high risk. By Japanese accounts, over 7,000 Koreans were killed during the March 1, 1919, independence movement demonstrations. Watchful authorities suppressed dissident ideas and incentivized pro-Japanese history, literature, and art.

With the end of Japan's colonization of Korea in 1945, cooperation with Japanese became openly disdained. In North and South Korea, interpretations of history and literature during the Japanese occupation claimed that popular opposition to Japanese officials was widespread. Social shame was heaped upon those who had collaborated with authorities.

There are ample contemporary indicators of the high value placed on a zero-sum, "strong," character against threats. Consider the place of willpower in national narratives. In North Korea, this includes a Kim personality cult and *juche*-style of self-reliance that deifies the leader's will and demands strict loyalty from the populace; invective rhetoric and threats in Korean People's Army and Korean Workers' Party propaganda; verbal escalation in negotiations with US and ROK counterparts;[21] and references to intellectual warfare—"wars of brains" (*dunoejeon*) and "wars of wisdom" (*jihyejeon*).[22] In South Korea, a dominant will manifests itself in a parallel moderate universe: personality-centered politics that reward strong leaders who demonstrate mental toughness and populism—the

Army Capital Maeng Ho ("brave tiger") Division's fearsome reputation in Vietnam (1965–1973), the steadfastness of South Korean officials facing hyperbolic North Korean counterparts, and the game of wits and passion played by student demonstrators and national police around military bases with US forces.[23]

Principled character is an enduring feature of Korean responses to aggression, but its effectiveness depends on competence in managing main power relationships. Certainly the North's antiforeign *juche* autarky and military brutality contrast with the South's interdependence and adherence to international norms. Despite these important differences, each state selects tools to turn constraints into advantages. Threats to both Koreas are perceived as emanating from intrusive dominant neighbors, reinforced by territorial issues: Japan and South Korea claim South Korean–occupied Dokdo (Takeshima, in Japan); China and North Korea claim North Korean–occupied portions of former Koguryo as exclusive heritage; North and South Korea contest the maritime boundary in the West Sea (the Yellow Sea, in China and Japan), and North Korea claims all of South Korea. Koreans are inclined to assess the cooperative and confrontational nature of main powers with resolute pragmatism. The United States is a temporary villain at times but is not seen as a permanent threat.

WHAT IS THE NATURE AND ASSESSMENT OF THE THREAT?

Korean leaders have judged threats from a practical and moral perspective that values sovereignty and willpower in righteous confrontation and cooperation with main powers. Responses to Chinese intimidation eked out variable-sum "protection." By accepting China's authority, Korean courts enhanced their own sovereignty over domestic rivals. In doing so, the Chinese world order became an acquired value, promising relative security. Particularly during the Ming dynasty, Confucian duties and obligations reinforced reciprocal respect and harmony, which maintained the social hierarchy. Add the coercive potential of Chinese troops, and a power-wise king stayed within the celestial Emperor's induced stability. The overall effect on threat assessment was transformational. Acceptance of Chinese cultural primacy by the Korean elite converted intimidation into loyalty.

In contrast, Japan's intervention was despised as a cultural threat. Meiji Japan's role in undermining the Chosŏn court and instigating the Sino-Japanese War radicalized the population. Subsequent colonization seeded bitter anti-Japanese sentiment. From a Korean perspective, the forty-year occupation was a replay of Japanese invasions during the 1590s.[24] Tokyo's handling of its "Korea problem" stole sovereignty, expropriated land and natural resources, controlled commerce and industry, and infused a deprecating historiography that suppressed a Korean identity.

For Korean elites and locals who collaborated with Japanese authorities, the threat provided variable-sum costs and benefits. At the time, it was unclear how long Japan's occupation would last and whether an independent Chosŏn would ever exist. This seemed to change in 1945. After the Soviet Red Army in North Korea and US Army in South Korea supplanted the Imperial Japanese Army, anti-Japanese narratives emerged with a vengeance. For a while, confronting Japan meant not cooperating with Japanese businesses or policies.

Koreans installed by the Soviet Union as leaders in the North, most notably Kim Il-sung, were touted as fearless guerrillas who fought against morally inferior Japanese. The fact that Kim fought for the Soviet army in northeastern China was omitted. The Korean War failed to unify the peninsula but served as a touchstone to boost Kim's influence, both domestically and toward China and the Soviet Union. North Korean defectors recount the use of imaginative nationalist stories to boost popular respect and public adoration of Kim Il-sung and his two succes-sors, regardless of historical accuracy:[25]

> In any event, if it is true that the North's Kim Il-song participated in partisan [activities], it is right to revere him. Judging from the fact that the real Kim Il-sung has not appeared, he could have

been an insignificant figure or it could have been an alias. What difference does it make, though, whether or not he is a true figure.

South Korea's founding political figures, Presidents Syngman Rhee and Park Chung-hee, were exiled to the United States and enrolled in Japan's Manchukuo Imperial Army respectively.[26] The absence of home-grown electable politicians is understandable given the moral rejection of Japanese authority. Historian Bruce Cumings captures this unvirtuous facet of *sadaejuui* as "treacherous collaboration," [27] without regarding it as a realistic national interest. At the presidential level, the moral authority deficit was handled by emphasizing Korea's security predicament, Rhee's arrest and imprisonment for sedition by colonial authorities, and Park's service in the South Korean military. Besides manufacturing anti-Japanese and anti-north/south credentials, Korean public diplomacy portrayed founding national leaders as stalwarts against the Japanese threat. In North-South meetings, each side tries to outdo the other in demonstrating their hatred for Japan.

Frequent visitors to Pyongyang have mentioned that North Korean officials remind them of their geostrategic reality: "keep those far away close, and those close to you keep at a distance."[28] At the time, the message was that North Korea desired US relations to counter the presence of China and Russia. The rise of South Korean economic power and alliance with the United States reinforces North Korean threat perceptions. It also presents Pyongyang opportunities to influence its relationship with China. So even as northern narratives refute the fact of its 1950 invasion that brought US and UN forces into South Korea, official messaging occasionally acknowledges the US presence as useful. Given stark differences in political, economic, and military conditions between North and South Korea, this common ground is easily overlooked.

So it should not be surprising that both Koreas seek to create influence through a relationship with a main power. We should expect to see shaping operations in relationships with the potential for undesirable effects. North Korean leaders mitigate US-led sanctions against it by garnering aid from Beijing, aware that China can devour North Korean autonomy. South Korea counters China's opposition to its reunification efforts by seeking US diplomatic support, knowing that a divergent ROK-U.S. position can undermine this goal.[29] A Korean proverb describes this vulnerability: "when whales fight, the shrimp's back is broken." For northerners and southerners, the classic question of security is *how can the shrimp survive among whales?*

The prevailing answers to this challenge have formed three patterns of main power management: (1) confronting a great power with the cooperation of a main power, meeting the latter's expectation of loyalty; (2) confronting and cooperating with a main power at the same time, expanding and defending territory; and (3) cooperating with more than one main power, especially during power transitions. We note that local rule on the Korean peninsula strengthened during periods of Chinese weakness. The 269-year interval between the Han (206 BCE–220 AD) and Sui (589–618) dynasties is proudly regarded as one of indigenous cultural development.

Among these patterns, unified Korea alternated among three strategic-cultural roles: tributary state, independent power, and colony. As tributaries to several dynasties, Koryŏ and Chosŏn were expected to conform to imperial priorities in exchange for military support and trade. As an independent power, Koryŏ exacted tribute from Jurchen tribes and the Khitan's Liao dynasty in northeastern China.[30] Chosŏn began the twentieth century as a colony of Japan.

These roles persisted as cultural images in the post–World War II period. The rise of authoritarianism in the North and democracy in the South led to different manipulations of rival powers. At the same time, both Koreas asserted a strong identity—*juche* in the North, and variants of global interdependence in the South. Kim Il-sung's nearly successful unification in 1950 illustrates the importance of outside support. The opportunity to strike was at hand—US Secretary of State Dean Acheson had declared Korea outside the US defense perimeter in January that year. Between then and the attack, Kim manipulated approvals from Joseph Stalin and Mao Zedong.[31] North Korean foreign policy targeted relations with China and the Soviet Union, gaining support while asserting independence from both. President Harry Truman's intervention against North Korea's invasion contrasted to Stalin's abandonment of it. During the conflict and for a decade thereafter, North Korea edged toward China. In the midst of China's Cultural Revolution (1966–1976) as Maoists criticized Pyongyang's bourgeois-style industrialization, Kim leaned toward Moscow. This posture stood through Deng Xiaoping's reforms until the Soviet Union's disintegration in 1991. Since then, China has been North Korea's only significant provider of aid. Despite assertions of self-reliance, without China's support North Korea would have to reinvent itself to survive.

While Pyongyang handled rival Chinese and Russian interests, Seoul managed US relations, also with Sillan skill. South Korean administrations redirected national history,[32] stretching American security assurances to influence the relationship. A few presidential examples of the latter underscore this aspect of Korean security culture.

During armistice talks in 1953, Syngman Rhee refused participation and released North Korean prisoners of war to compel US military aid.[33] In the 1970's Park Chung-hee attempted to acquire nuclear weapons, compelling Jimmy Carter to reverse his planned withdrawal of US forces from South Korea. He increased ROK military influence as the United Nations Command transferred operational control to Combined Forces Command.[34] In 1980, Chun Doo-hwan crushed student protests in Kwangju, compelling tacit support from the Carter administration. By 1994, Roh Tae-woo had persuaded Bill Clinton to relinquish US peacetime command of ROK forces. In 1997, Kim Young-sam broke through U.S.-North Korean bilateral negotiations with Four-Party Talks.[35] Kim Dae-jung's "Sunshine Policy" led to a summit in 2000 that countered George W. Bush's hardline. Roh Moo-hyun exploited the deaths of two South Korean school girls run over by a US armored vehicle to gain the presidency in 2003.[36] His successor Lee Myung-bak propounded "Global Korea" multilateralism and persuaded Barack Obama to transfer wartime control of ROK-U.S. forces to South Korea in 2015. Park Geun-hye's policies focus on rebuilding main power relationships, beginning with the U.S., then China, as levers against Japan.

Is Confrontation Effective in Achieving Outcomes and Eliminating Threats?

Korean leaders have employed limited force with other tools of influence to achieve political objectives. To fairly judge the effectiveness of confrontation, we need to recognize that diplomatic, informational, military, economic, and social actions all play confrontational and cooperative roles relative to desired effects. Generally, eliminating threats through confrontation alone has not been considered to be a realistic goal. For autocratic North Korea, that is not even desirable.

Under the influence of China and Japan, Korean confrontation was restrained and effective. Silla, Paekche, and Koguryo survived as relatively weak kingdoms through the judicious use of force. Yet, when Silla allied with China against Paekche and Koguryo, the latter two were eliminated. As we shall see in the case ahead, North Korea was able to develop nuclear weapons by gaining China's diplomatic and economic support and neutralizing that of the United States.

The consequential miscalculations have been about great power involvement. In this regard, Silla outmaneuvered Koguryo and Paekche. Kim Il-sung's invasion of South Korea in 1950 lined up Chinese and Soviet approval for a campaign confined to the peninsula, but failed to anticipate the US military response. Since then, the Cold War–style sponsorship of North and South Korea by main powers has deterred large-scale violence on the peninsula. Small-scale violence, however, helps legitimize the Kim dynasty in the North, and used to play a similar role for the military-dominated regimes of the pre-democratic South. At the same time, North and South Korean leaders typically agree that the involvement of larger powers is an obstacle to national reconciliation.[37]

To fathom how Korean rulers regarded the effectiveness of confrontation, we make three assumptions. First, preplanned use of force is a decision made at the highest level. This acknowledges the cultural and political role of vertical authority in these matters and permits us to judge strategic intent. Second, Korean use-of-force decisions take into account the risk of weakening relations with a main power—China, the United States, Russia, and Japan. This recognizes the importance of maintaining external power relationships filled with diplomatic, military, and economic ties. Third, justifiable responses to uses of force can sustain cycles of reprisal. Mutually mounting Han may induce escalation irrespective of great power involvement.

Considering North Korea's methods against American and South Korean targets since the armistice, we infer connections among domestic power arrangements and the external environment. North Korean goals have been to consolidate domestic support; demonstrate firm will and freedom to act; instill urgency, recklessness, and unpredictability; convey that North Korea does not care about what other powers think; seize opportunities for revenge; deter US and South Korean retaliation; and exploit legal vulnerabilities.[38] These desired effects are consistent with the assumption that main powers are interested in a relationship with North Korea. When Pyongyang perceives that vulnerability to be lacking, a forceful demonstration attracts attention.

Based on the following major episodes of North Korean aggression, we conclude: (a) North Korean attacks are designed to divide US and South Korean loyalties; (b) North Korean practices do not discriminate between non-North Korean military and civilian targets; (c) a twenty-year period of frequent North Korean attacks ending in 1987[39] was a deliberate campaign to combine force with political and economic actions. These coincided with the discovery of North Korean tunnels under the demilitarized zone (DMZ) that protruded into South Korea.

Figure 7. Major Incidents of North Korean Aggression 1967–2010.

Jan 1967	artillery destroys South Korean warship in the disputed West Sea
Jan 1968	31 commandos attempt to assassinate Pres Park, kill seven South Koreans
Feb 1968	patrol boats with fighter aircraft support capture *USS Pueblo* in international waters, coercing US apology and promise of bilateral talks
Oct 1968	130 commandos infiltrate ROK east coast; all but 12 killed or captured
Apr 1969	fighter aircraft shoot down US reconnaissance plane in international airspace
Jun 1969	agents infiltrate Huksan Island, are killed by South Korea forces
Dec 1969	agents hijack South Korean airliner, release 39 and detain 12
Jun 1970	would-be assassins of Pres Park pre-detonate bomb at memorial ceremony
Aug 1974	commandos kill Pres Park's wife, Yok Yeong-soo, while trying to kill him
Aug 1976	soldiers club to death 2 unarmed US officers sent to trim a tree in the DMZ
Oct 1983	agents assassinate 21 ROK officials in Burma, missing Pres Chun
Nov 1987	agents bomb a South Korean airliner, killing 115
Sep 1996	26 commandos from beached submarine kill 16 before killed or captured
Jun 1999	three patrol boats attack 8 South Korean boats; one North Korean boat sunk
Mar 2010	Submarine/mine sinks South Korean patrol boat in international waters, killing 46
Nov 2010	artillery shells Yeonpyeong Island, killing four

North Korea's recurring hostility has been marked by tenuous ties to main powers. Kim Il-sung obtained Chinese and Russian sponsorship of its invasion of the South, which failed to coerce reunification. After the departure of Chinese forces (1958) and reduced Soviet aid (1962), Pyongyang began more provocative operations.[40] The subsequent decision to develop nuclear weapons was partly a response to US nuclear threats in the 1950s and unreliable Soviet or Chinese allies.[41]

In contrast, South Korea's confrontational behavior has been restrained and organized within a credible alliance. South Korea utterly depended on foreign forces to defeat the North's invasion and thus maintained the relationship with their allies. Over time, the UN forces in Korea, and US Forces Korea in particular, came to be regarded as a source of foreign leverage and pressure on the South Korean government to strengthen its military forces.

At a cost of unwanted economic dependence on the Soviet Union and China, North Korea developed large forces and weapons of mass effect —notably informational, chemical, biological, nuclear, and cyber-attack capabilities. The Korean People's Army also serves to magnify the sense of external threat, particularly as citizens become more aware of a glaring North-South gap in living standards. External economic dependence is in many ways preferable to the internal threat of popular uprisings that easily could accompany real economic reforms.

South Korea developed smaller and eventually more modern forces through economic interdependence and reliance on US deterrence. The South's democratization reduced the threat of internal unrest as an existential threat to national security. So as repressive North Korean rulers asserted nuclear independence in a feisty relationship with its main power, South Korean governments negotiated even the shorter ranges of its future missiles with its superpower sponsor.[42] Both Koreas remain ultrasensitive to any perceived loss of sovereignty.

Finally, there is the obvious North-South difference with respect to initiation of confrontation and the actual use of force. Aside from early raids under military-dominated rulers and self-defensive reactions, South Korean use of force has been nonexistent. South Korean military readiness to retaliate further against the North, however, is ever present. After the North Korean shelling of Yeonpyeong Island, South Korean aircraft were poised to destroy selected targets in North Korea should Pyongyang reattack. President Park Geun-hye added her promise to respond quickly and strongly.

So far, South Korean reactions to North Korean aggression continue to be restrained. The potential for a tactical engagement to burst into a strategic miscalculation is always there. In May 2014, for instance, a South Korean patrol boat operating in the West Sea fired warning shots in response to what were apparently warning shots from its North Korean counterpart. This and other such confrontational incidents highlight the difficulty of attributing intent to North Korean behavior. We can say that the North has adhered to a general pattern of sudden uses of force in small doses of short duration, presumably to leverage other means.

In sum, Koreans have regarded limited force as effective confrontation, restrained in frequency and violence by their respective main power relationships. Both have sought to block and filter external inference. North Korean relations with main powers have been less constraining than in the case of South Korea, where US alliance and ROK acceptance of global norms minimize the use of force.

Next we describe the ongoing Korean nuclear crisis. Participants and observers continue to fill in historical details.[43] As we view the crisis in terms of combined effects, we will appreciate how Pyongyang has been able to act effectively as a strategic power.

NOTES

1. An ideographic decomposition of *sadaejuui*: first character's meaning is "thing" (item); the second means "big" (large); therefore "big thing" refers to "main power." The third character is "main" (primary); the fourth is system (way of doing). Together this becomes "the way of main power thinking," which acquired the meaning of appeasement.

2. On the interplay between geography and history of the Korean peninsula, see Edward A. Olsen, *Korea: the Divided Nation* (Westport: Praeger, 2005), particularly chapters 1 and 2.

3. On the construction of national identity to resist threats, see Andre Schmidt, *Korea Between Empires, 1895–1919* (New York: Columbia University Press, 2002), particularly Chapter 5.

4. See Lee's history of Wiman Choson as "confederated wall townstates" (near present-day Pyongyang) that resisted Yen, Chin and Han invasions. Ki-baik Lee, *A New History of Korea*, trans. Edward W. Wagner (Cambridge: Harvard University Press, 1984), 13, 16–17.

5. Lee, *A New History of Korea*, 19–25.

6. English language sources of the time include: Kim Pu-sik, *Samguk Sagi* (History of the Three Kingdoms) and Ilyon, *Samguk Yusa* (Legends of the Three Kingdoms, trans. Ha Tae-hung and Grafton K. Mintz (Seoul: Yonsei University Press, 2006).

7. Michael J. Seth, *A History of Korea: From Antiquity to the Present* (New York: Rowman & Littlefield, 2011), 38.

8. "The Unification of Korea Under Silla" and "The Peninsula Kingdom" in Seth, *A History of Korea*, 44–47, 49–50.

9. Examples from Jonathon W. Best, "Notes and Questions Concerning the Samguk Sagi's Chronology of Paekche Kings Chongji, Kuisin, and Piyu," in *Korean Studies 3* 1979: 125-34.

10. Kawazoe Shōji, "Japan and East Asia," in *Medieval Japan*, ed. Kozo Yamamura (Cambridge: Cambridge University Press, 1990), accessed October 9, 2012, DOI:10.1017/CHOL9780521223546.011.

11. On Mongol, Ming, and non-steppe Qing military technology, see Kenneth Chase, *Firearms: A Global History to 1700* (New York: Cambridge University Press, 2003).

12. John Dardess, "Shun-ti and the end of Yüan rule in China," in *Alien Regimes and Border States, 907–1368*, eds. Herbert Franke and Denis

Twitchett (Cambridge: Cambridge University Press, 1994), accessed October 10, 2012, DOI:10.1017/CHOL9780521243315.009, 581.

13. John W. Dardess, *Ming China, 1368–1644: A Concise History of a Resilient Empire* (Lanham: Rowman & Littlefield Publishers, 2011), 19.

14. Moral self-centeredness may help explain why Ming eliminated their seven fleets following an era of expansive maritime exploration. See Jurgis Elisonas, "The inseparable trinity: Japan's relations with China and Korea," in *Early Modern Japan*, eds. John Whitney Hall and James L. McClain (Cambridge: Cambridge University Press, 1991), accessed October 9, 2012, DOI:10.1017/CHOL9780521223553.007.

15. Seth, *A History of Korea*, 147.

16. Ibid., 149.

17. See Donald N. Clark, "Sino-Korean tributary relations under the Ming," in *The Cambridge History of China: The Ming Dynasty, 1398–1644, Part 2*, eds. Denis Twitchett and Frederick W. Mote (Cambridge University Press, 1998), 271–300, accessed October 4, 2012, DOI:10.1017/CHOL9780521243339.007.

18. On the impact China on Korean reforms, see James B. Palais, *Confucian Statecraft and Korean Institutions: Yu Hyŏngwŏn and the Late Choson Dynasty* (Seattle: University of Washington Press, 1996).

19. Japan's 1876 coercion of the Choson dynasty into signing its first foreign treaty (日朝修好通商条約, Japan-Korea Amity and Commerce Treaty) repeated US Commodore Matthew Perry's in 1853, which coerced Japan to sign its first treaty (日米修好通商条約, Japan-U.S. Amity and Commerce Treaty). Previous French (1866) and American (1866, 1871) attempts to coerce trade with Koreans had failed.

20. William T. Rowe, *China's Last Empire: The Great Qing* (Cambridge: Harvard University Press, 2009), 227–228.

21. On uses of *juche*, see B. R. Meyers, *The Cleanest Race: How North Koreans See Themselves--And Why It Matters* (New York: Melville House, 2010); and Victor Cha, *The Impossible State: North Korea, Past and Future* (New York: Harper Collins, 2012). On verbal escalation, see Lim Dong-won, *Peacemaker: Twenty Years of Inter-Korean Relations and the North Korean Nuclear Issue* (Stanford: Asia-Pacific Research Center, 2012), 38–39.

22. Narushige Michishita, *North Korea's Military-Diplomatic Campaigns 1966-2008* (New York: Routledge, 2010), xxv.

23. Activist groups protesting US military bases often feign the location of operations and strike ROK police to "draw blood," demonstrating commitment to their cause.

24. Japanese troops occupied Korea in 1905, though Japan's annexation was not formalized until 1910.

25. Interview of North Korean defector, July 2009.

26. President Yun Po Sun and Premier Chang Myon served for less than a year before Park's coup displaced them.

27. Bruce Cumings, *Korea's Place in the Sun: A Modern History* (New York: W.W. Norton and Co., 2005), 148.

28. Robert Carlin and John Lewis, *Negotiating with North Korea: 1992–2007* (Stanford University: Center for International Security and Cooperation, 2008), 3.

29. Scott A. Snyder, 'US Policy Toward the Korean Peninsula: Accomplishments and Future Challenges," *Kokusaimondai* (International Affairs) No. 614, September 2012, 14.

30. Dennis Twitchett and Claus-Peter Tietze, "The Liao," in *The Cambridge History of China 6: Alien Regimes and Border States 907-1368,* eds. Herbert Franke and Denis Twichett, (Cambridge: Cambridge University Press, 1994), accessed October 4, 2012, DOI:10.1017/CHOL9780521243315.001), 47.

31. William Stueck, ed., *The Korean War in World History* (Lexington: University of Kentucky Press, 2004), particularly chapters 2 and 3; Sergei N. Goncharov, John W. Lewis, and Xue Litai, *Uncertain Partners: Stalin, Mao, and the Korean War* (Stanford: Stanford University Press, 1993), 140–142.

32. See Alexis Dudden, *Troubled Apologies Among Japan, Korea and the United States* (New Yorl: Columbia University Press, 2008), 9–10.

33. Chong-Sik Lee, *Park Chung-Hee: From Poverty to Power* (Seoul: Kyung Hee University Press, 2012), 313–314; Uk Heo and Terence Roehrig, *South Korea Since 1980* (Cambridge: Cambridge University Press, 2010), 159.

34. The United Nations Command was established in July 1950 to repel the North's invasion. Combined Forces Command is a U.S.-ROK headquarters (est.1978) that directs military operations through a US commander and ROK deputy, each with specific peacetime and wartime authorities.

35. See Selig S. Harrison, *Korean Endgame: A Strategy for Reunification and US Disengagement* (Princeton: Princeton University Press, 2002), 210–211; and Charles Kartmann, Robert Carlin, and Joel Witt, *A History of KEDO 1994-2006* (Freeman Spogli Institute for International Studies: Stanford, June 2012), 46–52.

36. See Seung Ho-joo, "US-ROK Relations: The Political-Diplomatic Dimension'" in *The United States and the Korean Peninsula in the 21st Century*, eds. Tae Hwan-kwak and Seung Ho-joo (Hampshire: Ashgate, 2006), 39–60.

37. Yoo Gwan-hee, "Kim Jong-il, When Provoking the South, Will Hit US Military Bases in Japan and Pacific Fleet First," 5 May 2012, North Korean Strategic Information Center, accessed September 23, 2012, http://www.nksis.com; Lim, *Peacemaker*, 201.

38. The last two reasons are noted in Narushige Michishita, *North Korea's Military-Diplomatic Campaigns 1966–2008* (New York: Routledge, 2010), xxi–xxii.

39. For a longer list without context, see *CRS Report for Congress: 1950–2007*, Hannah Fischer Information Research Knowledge Services Group, http://www.fas.org/sgp/crs/row/RL30004.pdf (accessed May 20, 2015).

40. James F. Person, "The Cuban Missile Crisis and the Origins of North Korea's Policy of Self-Reliance in National Defense," Woodrow Wilson International Center for Scholars North Korea International Documentation Project. http://www.wilsoncenter.org/sites/default/files/NKIDP_eDossier_12_North_Korea_and_the_Cuban_Missile_Crisis.pdf (accessed June 2, 2014).

41. Kathryn Weathersby, "The Korean War Revisited," in *The Wilson Quarterly* 23 No. 3, Summer 1999; 91-5. http://www.jstor.org/stable/40259929 (accessed October 3, 2012).

42. "S. Korea 'Wins Permission to Extend Missile Range,'" *The Chosun Ilbo*, http://english.chosun.com/site/data/html_dir/2012/09/24/2012092400698.html (accessed October 14, 2012).

43. For a scholarly and practical overview, see William E. Berry, Jr, *Global Security Watch Korea: A Reference Handbook* (Westport, CT: Praeger Security International, 2008).

CHAPTER 5

KOREA'S NUCLEAR POLARIZATION

The security culture on the Korean peninsula developed in rough seams between major powers. The vexing challenge facing Korean strategists is the question *how do we gain external protection without admitting domestic interference?* Achieving these two effects separately seems insurmountable, especially during periods of weak governance and strong communities. Harmonizing them as a holistic synthesis, however, has proven only difficult.

With mixed success, Korean sovereigns have managed to achieve relative security in an environment dominated by larger powers—they have accomplished this by being flexible: aligning and opposing main powers' interests; contesting and acquiescing to disputed borders; suppressing and ignoring internal disorder; cultivating and switching loyalties to rival individuals, families, and factions. Confrontation and cooperation remains a vital combination to the management of threats to Korean territory and national identity. In this complex context, *sadaejuui* emerged as a way to deflect persistent pressure, at a cost of compromising independence.

Recall that early Chinese invasions were overland; the northwest frontier bore the brunt of these imperial penetrations. The Three Kingdoms were weak, failing to muster a common Defense against Chinese and Japanese ambitions. Silla allied with northern China. Koguryo aligned with southern China. Paekche tilted toward Japan. Silla's unification— that is, the defeat of Koguryo and Paekche—relied on China's support and ultimate desire to colonize the peninsula. Unified successors to Silla (Koryŏ and Chosŏn) managed to prevent annexation by China by accepting a tributary relationship.

In southern Korea, inhabitants felt the weight of northern influence as well as seaborne punctures and injections of foreign troops and mercantilists. Technology offered no respite. Except for a brief sixteenth-century naval edge over Japan, Korean weaponry lagged behind that of its invaders. There is little evidence of any grand strategy with which to counter threats, either. Japan's defeat of China in the late nineteenth century and subsequent colonization ravaged Korean resources and culture through superior organization and discipline.

The United States and the allies' subsequent victory over Japan in the Pacific War displaced Japanese influence, especially in the north where colonial administrators were not temporarily retained. Koreans were subject to Soviet and Chinese influence in the north and American influence in the south. Beginning with the imposed border that most Koreans ignored, main power ideologies divided the peninsula. Hybrids of communism, capitalism, and nationalism took root on either side of the 38th parallel. Kim Il-sung's invasion of the South, approved by main powers China and the Soviet Union, triggered unexpectedly strong US and UN responses. The "limited" war led to an armistice that rescued the Republic of Korea (ROK) from being absorbed into the Democratic People's Republic of Korea (DPRK), but this further polarized the peninsula.

The failure to conclude a peace treaty fit well with a *sadaejuui* security culture that blamed competition among the main powers for the conflict. North and South Korea were recognized as rival proxies for the main powers rather than independent Korean nation-states. Both Koreas were understandably anti-Japan. The presence of a U.S.-Japan security alliance guaranteed that China and the Soviet Union would support Pyongyang's anti-Japan behavior. At the same time, the separate U.S.-Japan and ROK–U.S. alliances restrained South Korea–Japan hostility. This facilitated business ties that began to nurture new patterns of cooperation and legitimate competition.

Both Koreas *Secured* main power support in similar ways up until the end of the Cold War. From Mao Zedong to Deng Xiaopoing, and Joseph Stalin to Leonid Brezhnev, Kim Il-sung and Kim Jong-il knew they could count on support for their frontline revolutionary role against capitalism. Given the competition between Beijing and Moscow, Pyongyang could triangulate a reasonably independent position that extracted benefits from both and resisted control by either. Similarly from Harry Truman to Ronald Reagan, Seoul's military administrations focused on maintaining US aid, Deterrence and Defense through successive US policies of containment, massive retaliation, and variations on flexible response. When American commitment wavered, the ROK sought to Secure it while considering other options. Then the relationships among the main powers began to transform.

CRISIS

Figure 8. Lines of Effect Logic.

Lines of Effect Logic	
Psychological:	intimidate will / neutralize capability to **Deter** D_t -- **Compel** C_p
	assure will / enhance capability to *Dissuade* D_s -- *Persuade P*
Physical:	punish will / deny capability to **Defend** D_f -- **Coerce** C_r
	demonstrate will / exercise capability to *Secure S* -- *Induce I*

Adjusting Strategies

By the end of the 1980s, Pyongyang and Seoul faced fundamental changes that called for strategic adjustments. Having watched capitalism transform China, Chairman Kim Il-sung now witnessed the collapse of his Soviet patron and communist bloc. Kim's top priority was survival of the Party-Army-State control system.[1] Maintaining that required suppressing dissent, Deterring main power influence, and Defending sovereignty. While the *juche* and Kim-legend myths were instrumental to social compliance, they failed to bend the will or reduce capabilities of external threats. A twenty-year surge of operations against the South had not produced the hoped-for rebellion there. As North Korea faced dwindling foreign aid, the value of an independent nuclear capability appreciated.

Uncertainty also amplified South Korea's vulnerability. In the aftermath of Pyongyang's attack on the Blue House and seizure of the *USS Pueblo*, President Park Chung-hee confronted waning American will and capability. The Nixon Doctrine, US withdrawal from Vietnam, and then President Jimmy Carter's plan to withdraw US troops from South Korea, impelled Park toward an independent nuclear option.[2] The U.S. Compelled and *Persuaded* Park to abandon the project through intimidation—threatening to end the alliance,[3] and assurance—reversing the troop withdrawal idea and acting again as a reliable ally.[4] Henceforth South Korean strategy sought more freedom of action.

Pyongyang confronted increasingly unreliable allies and growing potential threats. Soviet nuclear assistance did not attach a nuclear guarantee. Beijing provided diplomatic, ideological, and economic support, but its socialist improvisations undermined Kim's system of total control. In the wake of the US withdrawal from Vietnam, US Secretary of Defense James Schlesinger threatened nuclear retaliation against North Korea should it invade South Korea again. South Korea's GDP had caught up with the stagnating North Korean economy. Seoul's liberalizing trade and financial policies contrasted with Pyongyang's command economy that killed productivity. North Korea's bickering benefactors in Beijing and Moscow offered uncompetitive models of agricultural and industrial development, respectively. Sino-Soviet border disputes elicited a Soviet nuclear threat against Beijing that put China's nuclear forces on high alert. Mao Zedong's death unlocked Deng reformists who ended the Cultural Revolution and began capitalist-style modernization, which included mobile nuclear forces. At this point, a nuclear capability and policy of divided engagement toward main powers made strategic sense.

In the 1980s, Pyongyang's covert nuclear program and overt initiatives to split the main powers began to falter. Mikhail Gorbachev's glasnost-and-perestroika-headed Soviet Union *Persuaded* North Korea to sign the Non-Proliferation Treaty (NPT) in 1985. The treaty was administered by the International Atomic Energy Agency (IAEA), which monitored and inspected nuclear reactors, facilities, and reprocessing sites. Scrutiny from IAEA inspectors using advanced technology threatened to uncover North Korean production and reprocessing of spent nuclear fuel. From Pyongyang's perspective, nuclear weapons were needed to shape main power relationships. North Korea had uranium ore deposits to fuel nuclear reactors, which can be used to produce—or feign the production of—uranium-based or plutonium-based nuclear weapons. Centrifuges can enrich the amount of the explosive isotope uranium 235 to the 90 percent level needed for weapons-grade uranium. Or, plutonium can be separated out from reactor-grade uranium and reprocessed into a weapons-grade state.[5]

China also was becoming problematic as an ally after enacting market reforms. By 1985, Deng Xiaoping had traded off ideological purity to accelerate economic growth yet retain single-party political control. This was too revisionist for iconic Kim Il-sung to consider. With Japan out of the question, the United States was North Korean's only potential main power alternative at the time. As the Koreas joined the United Nations in May 1991, they faced a huge shift in US strategy.

President George H. Bush seized the global moment to assure the world of benign US intent, announcing unilateral reductions in nuclear readiness and missiles. This included the withdrawal of all US tactical nuclear weapons from South Korea. Toward North Korea, the Bush administration had concluded it could neither Deter the development of nuclear weapons nor Coerce NPT compliance via isolation. Rather than containing North Korea with Deterrence, Defense, and Coercion, the United States sought to improve relations "by maintaining a strong deterrent against North Korean aggression, promoting North-South dialogue, and locking Pyongyang into its nuclear nonproliferation obligations while preventing its access to dangerous enrichment or reprocessing technologies."[6]

The new US strategy effectively added *Dissuasion* of nuclear development based on reciprocal assurances, offering to withdraw American nuclear weapons in exchange for a North Korean halt of reprocessing uranium. As US ability to deliver on its assurances declined, American strategy shifted toward wishful Compellence by intimidating North Korean will and neutralizing its nuclear weapons-making capability, with words. Overall, post–Cold War strategy under the Bush and Clinton administrations focused on denuclearization. However, American political leaders seemed chronically divided over how to achieve it.

US strategy toward North Korea combined Deterrence and Defense, but it was inconsistently integrated with other desired effects. Deterrence was operational in scope, and Defense territorial. The military-economic elements were Deterrence, Defense, and Coercion, accompanied by political *Dissuasion* and Compellence ($D_t D_f C_r D_s C_p$):

> $D_t D_f C_r$: Deter development of nuclear weapons; Defend against an invasion of the South; and Coerce compliance by respectively intimidating political will, denying military objectives, and punishing political will and denying military-economic capabilities.
>
> $D_s C_p$: *Dissuade* the development of nuclear weapons; and Compel compliance by respectively assuring Pyongyang of US reci-

procity, intimidating Pyongyang's will, and neutralizing KPA military-economic capability.

The International Atomic Energy Agency (IAEA) was also an influential actor. Having failed to detect Iraq's Weapons of Mass Destruction program, the IAEA's institutional credibility was on the line. Operating within its UN charter and lacking any enforcement mechanism, the IAEA's desired effects became coopted by Pyongyang. Nevertheless, the IAEA sought to Compel (C_p) strict compliance with NPT standards:

C_p: Compel North Korea to comply with NPT standards by intimidating Pyongyang's will and neutralizing Pyongyang's capability to avoid nuclear inspections.

South Korean strategy reflected an ambivalent dependence on American forces. As in Washington, changing political priorities between Seoul presidential administrations generated versions of cooperation and confrontation toward North Korea. Overall, the combined effect of mounting South Korean economic and military power *Secured* by the US alliance presented Pyongyang a systemic dilemma: expand social, economic, and political ties with the South; or fall further behind. Both options undermined the Kim-centered Stalinist system of total control. *Secured* with a US commitment, South Korea consistently tried to *Persuade*, Deter, and Defend against North Korea ($P D_t D_f S$):

P: *Persuade* unification talks by assuring Pyongyang of economic benefits.

$D_t D_f S$: Deter and Defend against invasion and attack; and *Secure* the US commitment by respectively denying North Korean military objectives, and demonstrating and exercising its will and capability as a US ally.

Pyongyang's strategy claimed *juche*-style independence, but it relied on relationships with surrounding powers. The approach has been a multilayered, volatile mixture of cooperation and confrontation that achieved a combined effect of asymmetric envelopment. Pyongyang's nuclear promises/threats and sociopolitical linkages/breakages turned policy differences within the United States and South Korea—and among the United States, South Korea, Japan and China—into weaknesses. Pyongyang's behavior over time is consistent with the following desired effects, $C_p \, C_r \, D_t \, D_f \, P \, I$:

> $C_p \, C_r \, D_t \, D_f$: Compel and Coerce economic aid, US diplomatic recognition and reunification; and Deter and Defend against invasion and attack by respectively intimidating and punishing American and South Korean will to halt North Korean nuclear programs; and denying United States, South Korea, and International Atomic Energy Agency will and capability to seize the initiative.

> $P \, I$: *Persuade* and *Induce* US diplomatic recognition by assuring and demonstrating the will to pursue a nuclear option.

Shaping Lines of Effect

A welter of efforts from the United States, South Korea, and the United Nations opposed North Korea's nuclear programs with transitory results, Compelling nuclear inspections of North Korean sites and *Persuading* Pyongyang to negotiate with Seoul. These effects influenced North Korea's behavior, but not in the intended direction.

We can reasonably assume that competition among the Workers' Party of Korea (WPK), Korean People's Army, and government ministries shaped North Korean lines of effect. Attributing intent to leadership changes and to nuances behind vitriolic propaganda is a risky art. Nevertheless, we infer two closely related strategic-level lines of effect —nuclear development and aggressive dependency. These generated initiatives and relationships with main powers that were then held hostage to North Korean economic, political, and military demands. Divided internally and with respect to each another, the main powers' countervailing efforts were subsumed by Pyongyang's asymmetrically applied lines of effect.

In the hopeful thaw of the Cold War, North and South Korea signed ambitious agreements that enabled Pyongyang to lightly conceal nuclear development. The program was not so obvious as to be overt. This enabled Pyongyang to refute its very existence in the face of external pressure, thereby increasing domestic pride of independence while producing uncertainty externally. The mystery of nuclear programs cultivated main power interests in relationships with Pyongyang. This magnification of attention created leverage for Pyongyang's aggressive interactions, which promoted North Korean control and the cause of reunification.

North Korean nuclear strategy developed during a unique time— Kim Il-sung's singular standing within the party, army, government ministries, and the population segment that was aware of the situation. Kim was able to eliminate opposition through the party, intimidating and neutralizing resistance, and punishing and denying individual freedoms. The party also assured and demonstrated collective will of the Korean people through nationalistic propaganda and prestige. In the hostile environment that this system both bred and bore, a nuclear option that Deterred, Compelled, and Coerced main power threats to independence reinforced total control.

Before Pyongyang began to pursue aggressive dependency toward the United States and its allies, it continued to do what it could, Cold War style.

In 1987, North Korean agents blew up a Korean Airlines Burma-to-Baghdad flight, framing it as a Japanese terrorist plot.[7] If the plan had not been revealed as a North Korean operation, it might have operated as indirect Coercion, punishing South Korean will that sought closer relations with Japan. Due to the surviving assassin's confession, however—instead of dividing South Korea and Japan—the attack brought widespread outrage and condemnation of North Korea.[8] In 1990, Pyongyang tried to Deter Soviet recognition of South Korea by threatening to recognize former Soviet republics as independent states, support Japan's claim to the disputed Kuril Islands, and develop nuclear weapons. This produced two undesirable effects: Russia recognized South Korea earlier than it had planned and withdrew their nuclear and missile technicians from North Korea.[9] However, Moscow's response failed to intimidate Pyongyang's will or neutralize its nuclear capability. It did Compel North Korea to construct and exploit dependent economic ties with China, the United States, and South Korea. This dependency would envelop US and allied strategies by subjecting those tenuous relationships to North Korean threats. How did this work?

In 1992, Pyongyang welcomed Seoul's proposal for a North-South Agreement on Reconciliation, Nonaggression and Exchanges and Cooperation.[10] The stated aim, to achieve peaceful unification, was accompanied by a bevy of promises and obligations, joint committees, economic exchanges, dialogue and negotiations, and a ban on reprocessing and nuclear weapons. The North also agreed to sign the Safeguards Agreement of the Non-Proliferation Treaty which it had delayed for years. In these and other agreements, North Korean negotiators pressed every possible advantage to extract concessions and deny UN inspections. Pyongyang Compelled the provision of United States and South Korea economic enhancements, Deterred and then denied United Nations inspections, and *Persuaded* and *Induced* American officials to maintain a direct relationship. These effects were brought about via military intimidation; economic punishment and denial; and diplomatic assurances of mutually beneficial trade, investment, and peaceful reunification.

South Korean lines of effect seemed straightforward: military alliance with the United States and economic-moral *Persuasion* toward reunification. South Korea's security strategy was being formulated under increased public scrutiny and tighter military-economic interdependence with the United States. The presidency of Roh Tae-woo, the last of three consecutive generals and the first to be elected legitimately, sought more autonomy from US influence. In 1987, Roh began a Nordpolitik (northern policy) of expanding ties with the Soviet Union and former communist states. This diplomatic redirection meant to Compel Pyongyang into direct talks with Seoul and to *Induce* domestic reform in North Korea. As South Korea's politics became more inclusive and its economy more global, South Korean military capabilities increased. Within the bilateral alliance, South Korea was creating more tools and developing more national will to put its own twist on North Korea.

The South Korea–U.S. military alliance generated predictable routines to demonstrate common will for Defense, *Persuading* the South and Deterring the North. This *Secured* a credible US commitment to South Korea. Attempts to create a broader political-economic front against the North continue to be frustrated by national policy differences. Each year, military exercises replay a North Korean invasion scenario within political comfort zones.

Economic-moral suasion offered aid, humanitarian assistance, business deals, family contacts, cultural ties, and media coverage to Pyongyang to *Persuade* engagement. The idea was to coax relations for eventual reunification while *Dissuading* Pyongyang from nuclear weapons development. Seoul was divided on whether more contact with North Korea would collapse, transform, or strengthen the authoritarian regime.

The US lines of effect were simple: military alliance to Deter and Defend against North Korean attack, and incremental engagement to Coerce, *Persuade* and Compel denuclearization. Besides issues of having US bases such as burden sharing, labor agreements, and impact on landowners, a chronic challenge for the South Korean–American alliance is how to counter forward-deployed North Korean firepower that can devastate Seoul.[11] As the United States urged South Korea to modernize and take on US missions, North Korean nuclear provocations *Induced* political-economic engagement. US priorities were *Persuasion* and Compellence in support of denuclearization, in coordination with military exercises and operations. Denuclearization required patience across administrations and a consensus on ways and means that was utterly absent in Washington.

The International Atomic Energy Agency was creating its own nonproliferation line of effect to Compel North Korea through its high-tech intimidation tools of onsite monitoring and inspections. The IAEA targeted North Korean will to comply with Non-Proliferation Treaty obligations and therefore neutralized North Korean capability to hide its nuclear program. Interest in Pyongyang's historical record of plutonium production was motivated by the failure to detect Iraq's program, which was secretly pursued and then abandoned. The IAEA also aimed to regain its credibility and prevent future flouting of Non-Proliferation Treaty standards by verifying the absence of any plutonium production.

In contrast to Pyongyang's focused lines of effect, the scattered interests among United States, South Korea, and the International Atomic Energy Agency produced did not pose difficult choices. The efforts did Compel limited inspections of North Korean nuclear sites and *Persuade* Pyongyang to participate in talks with South Korea. However all of this operational-level activity fell rather nicely within the enabling conditions of Pyongyang's strategic lines of effect.

Setting Conditions

Pyongyang repeatedly turned American concessions into baselines for further demands. Creating divisive, and therefore negotiable, issues strengthened the power of the nuclear option. It remains unclear whether Pyongyang intended the program to be permanent, or to be traded away for concessions in a less hostile environment. Consistent with Korean security culture and the situation at hand, however, the stoking of a dependent US relationship gained some assurance of regime survival. One of the table-setting provocations was Team Spirit.

The US decision in 1992 to suspend its largest annual allied exercise, Team Spirit, presented an opportunity. North Korean negotiators insisted that the stoppage be permanent. South Korean officials feared being cut out of the peninsular picture. This was part of Pyongyang's plan—blocking the ROK from influencing North Korea's creation of mutual dependency with the United States. Condemning the exercise also enabled Pyongyang to shift the responsibility of abrogating the 1993 denuclearization declaration to the United States and South Korea.

While American and North Korean negotiators wrestled over the exercise, Pyongyang's Foreign Ministry cast it as a nuclear threat. Team Spirit imposed considerable costs on the North because it *Induced* the Korean People's Army to mobilize. US Ambassador Donald Gregg advocated cancelling Team Spirit as leverage for cooperation with the North. Ignoring this counsel, administration officials retained Team Spirit as a carrot and stick. Focused on Deterring, Coercing, and Defending, American tough-talk ignored *Dissuading* and *Inducing* as compatible elements of a grand strategy. In Pyongyang, however, arguments for nuclear development, and against inspections and negotiations, fit in as the dispensable *Persuasion-Inducement* piece of its broader combined effect. For the second year in a row, Kim Il-sung's New Year's message to political elites and diplomatic corps signaled assurance: Pyongyang wanted improved relations and trade.

Team Spirit had a double-effect advantage for North Korea: it helped Pyongyang maintain its strategic envelopment of American and South Korean strategies, and it was expendable. As long as the exercise continued, it triggered demands for compensation and helped retain a relationship with the United States. Team Spirit also provided observable hostile US intent that vindicated nuclear weapons development. If the exercise were canceled, it would be sounded as a victory against foreign interference. The notion that Team Spirit could Compel or Coerce nuclear compliance was not credible. Cancellation of Team Spirit, however, could have yielded mutually assuring political, military, and economic benefits—relative cooperation. In 1993 the new Clinton administration decided to keep Team Spirit on, for all the prudent reasons.

In February 1993, the International Atomic Energy Agency issued an ultimatum to Compel Pyongyang to accept special inspections, a short-notice procedure to uncover past deception. During the 30-day period before the deadline, senior US defense officials upped the ante to "a new position emphasizing a demand that North Korea freeze all future nuclear operations."[12] Secretary of Defense Les Aspin and his deputy William Perry meant to support the IAEA position by designing an independent policy. The initiative, however, was not focused on developing new tools to enhance UN and US effects. It was about using readily available tools. Subsequently, a military attack on Yongbyon was deemed to be too risky, as was enforcing economic sanctions.

Seeking an early breakthrough in North-South relations, the new South Korean administration of President Kim Young-sam advocated indirect liaisons rather than direct American talks with Pyongyang. Ambassador Gong Ro-myung offered a complementary stratagem to *Persuade* North Korea to abide by the Non-Proliferation Treaty and permit North-South denuclearization inspections.[13]

The first idea was to have the International Atomic Energy Agency act as a proxy for South Korean inspectors in North-South talks. Pyongyang rejected inspections from Seoul, claiming sole peninsular sovereignty. Another plan was to have the United States agree to North Korea's demands for more U.S.-North Korea meetings. This might assure Pyongyang of South Korean and US sincerity while preserving a South Korean diplomatic role. Washington declined, citing the urgency of getting Pyongyang to accept special inspections before the IAEA's deadline. This priority reflected a fixation that was killing US strategy: U.S.–North Korea talks would distract North Korea away from dealing with the IAEA.[14] From Seoul's perspective, Washington prioritized relations with North Korea and the United Nations over its alliance with South Korea.

Pyongyang exploited this difference and announced its withdrawal from the Non-Proliferation Treaty, a first for any member state. In accordance with NPT procedures, this would occur three months later. The global reaction was near-unanimous condemnation. Even Beijing reacted to this by restricting exports with nuclear weapons component potential. The IAEA's next logical step would be to report North Korea to the United Nations Security Council as noncompliant.

For Pyongyang, halting inspections preserved the mystery of its nuclear record, enhancing all of its combined effects. The big threat maintained the US relationship. Why didn't *juche*-minded North Korea "just go ahead and build bombs"[15] with its own uranium? A reasonable answer is that the timing was not right with respect to main power management. Two decades of economic decline, widespread famine, exposed military forces, and political isolation increased North Korea's vulnerability to Chinese and Japanese influence.

Having provoked a nuclear crisis, North Korea now demanded four conditions to end it: permanently cancel Team Spirit, open US bases in South Korea for nuclear inspection, guarantee no US nuclear attack on North Korea, and ensure IAEA impartiality.[16] The next day, North Korea had Compelled the United States to cancel Team Spirit. In doing so, the United States gained the probable support of China and the IAEA to Coerce compliance should Pyongyang continue to Deter further inspections. Yet this exchange of operational-level effects played into North Korea's strategy.

Subsequent negotiations generated an escalatory spiral. North Korea's line of effect neutralized inspections, attempting to Compel aid and normalization. In passionate fits of assurance and intimidation, Pyongyang initially granted permission for inspections, then rescinded them; then allowed inspectors to enter North Korea, then blocked their access to the site; allowed inspectors access to the site but not specifically to the fuel rods; then demanded an IAEA apology for causing the crisis; promised to abide by safeguards, then announced that it would not; assured negotiators of neither intent nor capability to possess nuclear weapons, then intimidated them with nuclear threats; and so on.

By comparison, the US conditions were low-key and vulnerable to fragmentation. The United States dangled carrots and prepared sticks until Pyongyang showed willingness to compromise in the North-South denuclearization talks. Washington also discussed economic sanctions with UN Security Council member states. All of this was supposed to Compel Pyongyang to accept inspections. The failure to strike a domestic consensus on economic enhancements to North Korea, or gain allied consensus on inspections and inter-Korean relations, strengthened Pyongyang's position.

Pyongyang's next shaping opportunity occurred when the International Atomic Energy Agency detected high levels of plutonium at Yongbyon. This called for additional inspections. Other North Korean reactors fueled by domestic uranium may have been able to produce thirty plutonium weapons annually.[17] Thus, escalation favored Pyongyang's asymmetric, two-track envelopment strategy, as long as it could intimidate and punish American will to stop the nuclear program. Destroying evidence of defueling and reprocessing was important to maintaining a nuclear narrative of responding to external pressure. The Defense of nuclear development became a just cause in North Korea. The IAEA posed a threat to this goal, but the relationship neutralized US diplomacy that sought economic sanctions to Compel inspections. As a result, Pyongyang maintained the strategic initiative. By cooperating with the IAEA, Pyongyang *Dissuaded* economic sanctions. By confronting the IAEA, Pyongyang Deterred nuclear inspections.

North Korea also sought a closer relationship with the United States to enhance its economic and military capability. In the absence of a credible counterstrategy, Pyongyang could be justifiably confident about using the possession of nuclear weapons to Compel normalized relations. Would normalization *Induce* North Korea to negotiate away its nuclear arsenal, however small? The lack of a united external power front reinforced the juche narrative and potential of an independent, nuclear-armed, unified Korea.

For the United States, the timing of the International Atomic Energy Agency inspections was premature. Unless the United States were willing to deny North Korea its nuclear capability (through successful attacks with persistent effects), it had to try psychological engagement. Yet, U.S.–North Korea preliminary negotiations and related ties with South Korea had barely begun. The United States was unprepared to offer assurances and enhancements, such as normalized relations and sustained economic aid, either in secret meetings or rounds of talks. Some seasoned negotiators advocated taking such risks to start developing trust through *Persuasion* and *Inducement*, rather than preventing it through Compellence and Coercion. However, Democratic President Clinton faced Republican majorities in both houses of Congress, and they were critical of conceding anything to North Korea. Intended or not, the operative assumption was that Pyongyang would bend to US pressure, or collapse. Furthermore, the first legitimately elected civilian leader of South Korea in three decades, Kim Young-sam, flip-flopped on inspections and concessions to enhance his diplomatic status and domestic support. US alternatives bounced between military action, containment through isolation, and "a strategy of coercive diplomacy that would require an integrated use of carrots and sticks."[18] The United States set itself on an incremental path of escalatory options subsumed by Pyongyang's broader strategy.

Over the course of sputtering U.S.-North Korea negotiations in 1994, and sporadic North-South talks, Pyongyang's voice quivered. Did this indicate internal discord? Messengers from the North Korean foreign ministry blustered and pled. The lengthy process was frustrating, but it developed a degree of rapport, mutual understanding, and a narrowing of differences on operational-level issues: types of inspections and timing, access to unloading of reactor fuel rods, costs and provision of Light Water Reactors (LWR), whether a nuclear freeze would precede or follow LWRs, and so forth. Throughout the ordeal, North Korean officials adhered to two positions: (1) United Nations authority to conduct special inspections was not acceptable; and (2) that the imposition of economic sanctions would be regarded as an act of war.[19]

If how American officials talked about the crisis reflects how they thought about it, the US strategy was reduced to games of temporary advantage: carrots and sticks, stacked card decks and bargaining chips, football with alternating turns of offense and defense, and "red lines" that threatened to end negotiations. Perhaps such analogies helped focus a divided government on how best to bargain smartly, but they also reinforced issue-generated routines with minimal effects. The US Department of State advocated getting the nuclear inspections started first to bring Pyongyang back into the Non-Proliferation Treaty where it could be diplomatically engaged. The US Department of Defense (DoD) insisted on North-South talks first to eliminate North Korea's plutonium-reprocessing capability; inspections and broader diplomacy would come later. Each side saw the other's priority as undercutting its own. Running inspections and denuclearization talks at the same time would have required coordination by the International Atomic Energy Agency and South Korea, and agreement on desired effects. While State and Defense disagreed on the timing of their own operational-level desired effects, they agreed on which North Korean actions were unacceptable. Instead of hard thinking about combinations of strategic-level desired effects in a united effort, negotiators focused on coordinating diplomatic, economic, and military means, hoping for North Korean compliance. As a combined effect, the American strategy was inert, little more than a tripwire of military occupation on South Korean territory.

Conditional "red lines" began to be crossed in 1994. In April, chief North Korean negotiator Kang Sok Ju informed chief US negotiator Robert Gallucci that Pyongyang would remove irradiated fuel rods from the Yongbyon reactor without International Atomic Energy Agency over-sight. This would destroy the historical evidence of plutonium extraction and prepare to reprocess the waste into weapons-grade plutonium. Defueling began the next month as US officials advocated phases of economic sanctions in the UN, which implied military enforcement.[20]

As the US military deployed more forces to the region and planned for conflict, the International Atomic Energy Agency and South Korea marched elsewhere. The IAEA avoided certifying North Korea as irreversibly noncompliant. This meant that North Korea could have reprocessed weapons grade plutonium, but there was no direct evidence that it did. Kim Young-sam's conditions for North Korean compliance were focused on asserting a US-*Secured* South Korean role, *Dissuading* North Korea from Non-Proliferation Treaty withdrawal, and *Persuading* North-South talks to happen. There was negligible public support for a military strike. These desired effects diverged from the US strategy of Compelling and Coercing nuclear inspections.

The United States and the International Atomic Energy Agency worked their separate ways of Compellence and Coercion, right up to imminent economic sanctions. The day after the president of the UN Security Council called for immediate North Korea–IAEA consultations over the discharge of the nuclear reactor core, Pyongyang test-fired an antiship missile into the Sea of Japan. The next month, the IAEA board of governors resolved to complain about Pyongyang's noncompliance and suspended nonmedical assistance to North Korea. While rebuffing UN inspections, Pyongyang offered to dismantle the nuclear reactor and demanded to see further evidence of its nuclear activity as claimed. Did these proposals indicate intent to negotiate a way to accept inspections without surrendering sovereignty? No one accepted that risk. So North Korea retained the secret nuclear program track while bringing the main powers, including China, to the brink of economic sanctions and the queasy question of military enforcement. Just as President Clinton was to decide how many and what types of forces to send to South Korea, former US president Jimmy Carter intervened.

President Carter's visit to North Korea and meeting with Chairman Kim Il-sung led to new conditions that stopped probable conflict and saved Pyongyang's two-track strategy. Carter provided Kim what Clinton deliberately withheld: North Korea's right to reprocess uranium into plutonium for peaceful nuclear energy. This assurance of a former president that the United States was committed to a nuclear-free peninsula gained Kim Il-sung's word to place the fuel rods into permanent storage.

In June, the death of Kim Il-sung delayed—but did not prevent—further negotiations and a written agreement. One of the Great Leader's sons, Kim Jong-il, had been selected to become the Dear Leader for some time. Over the mourning period, South Korean media labeled the dead leader a war criminal and President Kim Young-sam banned condolence visits. This killed inter-Korean relations until the next presidential administration.

The Agreed Framework

The gist of the Agreed Framework consisted of old North Korean promises and a new American assurance of Light Water Reactors (LWR) for nonnuclear weapons capable energy.[21] Under International Atomic Energy Agency oversight, Pyongyang would (1) freeze its nuclear facilities, dismantling them after receiving a complete LWR suite; (2) permanently dispose of the spent fuel rods; (3) implement the 1992 North-South Joint Declaration on the Denuclearization of the Korean Peninsula; and (4) and continue Non-Proliferation Treaty membership, including the Safeguards Agreement. The United States pledged new levels of energy assistance and progress toward normalized relations, the details of which Pyongyang negotiated as intensely as its previously broken agreements.

Each of these provisions contained known disagreements, papered over with the conviction they would be overcome by events, or ignored. Pyongyang still rejected IAEA monitoring and inspecting to verify the freeze, dismantlement of graphite-moderated reactors and facilities, and placement of fuel rods into permanent storage. This enabled defueling and reprocessing. The symbolic utility of disagreeing over North-South talks, which Seoul wanted before implementing the Agreed Framework and which Pyongyang did not want at all, is illustrated by a mutually agreed sentence involving the meaning of the word *as*: "The DPRK will engage in North-South dialogue, as this Agreed Framework will help create an atmosphere that promotes such dialogue." [22] If "as" meant "at the same time," North Korea would receive light-water nuclear reactors while the talks were going on. If, however, "as" meant "because," South Korea would participate as an equal in bilateral North-South talks before the North received benefits. This contested issue aided North Korea's suppression of equal status for South Korea to Coerce a direct relationship with the United States. Finally, North Korean Non-Proliferation Treaty membership included a new international standard that Pyongyang opposed. Model Protocol INFCIRC/540 expanded IAEA inspections to cover suspected nuclear facilities, but it was not yet accepted by most Non-Proliferation Treaty members.[23] These disagreements protected Pyongyang's broad strategy.

For the next eight years, the Korean Peninsula Energy Development Organization (KEDO) helped preserve North Korea's strategic lines of effect and busied the U.S., ROK, and Japan in their own divisive operational lines. KEDO's goals were to finance and supply two Light Water Reactors, interim energy alternatives, and other measures needed to carry out the Agreed Framework.[24] Yet KEDO was a source of division between South Korea and Japan. Even though the organization emerged from the bilaterally negotiated U.S.-North Korea Agreed Framework, South Korea covered 70% of the costs and Japan 20%. European partners joined later, expecting to influence the project in proportion to their contributions. The Agreed Framework, however, specified US leadership, a criterion on which Pyongyang shrewdly demanded compliance. Because both the KEDO Charter and KEDO Supply Agreement required detailed negotiations, squabbles over financial entitlements neutralized an integrated effort.

In addition, the South Korea government used KEDO to enhance ties with North Korea at the expense of nuclear compliance. This difference between South Korea's economic-moral suasion and US incremental engagement widened when the George W. Bush administration took over in 2001. The George W. Bush administration was all about KEDO forcing North Korean nuclear compliance, disdaining expanded ties while obligated to provide Light Water Reactors to Pyongyang. The failure to integrate KEDO into US strategy crippled both efforts.

In December 1994, a US helicopter strayed five kilometers over the North Korean border and was shot down, killing one of the pilots. North

Korea held the survivor to extract a US apology, direct military talks, and the return of prisoners held in South Korea. The pilot was released after the United States expressed regret. To North Korea the incident provided evidence of US military Coercion; to the U.S., this was evidence of opportunistic North Korean Coercion. Congressional support for the newly signed Agreed Framework disappeared.

In 1996, the North Korean submarine incursion at Kangnung emboldened South Korean President Kim Young-sam's hardline approach to Pyongyang. Like the helicopter incident, which the United States attributed to navigational error, this could have been a live-training error. Thereafter the Kim administration demanded more reciprocity from the North—not related to the Korean Peninsula Energy Development Organization—to deepen bilateral socioeconomic ties.

Exploiting Fractures

In 1998, North Korea fired a three-stage Taepodong-1 missile over Japan, with several repercussions. The impact *Induced* Tokyo to withdraw from KEDO before being *Persuaded* back in by Clinton administration officials. Perhaps the shot also meant to Coerce Washington into relaxing economic sanctions by showing Pyongyang's resolve to develop missiles for export. Clearly, the action demonstrated that all of Japan was now within range of a North Korean strike. Initial reports from Tokyo insisted that the launch was a preattack test, while Washington assessed it as a satellite launch. Seoul downplayed North Korean hostility, citing domestic motivations— the bolstering of Kim Jong-il's status as he announced fiftieth-anniversary economic reforms. In the U.S., the Republican-controlled Congress voted against ratifying the Comprehensive Nuclear-Test-Ban Treaty (CTBT), preferring to develop a national missile defense and ensure the reliability of its nuclear force with nuclear tests. To promote unity toward Pyongyang, in April 1999 the U.S., Japan, and South Korea established the Trilateral Coordination and Oversight Group headed by deputy foreign ministers and an assistant secretary of state. This group had its limitations.

In June 2000, the historic Kim Dae-jung–Kim Jong-il summit produced a joint declaration and surge in inter-Korean relations. Seoul's soft line of *Dissuasion* and *Persuasion* now included *Inducement* as linked economic, social, and military issues began to yield political cooperation.[25] At the same time, Washington's hard line of Compellence and Coercion became more confrontational.

As North Korea's deputy representative to the United Nations urged continued engagement, the new George W. Bush administration filled key positions with hardliners who derided engagement and peace talks as strategies. National Security Presidential Directive One placed the National Security Council's non-proliferation office in charge of a policy review that squelched rapprochement and accommodation.[26] While Kim Dae-jung attempted to *Persuade* North Korea to open diplomatic, economic, and cultural ties, George W. Bush rejected these as immoral.

President Kim Dae-jung took Roh Tae-woo's Nordpolitik to the next level of independent diplomacy. He strengthened his relationship with Russian president Vladimir Putin during a February 2001 summit that endorsed the bilateral Anti-Ballistic Missile Treaty, ratification of the Strategic Arms Reduction Talks II, and the Comprehensive Nuclear-Test-Ban Treaty. This conflicted with President Bush's desire to eliminate the Anti-Ballistic Missile treaty because it limited US plans to expand missile Defense. The Bush-Kim March 2001 summit in Washington went badly. As Bush administration officials began to speak out more against an already-isolated North Korean regime and advocate its collapse, the Kim administration pushed for engagement.

The 9/11 terrorist attacks on the United States led to more South Korean–American divergence. American fears of nuclear proliferation to "rogue" states reinforced Compelling and Coercing North Korean compliance with the Non-Proliferation Treaty. It also reinforced Pyongyang's need for regime survival. Seoul and Pyongyang quickly condemned the attacks, but President Bush's State of the Union address labeled North Korea, Iran, and Iraq an axis of evil. The demonization of intent strengthened Pyongyang's hardliners.[27] North Korea faced a self-righteous American policy backed up by nuclear weapons and a preemptive strike policy against Weapons of Mass Destruction–capable actors. South Korea's participation in North-South ministerial talks yielded railroad connections, South Korean tourism at Mount Kumgang, and the construction of the Kaesong Industrial Complex.

South Korean attempts to develop cooperation continued during U.S.–North Korea confrontations. South Korea's special advisor to the president for national security and unification, Lim Dong-won, doubted the North would accommodate Seoul's proposal for a joint antiterrorism statement and that the United States would act on the U.S.–North Korea joint statement on antiterrorism.[28] As Pyongyang and Washington continued mutual intimidation, Seoul under Kim Dae-jung and Kim's successor Roh Moo-hyun provided assurances of accommodation. Rejecting the potential of allied cooperation with confrontation, President George W. Bush announced in March 2002 that the United States would not certify North Korean compliance with the Agreed Framework.

South Korean and American lines of effect operated respectively to *Persuade* and *Induce*, and Compel and Coerce, North Korean behavior. South Korean administrations found it difficult to mix confrontation with cooperation toward the North and were out of synch with their divided American counterparts. Without South Korea–U.S. agreement on the priority and timing of International Atomic Energy Agency inspections, reprocessing stoppages, and improved relations, Pyongyang could target the will and capability of one ally to bring about desired effects on the other. Pyongyang would engage South Korea on eventual reunification to Deter the nuclear compliance demanded by the United States, and engage the United States on denuclearization to Deter the independent political-economic role that South Korea sought. Pyongyang basked in Seoul's Sunshine Policy that assured access to separated families and government ministries, and shaded itself from US demands of special inspections that assured access to stored fuel rods. North Korean "coopfrontation" bought time to develop its nuclear capability. Allied failure to coordinate an effective counterstrategy is evident in the issue of North Korea's Highly Enriched Uranium (HEU) program.

Nuclear North Korea

In February 2002, a Central Intelligence Agency-led task force estimated North Korea's Highly Enriched Uranium potential based on historical indicators. US Special Envoy to North Korea Jack Pritchard concluded that North Korea "had embarked on a program to create nuclear weapons by using highly enriched uranium,"[29] a clear violation of the Agreed Framework. Preoccupied with operations in Afghanistan and considering an invasion of Iraq, the George W. Bush administration decided to handle the problem by confronting Pyongyang with the facts—in North Korea. Department of State Director of East Asian Affairs James Kelly was selected to travel to Pyongyang and issue an ultimatum. The administration's idea of stern signaling was to eliminate the usual US-hosted (funded) reciprocal dinner the second evening and to prohibit Kelly from toasting the North Koreans during their dinner.[30]

North Korea's sinking of a South Korean patrol boat in June delayed the trip until October. Washington called for confidence-building measures and nuclear compliance, while Pyongyang demanded the withdrawal of all US forces from the South before talks could resume. South Korean diplomats urged their American counterparts to ignore the naval attack.[31] Kelly personally delivered the message in Pyongyang: the United States had irrefutable intelligence of a Highly Enriched Uranium program and until it was resolved, there would be no dialogue.[32] Vice Foreign Minister Kim Gye-gwan, accompanied by Kang Sok-ju (later First Vice Foreign Minister), immediately denied this. The next day, Kim reiterated the denial. In a separate meeting, Kang admitted that North Korea had a HEU program and was prepared to produce weapons that were much easier to construct as well as much more difficult to detect than high-radiation-emitting plutonium warheads. Pyongyang's second track was exposed.

Over the next several weeks North Korean officials denied possessing nuclear weapons while insisting they were entitled to have them.[33] US officials split on whether this was a North Korean tactic or position. The public, Congress, and key Bush administration officials were united in not negotiating about it. In November, President George W. Bush charged that North Korea was actually enriching uranium to develop nuclear weapons even though information indicated only the capability to enrich it.[34] On such tenuous intelligence, the administration began requiring "complete, verifiable and irreversible" elimination of North Korea's nuclear programs, including long-range missiles. The escalation of US demands disregarded the possibility of providing Pyongyang Light Water Reactors per the Agreed Framework. Indications that economic reforms had gained a foothold in North Korea were not regarded as a strategic opportunity.[35]

The Kim Dae-jung administration was unconvinced that its neighbor had a Highly Enriched Uranium program. Different South Korean and American priorities regarding reunification and denuclearization provided incentives for divergent assessments. Pyongyang's uncertain strategy fed this, too. A key question was whether a uranium enrichment facility was being built and, if so, how long would it take to produce nuclear weapons? Indicators of a capability, such as components of enrichment technology and construction activity, generated competing hypotheses. North Korean purchases of Pakistani-designed centrifuges and German-made aluminum tubes might be used to modernize existing facilities, upgrade conventional rockets, or enrich uranium. Behavioral patterns and anomalies were prone to alternative explanations and required deep cultural insight. Seoul therefore viewed Washington as casting suspicions to inhibit inter-Korean relations. In his role as South Korea's Director of National Intelligence, Lim Dong-won agreed to convey, but not fully support, the US message to North Korea: Abandon your HEU program in order to gain talks with the United States.[36]

In November 2002, North Korean officials declared the Agreed Framework null and void. The next month the Korean Peninsula Energy Development Organization cut off the next planned heavy oil shipment to North Korea in accordance with the latter's breach of the 1994 Agreed Framework. Pyongyang expelled United Nations inspectors, dismantled surveillance equipment, and broke storage seals of plutonium rods. Subsequent threats in 2003 included conducting a preemptive attack on US forces and pulling out of the 1953 Korean Armistice Agreement. It worked.

The Bush administration's principled refusal to conduct bilateral negotiations withered. Multilateral talks became the realistic alternative to a nuclear North Korea—a conflict the United States would not risk. As far back as October 2002, President George W. Bush recognized that the United States needed China to moderate North Korea's nuclear ambitions.[37] Following a year of entreaties from American diplomats, China agreed to host Six-Party Talks involving China, the United States, North Korea, South Korea, Japan, and Russia. After *Persuading* North Korea to attend, China scheduled the first round for August. The second and third rounds in February and June 2004 occurred as the United States deepened its military occupation of Iraq; subsequent talks lasted until March 2009.[38] For the first three years, negotiating positions from Washington reflected Compellence and Coercion; from Seoul, *Persuasion* and *Inducement*; and from Pyongyang, a paradoxical yet effective combination of all four.

Episodes of North Korean negotiators pulling out of talks, then being *Persuaded* and *Induced* back in, and on-off talks with US and other states' negotiators bought Pyongyang more time. In September 2006, a breakthrough agreement was at hand. Ambassador Chris Hill had negotiated a draft joint declaration resembling the Agreed Framework, but with more incentives for Pyongyang. North Korean promises were the same as before—abandonment of all nuclear weapons and programs, and a return to the Non-Proliferation Treaty and International Atomic Energy Agency safeguards. The differences in the new proposal were the assurances and enhancements provided to North Korea by the main powers. The United States would take steps to normalize relations; and the United States, China, South Korea, Japan, and Russia agreed to provide energy assistance and later engage in discussions on the provision of a Light Water Reactor.

The same month, rumors surfaced that the Bank of China and two banks in Macau were financing illicit North Korean activities. Instead of regarding the news as potential leverage with which to confront North Korea, the Department of State and Six-Party Talks negotiators were concerned about derailing cooperation. The US Department of Treasury created its own effect aimed at dismantling terrorist financial networks. After announcing that Banco Delta Asia of Macau had accepted huge deposits from North Korea, American officials imposed sanctions on North Korean companies charged with money laundering and weapons proliferation. Observers speculated that this included a personal account Kim Jong-il used to *Persuade* loyalty among his inner circle. If true, seizing the funds might have denied hard currency to Coerce inspections compliance, the halt of reprocessing, or improved Korean relations. US strategy was again divided. Korea experts in the US Department of State were focused on retaining North Korean participation in the talks, unmoved by intelligence analyses.[39] US Department of Treasury accusations and investigations led to Macau authorities freezing the assets.

North Korean officials charged that the United States fabricated the money-laundering issue to influence the nuclear disarmament talks. American negotiators framed the issues separately. North Korea responded with Coercion and *Persuasion* by: (1) threating to increase its nuclear arsenal unless its funds were released and (2) getting the International Atomic Energy Agency to announce Pyongyang's offer to shut down a reactor when the funds were released. The United States kept its financial-punishment line of effect separated from those of inspection Compellence and denuclearization *Inducement*. How did this failure to combine effects happen?

Viewing the issue as a terrorist crime, the Department of Treasury operated under the post-9/11 US Patriot Act, Section 311. This produced an international investigation of Banco Delta Asia for money laundering, which led to freezing of US$24 million of North Korean assets. The Bank of China's response was to buy Banco Delta and request that the US Treasury Department replace its comprehensive ban with limited restrictions.

As American officials sparred over whether to cooperate or whether to confront, North Korea Deterred and Defended the viability of its nuclear weapons development program. Demonstrations of will and capability Coerced allied acquiescence. The year 2003 was filled with North Korean attempts at intimidation and punishment of allied will. In February, North Korea launched antiship missiles in the East Sea just before South Korean president Roh Moo-hyun took office. In March, preceded by several days of warnings, North Korean fighter aircraft ran intercepts on a US reconnaissance plane in international airspace. The same month, the North Korean representative to the United States, Pak Gil-Yon, informed Special Envoy Jack Pritchard and David Straub that North Korea had restarted reprocessing spent fuel rods.[40] In August, the North Korean representative at the Six-Party Talks insulted Russian and Japanese representatives and made nuclear threats following US remarks.[41]

Throughout the fourth round (2004–2006) of the Six-Party Talks, Pyongyang continued to spew disinformation about external threats, demanding energy assistance before any nuclear dismantlement. For the first time, the United States, South Korea, and Japan called for North Korea's complete, verifiable, and irreversible dismantlement of North Korea's nuclear program on the basis that it did not match a civil-only use. Conservative influence in Washington and Japan's outrage over North Korea's abduction of its citizens led to tough talk about human rights abuses, missile proliferation, and criminal activity. From this, Pyongyang sensed increasing allied support for regime change. On July 4, 2006, North Korea launched several missiles into the East Sea. In October

2006, Pyongyang detonated its first nuclear device, estimated to be a one-kiloton explosion. North Korea now regarded itself as a nuclear power, better able to confront and cooperate with main powers to survive and expand its influence.

The UN Security Council denounced the nuclear detonation as a threat to international peace and security, and demanded that North Korea halt its production of nuclear weapons and long-range missiles. Chinese Prime Minister Hu Jintao condemned the event and called for North Korea to return to the Six-Party Talks. This happened briefly in February; then the North Korean delegation walked out after demanding resolution of the Banco Delta issue. By June, Pyongyang had Compelled the United States to resolve the issue in its favor as a precondition to return to the Six-Party Talks. North Korean elites regained access to their funds in a North Korean foreign trade account in the Bank of China in return for their pledging to use the funds solely for the betterment of the North Korean people. US officials gained Chinese cooperation in anti-money-laundering and other antiterrorism issues. Days after the Banco Delta funds were transferred back to the North Korean account, Pyongyang permitted UN inspectors to visit Yongbyon. In July 2007, Pyongyang shut down the reactor, again temporarily.

In September 2007, the Israeli Air Force destroyed nuclear facilities in Syria that had been provided by North Korea. This activated American and North Korean hardliners against the Six-Party Talks. A letter from President Bush to Kim Jong-il and the other heads of state of the Six-Party Talks would have returned North Korea to the Agreed Framework of the Clinton administration. However, now that it was clear North Korea had concealed the extent of its nuclear programs, the administration would not remove North Korea from its list of terrorist groups. Secretary of State Condoleezza Rice demanded tougher verification standards. President Bush restated his distrust of North Korean rule and its nuclear proliferation. US-promised energy aid to North Korea stalled.

The Six-Party Talks resumed again in December 2007 with Pyongyang demanding that Washington end its financial sanctions and threatening another nuclear test. The United States gave January 2008 as its deadline for North Korea to disable its nuclear reactors. Before leaving office, President Bush offered normalized ties if North Korea dismantled its nuclear reactors and weapons in an irreversible, verifiable manner. December also saw the election of Lee Myung-bok as president of South Korea with 49% of the vote. In February 2008, Lee stiffened South Korea's policy toward North Korea, prompting North Korea to threaten the South with a "sea of fire." After missing the January deadline, North Korea announced it would strengthen its war Deterrent. Meanwhile reports circulated that Kim Jong-il was on his deathbed.

The year 2009 marked a change in South Korean and American strategy while Pyongyang pressed with nuclear detonations of increased sophistication. After ten years of allied concessions and no diplomatic or nuclear reciprocity from the North, President Lee announced that aid to the North would depend upon Pyongyang's progress toward denuclearization. Newly elected Barack Obama had picked up where President George W. Bush finally left off—both presidents advocated what resembled the strategy under President Bill Clinton. The United States provided diplomatic assurance—normalized relations—if North Korea eliminated its nuclear weapons. Economic enhancements became economic punishments as the US Department of State announced a halt of fuel-oil shipments unless Pyongyang signed a nuclear-verification agreement.

In response to this and a more united approach from South Korean and Japanese leaders, North Korea maintained asymmetric advantage by demanding energy aid and increasing the frequency of border incidents, missile firings, maritime attacks, and nuclear tests. Another nuclear test in May 2009 estimated at two kilotons, and a third in February 2013 of six kilotons, asserted North Korea's nuclear status and suggested successful miniaturization of a nuclear warhead.[42]

US strategy has avoided engagement and the potential of cooperation, calling for North Korean compliance with UN and Non-Proliferation Treaty responsibilities. The Obama administration's approach to the Koreas has been to cultivate coalition support among leaders in Japan, South Korea, and China. Ambassador for North Korean Policy Glyn Davies described a strategy of engagement and pressure that will not tolerate a nuclear North Korea. His successor, Sung Kim, advocates enhanced sanctions.[43] The expectation is that regional powers will develop a neighborly interest in nuclear nonproliferation. Since the death of Kim Jong-il in December 2011, Pyongyang's internal control system continues in raw form under Kim Jong-un, who conveniently resembles Kim Il-sung.

The young leader appears intent on managing external relationships with *byeongjin* (parallel progress)—nuclear weapons and economic growth. We can expect to see confrontation and cooperation to Defend and Deter threats to the hereditary regime, nuclear status, and, problematically, economic independence. Pyongyang's cyber attacks on South Korean banks in March 2013,[44] Sony Pictures Entertainment USA in November 2014,[45] and landmine, rocket, and artillery attacks against South Korea in August 2015[46] reflect the regime's aggressive-dependent security culture. Attempts to Coerce and Compel main power behavior are likely to continue as a compatible complement to Pyongyang's combined-effects strategy.

COMBINED-EFFECTS ANALYSIS

Figure 9. Lines of Effect Logic.

Lines of Effect Logic	
Psychological:	intimidate will / neutralize capability to **Deter** D_t -- **Compel** C_p
	assure will / enhance capability to *Dissuade* D_s -- *Persuade P*
Physical:	punish will / deny capability to **Defend** D_f -- **Coerce** C_r
	demonstrate will / exercise capability to *Secure S -- Induce I*

Korean security culture provides an instructive context for understanding cooperative and confrontational strategies in a security environment dominated by interventionist powers. Pragmatic *sadaejuui* and traditional virtues play out in disparate social systems. In the North, independent brinksmanship occurs in main power relationships that are at once confrontational and cooperative. An oppressive political dynasty pursues zero-sum security with an integrated strategy of aggressive main power management and nuclear self-reliance. In the South, political-economic statesmanship operates in main power relationships that are either confrontational or cooperative. A nationalistic democracy achieves variable-sum security through a coordinated strategy involving an interdependent main power alliance. So far, Pyongyang's strategy has managed to envelop Seoul's combined-arms alliance and resist its domestic influence, as well as exploit divisions among Russia, China and the United States. How has this happened?

With respect to Russia, Moscow's normalization of ties with South Korea and withdrawal of nuclear scientists from North Korea did not Compel Pyongyang in favorable ways. Instead, it led to expanded North Korean ties with China and the United States. For its part, Pyongyang failed to anticipate Russian firmness, or simply disregarded it. Instead of trying to intimidate Moscow away from recognizing Seoul, Pyongyang might have tried to assure Moscow with alliance at the time, *Persuading* additional nuclear assistance to Deter South Korea–U.S. capability. We assume that the Kim dynasty could not tolerate being seen as giving in to any main power.

In the case of China, Pyongyang was able to use Beijing as the host of the Six-Party Talks. This permitted two strategic maneuvers. First, negotiators engaged all participants, including those with otherwise-banned bilateral interactions with the United States. Second, the process prolonged the nuclear-development timeline. The provision to North Korea of a main power forum and the inability of non–North Korean participants to agree on a combination of effects enabled Pyongyang to execute its two-track strategy of warfare.

In contrast to an underperforming American strategy split between Coercion and *Inducement*, and Compellence and *Dissuasion*, North Korean strategy maintained its structural integrity. There were no moral compunctions against combining nuclear Coercion and diplomatic Compellence. Just as righteously, the United States failed to combine cooperation and confrontation—such as *Persuading* and *Inducing* change in the security environment to *Dissuade* development of nuclear weapons. Examples include the Clinton administration separating International Atomic Energy Agency Compellence from US Coercion, former president Jimmy Carter rescuing Kim Jong-il's Coercive strategy by again promising civilian nuclear energy against President Clinton's instructions, the George W. Bush administration undermining South Korean efforts at *Persuasion* during a period of US Compellence, and the Obama administration abandoning cooperative stratagems after Pyongyang's 2009 nuclear detonation. In this competition, North Korea won nuclear power status against a narrow-minded and weak-willed adversary.

We saw North Korea's strategic-level lines of effect intersect, collide, careen, and conjoin with those of its competitors. When lines intersected, they proceeded along the same paths as before but seeded future outcomes not immediately apparent. A prime surprise was the North Korean nuclear detonation in October 2006, which occurred during the Banco Delta Asia issue. At the time, North Korea's nuclear development and aggressive dependency lines continued unchanged as they crossed paths with the US alliance and engagement lines. The South Korea–U.S. alliance had increased antiterrorism cooperation, but this was separated from the US Department of Treasury's antiterrorist law enforcement operations. Neither was linked to the US Department of State's denuclearization efforts. No one took the initiative to combine US Department of Treasury's Coercion and Compellence, and US Department of State's *Persuasion* and *Inducement*, against Pyongyang's same effects. The United States and South Korea did have impressive combined-arms capabilities, however.

As a strategic intersection, the Banco Delta Asia case was a missed opportunity for the United States to punish Kim Jong-il's will and deny him a specific financial capability after the first nuclear detonation, while advancing cooperation with other members in the Six-Party Talks. President Bush might have assured Pyongyang of conditional diplomatic recognition and economic enhancements. Ambassador Chris Hill was negotiating these at the time. Instead, the United States pursued the issue as an international crime. If the White House, along with the Department of Treasury and the Department of State, had anticipated the nuclear detonation and worked together to create a combined financial and diplomatic effect, the issue could have provided traction to denuclearize North Korea through sustained contact.

Strategies collided when the United States demanded special inspections and North Korea demanded special sovereignty. Confrontation escalated until Washington conceded. Pyongyang never accepted special inspections, although there were indications that negotiators might do so under a different label and less threatening conditions. Instead of improving the atmospherics of the Six-Party Talks, the George W. Bush administration demanded access to North Korean nuclear facilities beyond that which Ambassador Hill had negotiated. This and the failure to deliver promised heavy fuel-oil contributed to the final breakup of the Six-Party Talks in February 2009. Three months later, Pyongyang conducted another nuclear test, and the new Obama administration's open hand closed.

North Korean and American strategies careened when they interacted and altered courses in different directions. North Korean Coercion through the development of its nuclear capability, and Compellence via alternating episodes of intimidation and assurance, interacted with US Coercion through economic denial, and *Persuasion* through economic and political enhancements. While North Korean Coercion and Compellence created a nuclear main power relationship, US Coercion and *Persuasion* did not even have a combined effect in mind. The result was a nuclear North Korea facing a superpower that lacked both credible confrontation and cooperative engagement.

Conjoined strategies have been flashes of cooperation undone by domestic changes or international events. The September 2008 agreement negotiated during the Six-Party Talks was similar to the Agreed Framework of 1994 and met a similar fate. After North Korea received US assurance of diplomatic relations and the United States received North Korea's assurance of a reactor shutdown, Washington failed to take the initiative or exploit the next move. Pyongyang's provision of nuclear weapons technology abroad in contravention of previous agreements, and Washington's confrontational response, activated reactionaries in both countries to derail the deal. Instead of anticipating and shaping interactions, the United States and its partners sleepwalked through sequential routines that precluded combined effects.

What would nonlinear thinking have required? Even a low-bar national strategy needs to resolve internal divisions among administrations to coordinate external lines of effect—such as US *Persuasion* and International Atomic Energy Agency Compellence. Then, the participants in the Six-Party Talks, as well as the International Atomic Energy Agency, need to agree on desired effects, such as a nuclear weapons-free Korean peninsula under Non-Proliferation Treaty standards, and negotiate within those restraints. Overt and covert lines of effect undoubtedly challenge the ability of organizations to adapt. Through individual effort, negotiators may achieve flexibility and strike deals, but they need leadership support to follow through on them. Strategists need the capacity to orchestrate decentralized diplomatic, informational, military, economic, and social lines of effect.

Negotiators might have agreed on combined effects if they had been empowered to act as strategists. Instead of framing IAEA–North Korea and U.S.–North Korea interactions as two lines of effect that ran separately because they competed for North Korean attention, the United States and IAEA could have tried for *Persuasive* Compellence. Granted, this would mean resolving U.S.-IAEA operational-level disagreements, such as whether to push special inspections or an immediate freeze, and holding Pyongyang accountable or keeping Pyongyang in the talks. If this were made a priority, then agreement on strategic-level outcomes is feasible, such as North Korea's peaceful integration into the global economic and political system. The extent to which national leaders have the will or capability to make the latter a sustainable priority profoundly affects strategy.

In the absence of such strategic capacity, differences in national priorities sabotaged allied effectiveness. From a South Korean perspective, Washington prioritized relations with North Korea and the International Atomic Energy Agency over the South Korea–U.S. alliance. Likewise, American officials viewed Seoul's Nordpolitik, Sunshine Policy, and KEDO-related policies as undercutting denuclearization. The failure to work out an allied combination of effects resulted in divergent national lines of effect. Pyongyang was keen to exploit these by constructing its own combined effects—directly with its own operatives or indirectly via surrogates. The United States, International Atomic Energy Agency, and South Korea were able to coordinate their operations at times, but they all missed opportunities to combine denuclearization, inspections compliance, and economic integration. Fixated on combined arms, the US government failed to consider alternative effects. Instead of using its enhancement of North Korean economic capability to *Persuade* Pyongyang to accept nuclear inspections, the United States conditioned a potentially powerful tool—the provision of economic assistance—on its target's will to make progress in North-South denuclearization talks. Denuclearization clashed with reunification. Particularly during the Clinton–Kim Young-sam administrations, this grand failure of a main power ceded the initiative of generating effects to Pyongyang and Seoul.

By comparison, we note two North Korean mistakes that were subsequently corrected, and strengthened Pyongyang's confrontational lines of effect. First, in 1990 Pyongyang failed to anticipate Russian will with respect to normalizing relations with Seoul. Instead of trying to intimidate Moscow into nonrecognition of Seoul, Pyongyang might have assured Moscow with alliance and thereby *Persuaded* more nuclear assistance to Deter South Korea–U.S. capability. Pyongyang realized it was being isolated by Moscow and turned toward China. Second, in 1994 President Clinton was about to follow through on the military enforcement of economic sanctions, a will that Pyongyang miscalculated its capability to intimidate. North Korean actions did *Induce* President Carter's intervention, however, enabled by a standing annual invitation that preserved the North Korean lines of effect that endure today.

Viewing the nuclear crisis in the context of Korean security culture helps us anticipate synergistic lines of effect and shape future conditions. When Pyongyang detonated its first nuclear device, US observers saw this as an event that could have been prevented. Through conservative eyes, this meant confrontation such as enforcing economic sanctions. Liberals, however, advocated cooperation such as a path with milestones toward normalization. By orienting on Korean security culture, even politicians could have anticipated two lines: (1) Pyongyang's main power management and nuclear weapons development; and (2) Seoul's strategy of seeking more autonomy from the United States while retaining its nuclear guarantee. The tendency of the Koreas to seek security through these lines should lead us to focus on relationships as much as particular weapons. How did these preferences play out from North and South Korean perspectives?

Pyongyang needed to confront and cooperate with the United States to achieve a nuclear capability. The basic confrontational line of effect was to Compel and Coerce the United States into accepting a nuclear-armed North Korea as the price for normalization. Given the gap in North Korea–U.S. military-economic capability, North Korea targeted weak US government will to escalate and weak US diplomatic capability to lead a countervailing consensus. Pyongyang's cooperative line was to *Persuade* and *Induce* the United States into guaranteeing North Korea's regime survival. Based on its record of violence and threats, this was not a credible strategy because it would require Americans to believe that North Korean hostility would abate, mutual disarmament would begin, and intra-Korean relations would improve. It would also require a great leader indeed to dismantle the nuclear program over party and army objections. That is unlikely today under Kim Jong-un, whose awkward efforts at Coercion sustain the venal regime. As we interpret the significance of executed changes among senior leaders, younger replacements are populating the new Kim network. Overall, North Korea has combined confrontation and cooperation with relative success primarily due to US and allied strategic incompetence.

Seoul's cooperative line of effect during the Kim Dae-jung and Roh Moo-hyun presidencies was to *Persuade* and *Induce* Pyongyang to improve Korean relations and so moderate its behavior over the long run. Differences between these South Korean and their corresponding American administrations undermined the credibility of what might have been a systemic allied dilemma on Pyongyang. The confrontational line under Presidents Kim Young-sam, Lee Myung-bak, and Park Geun-hye, however, has withheld aid to Compel reciprocity from the North. So far this has not worked. The democratic hope is that Pyongyang will eventually have to react to the sustained rise of South Korean power. That is, in order to outperform the US-*Secured* South militarily, the North will have to adjust its political and economic processes. So far, the Kim-centered control system does not care, impoverishing its own people and threatening nuclear war for the sake of ideological control.

Unless the main powers provide assurances and enhancements to Pyongyang to cooperate, further confrontation is inevitable. Such options require thinking about strategy broadly. This could involve coordinating financial and military tools to neutralize and deny North Korean nuclear capability while offering diplomatic recognition and social prestige to enhance and assure Pyongyang leaders' personal stakes. Compared to such combined-effects strategies, are the US and its allies willing to "out-escalate" North Korea with combined arms? Based on Korean security culture and the current environment, North Korean leaders see little efficacy in cooperation—at least until (1) China withdraws support, (2) the United States offers to eliminate threats, or (3) Pyongyang acquires a sufficient nuclear capability to *Persuade* and *Dissuade, Induce* and *Secure*.

With respect to the first possibility, there is evidence that China has drawn a line on North Korean Coercion. We know that China is also interested in reclaiming its lost imperial boundaries all around. Pyongyang's pattern of nuclear tests and missile firings during leadership transitions—its own, US, South Korea, or China—has become a trend. The standdown of missile alert in May 2013 after weeks of preparatory bluster, however, seems an anomaly. This may be an indicator of losing Chinese support. Will main power competition hand North Korea a Russian or American partner? Will there be external solidarity to denuclearize the peninsula?

Sino-American unity is more likely when South Korea, the United States, and Japan agree on a common approach. We know this is possible because the Six Party Talks were able to forge a China-Japan-Russia-South Korea-U.S. consensus on an Agreed Framework–like package, only to be undone in the White House. The likelihood that the current American administration would offer to reduce the threat to North Korea must be judged in the context of South Korea–U.S. alliance. The Obama-Park 2013 summit announced that North Korea would not be permitted to "create a crisis and elicit concessions."[47] All indications are that US "strategic patience" means following the lead of President Park Geun-hye, whose double-edged policy promises retribution for any North Korean attack, and substantial aid for a change in course. The daughter of separately assassinated parents, her proposal for a park in the demilitarized zone seems to be the only engagement on the table. As a result, the current strategy seeks to break North Korean will, then reengage Pyongyang with tit-for-tat rewards and punishments.

In a security environment with minimal diplomatic, informational, economic, and social interactions, both Koreas will see threats as zero-sum rather than variable-sum opportunities. Likewise, if Pyongyang or Seoul encounters confrontation without the credible will to Coerce or Compel, either state is likely to escalate with enough force to charge its basic strategy. Seoul will pursue global interdependence and cooperation while relying on the US nuclear guarantee to confront Pyongyang. Nuclear Pyongyang will confront and cooperate its way toward peninsular unification and regional power status. Meanwhile China bides its time, building capability and influence to reassert control over the peninsula. Across the East Sea lies Japan with a similar legacy. The need to engage North Korea with a strategy of combined effects, to idealize a notion from Clausewitz, ought to be simple to recognize even if difficult to do.

Figure 10. Combined Effects Summary of *Korea's Nuclear Polarization*.

Combined Effects Summary of *Korea's Nuclear Polarization*

North Korea

    Strategy $C_p\,C_r\,D_t\,D_f\,P\,I$ Asymmetric Envelopment

        (**Compellence-Coercion-Deterrence-Defense-***Persuasion-Inducement*)

    Lines of Effect   Nuclear Development to **Deter**, **Compel** and **Coerce** main powers for economic concessions, reunification and control

        Aggressive Dependence to **Deter** and **Defend** against nuclear inspections, **Compel** and **Coerce** economic aid, and *Persuade* and *Induce* US relations

South Korea

    Strategy $P\,D_t\,D_f$ Secured and Systemic Dilemma

        (*Persuasion*-**Deterrence-Defense-***Security*)

    Lines of Effect   Military Alliance with the US to *Persuade* South Korean citizens, **Secure** US commitment, and **Deter** and **Defend** against North Korean attack

        Economic-Moral Suasion to *Persuade* North Korea into peaceful engagement

United States

    Strategy $D_t\,D_f\,C_r\,D_s\,C_p$ Operational Deterrence and Territorial Defense

        (**Deterrence-Defense-Coercion-***Dissuasion*-**Compellence**)

    Lines of Effect   Military Alliance to **Deter** and **Defend** against attack

        Incremental Engagement to **Coerce**, *Dissuade* and **Compel** North Korea

International Atomic Energy Agency

    Strategy C_p Coopted Compellence

        (**Compellence**)

    Line of Effect   Nuclear inspections to **Compel** North Korea compliance with the Non Proliferation Treaty

Notes

1. See Sung Chull Kim, *North Korea under Kim Jong Il: From Consolidation to Systemic Dissonance* (Albany: SUNY Press, 2006).
2. For differences in ROK-U.S. threat perceptions, see Christian F. Ostermann and James F. Person, *Crisis and Confrontation on the Korean Peninsula: 1966–1969 A Critical Oral History* (Washington, DC: Woodrow Wilson International Center for Scholars, 2011).
3. See Peter Hayes, "The Republic of Korea and the Nuclear Issue," in *Asian Flashpoint: Security and the Korean Peninsula*, ed. Andrew Mack, (Canberra: Allen and Unwin, 1993).
4. Peter Hayes and Chung-in Moon, "Park Chung Hee, the CIA and the Bomb," in *Global Asia* 6 No. 3, Fall 2011. http://www.globalasia.org/V6 N3_Fall_2011/Peter_Hayes&Chung-in_Moon.html (accessed November 3, 2012).
5. For an informative report that estimates North Korea's fissile materials, see David Albright, "North Korean Plutonium and Weapons-Grade Uranium Inventories," Institute for Science and International Security. www.isis-online.org/uploads/isis-reports/documents/North_Korean_Fissile_Material_Stocks_Jan_30_2015_revised_Oct _5_2015-final.pdf (accessed April 13, 2015).
6. National Security Review 28, cited in Joel S. Wit, Daniel B. Poneman, and Robert L. Gallucci, *Going Critical: The First North Korean Nuclear Crisis* (Washington, DC: The Brookings Institution Press, 2004), 13.
7. Yoichi Funabashi, *The Peninsula Question: A Chronicle of the Second Korean Nuclear Crisis* (Washington, DC: Brookings Institution Press, 2007), 21.
8. The surviving agent was pardoned for political effect. See her autobiography: Kim Hyun-lee, *The Tears of My Soul* (New York: William and Morrow, 1993), the film *Mayumi* (1990) and appearances on talk shows in South Korea.
9. Yoichi Funabashi in Funabashi, *The Peninsular Question*, 172–173.
10. See the appendix in Lim, *Peacemaker*, 377–381.
11. For a broad study on issues associated with US bases overseas to include those in South Korea, see Kent E. Calder, *Embattled Garrisons: Comparative Base Politics and American Globalism* (Princeton: Princeton Uni-

versity Press, 2007), particularly Chapter 8, "The Financial Equations," 188-208.

12. Ashton B. Carter and William B. Perry, *Preventive Defense: A New Security Strategy for America* (Washington, DC: Brookings Institution Press, 1999), 127.

13. Gong Ro-myun was ROK ambassador to the Joint Nuclear Control Commission attempting to implement mutual obligations of the North-South Denuclearization Agreement.

14. Wit, Poneman and Gallucci, *Going Critical*, 30.

15. Leon Sigal asks this question and argues that economic stagnation led Pyongyang to negotiations. Leon V. Sigal, *Disarming Strangers: Nuclear Diplomacy with North Korea* (Princeton: Princeton University Press, 1998), 21.

16. Wit, Poneman and Gallucci, *Going Critical*, 40.

17. Uranium Information Centre, Ltd., Canberra, Australia, www.uic.com.au/nip15.htm (accessed March 11, 2015).

18. Wit, Poneman and Gallucci, *Going Critical*, 5.

19. *North Korean Nuclear Crisis February 1993-June 1994*, Federation of American Scientists website, www.fas.org/man/dod-101/ops/dprk_nuke.htm, (accessed January 27, 2013).

20. Wit, Poneman and Gallucci, *Going Critical*, 77–181.

21. "Agreed Framework Between the United States of America and the Democratic People's Republic of Korea," October 21, 1994, www.ceip.org/files/projects/npp/resources/koreaaf.htm (accessed December 7, 2012).

22. On "as" as either "at the same time" or "because," see Wit, Poneman and Gallucci, *Going Critical*, 341–344.

23. Harrison, *Korean Endgame*, 262.

24. Appendix 3, KEDO Charter, in Kartmann, Carlin and Wit, *A History of KEDO*, 171-79.

25. For examples see Lim, *Peacemaker*, 86–87.

26. Mike Chinoy, *Meltdown: The Inside Story of the North Korean Nuclear Crisis* (New York: St Martin's Press, 2009), 74.

27. See "Part I, The Role of Rhetoric," in Charles L. Pritchard, *Failed Diplomacy: The Tragic Story of How North Korea Got the Bomb* (Washington, DC: Brookings Institution Press, 2007).

28. Lim, *Peacemaker*, 285.

29. Pritchard, *Failed Diplomacy*, 28.

30. Ibid., 34.

31. Interview with senior US official, November 2012.

32. Chinoy, *Meltdown*, 146.

33. "N. Korea Report steps back from nuclear claim," *The Boston Globe*, 19 November 2002, www.boston.com/dailyglobe2/323/nation (accessed December 8, 2012).

34. The American Presidency Project, President's News Conference 7 Nov 07. http://www.presidency.ucsb.edu/ws/index.php?pid=63868 (accessed November 28, 2012).

35. See Robert L. Carlin and Joel S. Wit, "North Korean Reform: Politics, economics and security," Adelphi Paper 382 (London: The International Institute for Strategic Studies, 2006), 38–52.

36. Lim, *Peacemaker*, 326.

37. Testimony by Christopher Hill, "The North Korean Six-Party Talks and Implementation Activities," Hearing before the Committee on Armed Services, 110th Congress, 2d Session, 31 Jul 08. http://www.gpo.gov/fdsys/pkg/CHRG-110shrg46091/pdf/CHRG-110shrg46091.pdf (accessed December 3, 2012).

38. Iterations of the Six-Party Talks: August 2004 (4th round, phase 1); September 2004 (4th round, phase 2); November 2005 (5th round, phase 1); December 2006 (5th round, phase 2); February 2007 (5th round, phase 3); March 2007 (6th round, phase 1); July 2007 (6th round, phase 2); September 2007 (6th round, phase 3). In March 2009, Pyongyang vowed to never again participate.

39. Chinoy, *Meltdown*, 288.

40. Yoichi Funabashi, *The Peninsula Question: A Chronicle of the Second Korean Nuclear Crisis* (Washington, DC: Brookings Institution Press, 2007), 148.

41. Funabashi, *The Peninsula Question*, 343.

42. Shuji Sue, Katsuya Tsukamoto and Hiromu Arakaki, "The Role of the Ministry of Defense and Self-Defense Forces in Nonproliferation of Weapons of Mass Destruction (WMD): Toward Strengthening WMD Intelligence," *National Institute of Defense Studies Bulletin* (2010): 3-44, 7-8. http://www.nids.go.jp/english/publication/east-asian/e2011.html (accessed October 18, 2012).

43. Presentation by Ambassador Glyn Davies, Korbel School of International Studies, University of Denver, CO, January 18, 2013.

44. See Johee Cho, "North Korea Eyed in Huge Cyber Attack on South Korea," *ABC News*, 20 March 2013. http://abcnews.go.com/International/north-korea-eyed-huge-cyber-attack-south-korea/story?id=18769664;

and "North Korean cyber-rattling," *The Economist*, 17 May 2013. http://www.economist.com/blogs/babbage/2013/05/digital-warfare (both accessed November 9, 2012).

45. "A Breakdown and Analysis of the December 2014 Sony Hack," Risk-Based Security. https://www.riskbasedsecurity.com/2014/12/a-breakdown-and-analysis-of-the-december-2014-sony-hack/ (accessed September 19, 2015).

46. "South Korea fires at North Korea in retaliation for loudspeaker attack," *theguardian.* http://www.theguardian.com/world/2015/aug/20/south-korea-north-korea-border-attack-loudspeaker-retaliation (accessed September 19, 2015).

47. Robert A. Manning, "Park-Obama summit bolsters US-ROK alliance," *East Asia Forum*, 16 May 2013. http://www.eastasiaforum.org/2013/05/16/park-obama-summit-bolsters-us-rok-alliance/ (accessed January 3, 2016).

CHAPTER 6

JAPANESE SECURITY CULTURE

Japan, a society whose exclusive economic zone is five times the size of China's, looks outward for 80 percent of its energy needs. Its self-defense force, however, is supposed to operate decidedly inward under an American-imposed constitution that forever renounces war, the use or threat of force to settle disputes, military forces, and war potential.[1] Japanese air, ground, and maritime forces contribute to international peacekeeping operations while rejecting collective defense[2] and restricting their weapons to "the minimum necessary for self-defense."[3] What kind of security culture permits such unrealistic defense? There are two defining features.

The first is unique-ism, a national myth rooted in a cultivated legend of single-dynasty rule.[4] Threat perceptions portray Japan as distinctly different, reinforced by self-imposed isolation, then unwanted recontact, with outside powers in the mid-nineteenth century.[5] This constructed identity is remarkably persistent, manifesting itself in idiosyncratic art, *nihonjin ron* (Japanese-ness theory), indigenous and assimilated religions, and assorted special exceptions in government and private decisions.[6] As in Chinese centrality and Korean self-reliance, societal beliefs in national characteristics do not neatly coincide with reality, but do affect strategic choices about security.

The second value is ambivalence in foreign relations—how isolated and how engaged should Japan be? A pervasive reminder of this dualism is the prevalence of outsider-insider distinctions found throughout the Japanese language such as *soto* 外 (outside) and *uchi* 內 (inside), *honne* 本音 (true, sound = real intention) and *tatemae* 建面 (constructed face = public face), and *ura* 裏 (hidden side) and *omote* 表 (visible side).[7] Group decisions seek to harmonize such differences in a common context,[8] while national security-related programs and policies habitually frame actions as reactions to *gaiatsu* 外圧 (outside pressure).[9] Uncertainty can help account for this variation in shaping the environment, but why do these uniquely regarded reactions matter?

Japanese security culture institutionalizes special isolationist policies that engage the world with reactive strategies. This tendency makes it difficult for Japanese leaders who anticipate future threats to implement long-term strategies to shape desired outcomes. Consider the present situation of China's territorial coercion and North Korea's nuclear intimidation. On the one hand, how can Japan expect to resolve long-standing disputes with minimal confrontation and total avoidance of force? On the other, how can Japan use confrontation in proactive ways as practiced by other states? We turn to our first question of security culture.

What is the Role of Confrontation and Cooperation in Security?

Historically Japanese confrontation is competitive and cooperative, shaping identity and gaining resources. As early as the third century, the Yamato kingdom's agro-military advantages fueled its expansion from the Inland Sea. Trade sent Yamato to the continent, allying with Paekche to counter Sillan dominance.[10] When Koguryo and Silla sided with China's Northern Song dynasty, Yamato and Paekche stood with the Southern Song . Yamato's military campaigns acquired raw materials, but stirred fears of a retaliatory Chinese invasion of Japan. Defeats abroad and rebellions at home forced Yamato to retreat from its first foreign encroachment. Tang China and Silla then destroyed Koguryo and Paekche.

During the Asuka (538–710) and Nara (710–784) periods, Japanese emperors coopted Shintoism and Buddhism to align local loyalties to higher royal duties. Shintō beliefs in gods connected sacred spots to the Tennō (Emperor, " heavenly luminescence") who represented the sun goddess (Amaterasu). A Department of Imperial Shrines assured this supreme linkage. Courts induced obedience through provincial Buddhist temples where appointed priests worshipped national deities.[11] Upward Confucian obligations accommodated the hierarchy, a bond that helped colonize Japan.

Throughout the Heian period (784–1180), priests and warriors manipulated imperial control. Buddhist monks used social status and court subsidies to command their own armies. Hiring of samurai (servant) led to the proliferation of daimyō (great name) families and internecine wars. Fujiwara regents fell to Taira aristocrats, defeated in turn by the Minamoto who induced loyalty with land rights and shōgun (supreme commander) status. Two capitals emerged—inland Kyoto, where the emperor ruled, and Kamakura (protected harbor), where a military bakufu (tent office) governed fiefdoms and local communities. Kyoto's flat terrain led to the construction of heavily fortified castles, while Kamakura became an enclave protected by defensible mountain passes and a heavily armed bay.

In the 1200s the bakufu defended Japan against Mongol invaders and in the process strengthened their domestic influence. China's Yuan dynasty subjugated Koryŏ and sent official delegations to compel Japanese submission. The court was inclined to compromise, but the bakufu purged internal rivals and prepared fortifications. In 1274, nine hundred warships and 23,000 warriors landed in Hakata Bay. They battled pockets of samurai and returned to their ships, where one-third perished in a storm henceforth referred to as kamikaze (divine wind).[12] Afterwards the bakufu expanded their political jurisdiction. Plans for retaliation were drawn up, but not executed. They did execute another delegation of Yuan envoys who reiterated previous demands. In 1281, China's Kublai Khan sent over 4,400 warships and 140,000 soldiers toward Japan, only to be encounter another storm that killed 100,000. Blustering bakufu threatened counterattack, but left it at that.[13]

Under the specter of foreign invasion, military factions and court intrigues disrupted Japan for 500 years. Conspiracy in Kyoto prompted the bakufu to dispatch Ashikaga Takauji to suppress it. Instead of doing so he installed his own lineage, the Muromachi (1336). Prominent families cultivated key relationships among warriors, daimyō, and the court.[14] The major confrontations during the Sengoku (war country) period may be understood in terms of these turbulent triangles.[15]

The subsequent conquest of lands and loyalties under warlords Oda Nobunaga (1568–1582), Toyotomi Hideyoshi (1583–1598), and Toku-gawa Ieyasu (1603–1616) ordered Japanese society. Samurai and farmers became separate classes; merchants were progressively taxed. Officially esteemed, nobles and priests were controlled through stipends. Martial arts became idealized as warfare mobilized vassals to serve lords.[16] Disas-trous invasions of Chosŏn in 1592 and 1597 were justified as defensive wars that affirmed Japan's sacred identity.[17]

The House of Tokugawa completed Japan's unification but ignored external threats and internal grievances. The shogunate relocated to Edo (within present-day Tokyo), closing ports to all but a few envoys.[18] Bushidō (the way of the warrior) became formalized, admitting a ritualized form of mobility as gekokujo (vassal supplants lord) samurai overpow-ered some of higher status. Reformists urged change, but the conserva-tive-minded bakufu stuck to "obligations of the past."[19] By the mid-1800s, Western missionaries and merchants pressed into Japanese ports.

The treaty system arrived in Japan from America. Commodore Matthew Perry's squadron of steamships darkened Edo Bay in 1853, coercing access that led to Japan's first treaty with a foreign power (1858). Ensuing agreements promised outposts and extraterritorial rights to fifteen more states.[20] The crucial dilemma for Japan became how to confront outsiders without submitting. "Expelling the barbarians" (jōi) seemed well beyond Tokugawa capabilities. Imperial authority might strengthen resolve, but that threatened the main lineages of bakufu control. Unsurprisingly, no new strategy developed.

Humiliating defeats forced change as cultures clashed. In 1862, a British merchant who refused to dismount from his horse for a passing samurai was summarily slashed to death, for which Great Britain demanded reparations and bombarded Kagoshima when these went unmet. After a rash of assassinations, Emperor Kōmei finally enacted the unequal treaties in 1866. He died of smallpox the next year, after which loyalists and reformists overthrew bakufu rule. The new Emperor's era was entitled Meiji (enlightened rule).

From its new tōkyō (eastern capital), the Meiji Restoration pushed modernization. Land taxes eroded local influence. Market incentives increased revenue for industrialization. Governors replaced daimyō. Compulsory education instilled state loyalty as "civilization and enlightenment" (bunmei kaika). Conscription mobilized a national army that suppressed rebels. A constitution (1881) equated imperial authority with state sovereignty, undercutting a "freedom and people's rights" (jiyū minken) movement. Overseas delegations learned foreign politics and technology and urged renegotiated treaties. Somehow Japan's normal drive for influence was seen as exceptional.

Japan's territorial expansion began in the Ryūkyū (Liuqiu, in Chinese) islands also claimed by China. The beset Ryukyu Kingdom had paid tribute to China, Chosŏn, and the Satsuma clan of Japan.[21] In 1871 the killing of shipwrecked Ryukyu fishermen by aborigines in Taiwan presented an opportunity to exercise sovereignty. The morality of exacting satisfaction was not an issue. Punitive missions were common international practice, particularly against people deigned to be barbarian, uncivilized, or savage.[22] Besides, China had no embassies to influence, so...what to do? Japan's 3,600-strong Taiwan Expedition in 1874 killed dozens of native people on Taiwan, suffered hundreds of Japanese casualties due to malaria and other endemic diseases, and returned home.[23] In 1874 after months of negotiations, China provided Japan compensation and equal international status in return for Japanese withdrawal. Four years later, Japan annexed the Ryukyu Kingdom.[24] Next the Meiji Cabinet endorsed opening Korea for trade. The plan was to administer reforms and reorient resources toward Japan. In 1875, the Japanese ship *Unyō* trespassed deliberately to draw fire from Ganghwa Island and in response invaded it.[25] The Treaty of Ganghwa Island (also known as the Japan-Korea Treaty of 1876) coerced the opening of chosen ports and extracted extraterritoriality. Stirred by a modern Japanese press, peasant uprisings, and an army mutiny in Korea, the Chōsen mondai (Korea problem) roiled into war.[26]

Factional fighting in Korea led to a coup crushed by Chinese troops, after which Tokyo negotiated equal rights to intervene as reflected in the Convention of Tientsin, 1885.[27] When Seoul obtained Chinese troops to suppress the Tonghak Rebellion (1894), Tokyo ordered its troops to initiate the Sino-Japanese war. Japanese forces prevailed on the Korean peninsula, then seized Port Arthur, Weihaiwei, the Pescadores Islands (Penghu), and Taiwan. In the Treaty of Shimonoseki (1895), Japan replaced China's suzerainty over Korea, gained access to Chinese ports, and acquired Taiwan and the Liaodong Peninsula (which was later retroceded).

Tokyo also instigated the Russo-Japanese War in Korea after failing to contain Moscow diplomatically. Bargaining had worked before—the Treaty of Saint Petersburg (1875) gave Russia Sakhalin and Japan the Kuril Islands. But now both empires sought Manchuria and Korea. Japan first neutralized British sea power with the Anglo-Japanese Alliance (1902). Two years later, Japanese destroyers torpedoed Russian Pacific Fleet battleships anchored near Port Arthur. Tokyo declared war, captured Seoul, and advanced into Manchuria where both Japanese and Russian soldiers suffered heavy losses. Japan's armored cruisers broke the stalemated land war by annihilating a hopelessly outranged Russian Baltic Fleet transiting the Tsushima Strait. This victory combined with rebellions against the czar to force negotiations.

In a preparatory Japan-U.S. rendezvous, Prime Minister Katsura assured Secretary of War Taft that Japan would not attack the Philippines, thus obtaining acceptance of Japan's occupation of Korea. The Treaty of Portsmouth (1905) hosted by President Theodore Roosevelt awarded to Japan southern Sakhalin Island and Russian rights in Manchuria and the Liaodong Peninsula. Western powers rewarded Tokyo by upgrading their legations to embassies. Still debating strategic priorities, Japan annexed Chosŏn in 1910.

Domestic politics facilitated Japan's national reactions. Prime ministers and cabinets changed out every two years. Factions riddled the elected Lower House while genrō (senior statesmen) controlled the court-appointed Upper House. As political parties populated the cabinet, policies swung from a "world without war"[28] (1924–1927) that respected China's sovereignty, to "Manchuria-Mongolia separation" (Man-Mō bunri) which repudiated it.[29] While the Japanese emperor acted above such mundane matters, ministries and the general staff vied for imperial authority.[30] As gunbatsu ("military factions") gained influence, the Japanese foreign ministry supported territorial expansion.

Reactively put, opportunities for warfare were exploited by Japan. The collapse of Qing China (1911) released Japanese troops into Mongolia. Germany's losses after World War I enabled Japan to garner portions of Shandong Province and the Pacific. President Yuan Shih-kai's assumption of power in the new Republic of China unleashed the Twenty-One Demands. Japan's new holdings withstood the Paris Peace Conference of 1919, the Washington Naval Conference of 1921–1922, and related attempts to contain Japan. As foreign opposition mounted, so did Japanese support for an equal share of Asia. In June 1928, Kwantung Army soldiers assassinated China's Marshal Zhang Zuolin in Mukden by detonating a bomb underneath his railroad car. Punishment for the colonel in charge:

early retirement.[31] When the global depression of 1929 disrupted Japan's economy, culturally characterized as uniquely so, the Manshū mondai (Manchuria problem) became urgent.[32]

Another incident near Mukden led to disproportionate effects. In September 1931, a lieutenant detonated a bomb that failed to derail the targeted train.[33] It did engineer the dispatch of more Japanese Kwantung Army troops. The foreign ministry announced the new state of Manchukuo. When the League of Nations refused to recognize it, Japan withdrew from the league rather than from Manchukuo. National policy switched to "autonomous strength and defense."[34] By 1937, China and Japan were at war. Under special imperial authority, the gunbatsu sought battlefield victories and, as those became elusive, military occupation.

Behind a harmonious face, Japan's wartime cabinets drifted in indecision. Early victories won domestic support, but operational momentum stalled against costly defeats and prolonged resistance. The rivalrous army and navy, each with its own air force, failed to prioritize their campaigns. Forces became scattered in an under-resourced war of attrition. The defense of the homeland was an afterthought; it was finally approved in January 1945.[35]

In July 1945, the Potsdam Declaration issued by the United States, Great Britain, and Republic of China demanded Japan's unconditional surrender. The ultimatum made explicit that Japan would be occupied and democratized. Japan's reply from the deadlocked Supreme War Council[36] was ambiguous, translated negatively as "not worthy of comment."[37] In ten days, the first atomic bomb detonated over Hiroshima; three days later, another devastated Nagasaki. The next day Emperor Hirohito broke the impasse. On August 15, the populace heard his voice for the first time as a rescript that directed acceptance of the Potsdam Declaration's terms.

Remarkably, the occupation of Japan was a compatible merge of exceptionalist security cultures. Despite a late crash campaign for homeland defense, half of Japan's cities destroyed, and more than two million dead, the Japanese people offered a non-hostile environment. Some attributed this to war fatigue. Others credited the emperor's unique broadcast. As occupation forces arrived, Japanese commanders sent emissaries to broker Japanese compliance. US forces encountered deferential military and police, and an obedient population. Under the orders of General Douglas MacArthur, Supreme Commander for the Allied Powers (SCAP), occupation forces were to supervise, not rule.[38]

As SCAP headquarters outlined expectations for demilitarization and democratization, Japanese authorities administered the details. By and large, only military leaders were tried for war crimes. The emperor renounced his divinity to serve as a constitutional monarch. MacArthur's staff drafted the new constitution that placed sovereignty with the people, forbade military forces, and renounced war. Individual rights replaced paternalism. Compulsory education was lengthened, and more universities established. Land, finance, and industrial reforms weakened monopolies and empowered unions. A National Police Reserve (1950) and National Safety Force (1952) became forerunners of the Self-Defense Force (1954). American economic assistance helped Japan rebuild its manufacturing, trade, and finance sectors.

The Bilateral Security Treaty between the United States of America and Japan signed in 1951 and the San Francisco Peace Treaty signed on the same day ended the occupation but did not begin a new security culture. Beliefs in uniqueness and ambivalence about foreign relations persisted. The Japanese struggled with national identity after starting and losing the Greater East Asia War, but nevertheless they transformed their economy and political system. Democratic Japan certainly intended to keep disputed territories. Estranged from other partners, Japan's best choice was to offer military bases for an external US security guarantee. US collective defense fit Japan's self-defense restraints.

The security relationship developed ambivalently. As UN forces defended South Korea (1950–1953), Japan's Special Procurement Agency provided logistical support against the North Korean offensive.[39] This also garnered tokujū (special income) benefits to Japan.[40] Japan's National

Diet refused to fund its own defense forces, so US Congressional appropriations established the Japan Self-Defense Force (JSDF; 1954). As the United States urged rearmament, Japanese leaders pushed economic recovery. Japan's Basic Policy on National Defense (1957) established four principles: an exclusively defense-oriented policy; not becoming a military power; not possessing, producing, or permitting nuclear weapons; and civilian control of the military. Quantum changes to this original formula have been political poison in Japan.

The relationship's resilience reinforces the myth that Japan is unique. A mainstream thread goes: Japan is a war-renouncing country with a special non-belligerent model for security. A countervailing response: Japan needs normal offensive military capability. Mounting tension is abetted by unresolved territorial issues.

The San Francisco Peace Treaty required Japan to return most, but not all, of its forcibly acquired possessions. Tokyo renounced the Kuril Islands, Sakhalin and adjacent islands gained in the Treaty of Portsmouth, Korea, Formosa (Taiwan), the Pescadores, the Spratlys, and the Antarctic area. Exactly which islands constituted the Kuril Islands were not specified. The Soviet Union had not signed the treaty, so a separate peace agreement was needed. Signed in 1956, both sides agreed to resolve territorial issues later. Japan still claims four "northern territory" islands occupied by Soviet troops after hostilities ended.[41] These were not part of the Treaty of Portsmouth and are not considered by Japan to be part of the Kuril Islands.[42] Summit talks and domestic assertions of ownership have failed to settle the dispute, but these have not generated any sustained crisis either. In the Koreas, it's a different story.

About halfway between Japan and Korea in the Sea of Japan (East Sea) sits the islet of Takeshima (Dokdo). In South Korean hands since 1954, the disputed territory delayed Japan–South Korea diplomatic relations until 1965. It remains a touchstone of nationalism, particularly after 1982 when the United Nations Convention on the Law of the Sea permitted 200 nm exclusive economic zones (EEZ) around such high-tide specks.[43] South

Korea argues that Japan wrongfully declared the island terra nullius in 1904 and had seized it on the way to occupy Korea. Japan counters that its merchants charted the island in the sixteenth century before anyone else, and the San Francisco Peace Treaty does not specify it as part of Korea. Today Seoul maintains a 12 nm zone of control.

In the Treaty of Taipei (1952), Japan renounced its 1895 claim to Taiwan, the Pescadores, the Spratlys and the Paracels, and "all treaties, conventions, and agreements concluded before 9 December 1941 between Japan and China."[44] The 1972 Japan-China communiqué specified Taiwan as part of China, but it also referred to the Potsdam Declaration, which limited Japanese sovereignty to the four main islands "...and such minor islands as we determine."[45]

None of these agreements affected the Ryukyu archipelago, where the San Francisco Peace Treaty handed the United States sole administrative authority. As the Japanese self-defense force developed capabilities, the United States progressively returned control to Japan in 1953 (Amami, north of Okinawa), 1968 (Ogasawara, east of Okinawa, and mainland Japan), and 1972 (Ryukyu, including Okinawa).

This review of Japanese confrontation and cooperation ends where it began—the quest for identity and resources. Prevailing beliefs about both goals perpetuated conflict and unified Japan. Continental expeditions were an extension of the latter, and they failed. When pressed by Western contact, Tokugawa Japan responded with seclusion that proved similarly ineffective. Meiji Japan modernized and pursued empire through unsustainable warfare. After that defeat, postwar Japan focused on economic development and an asymmetric, interdependent alliance. Today's ambivalent proportion of isolation and engagement is also regarded as unique. In a dynamic threat environment, there is considerable uncertainty about whether it should continue to be so.

What is the Nature and Assessment of the Threat?

Traditionally, securing Japan has meant countering threats from the continent and adjacent seas. Japanese chronicles note Yamato alliances and rivalries with Korean kingdoms, as well as concerns about coastal trade.[46] Curiously, the rise of the Soga clan in the sixth century coincided with an influx of Chinese traditions. Initially a variable-sum "threat," Chinese-style reforms began the century of Asuka Enlightenment.

The Mongol invasions of the thirteenth century presented a stark, zero-sum threat—defeated Japan would have become a tributary kingdom of the Yuan dynasty. But the "divine wind"-aided defense held, and plans to counterinvade Chosŏn were prudently postponed. Periodic pirate raids aside, Japan was free of external interference for nearly four centuries. Threat assessment during this turbulent Sengoku period was shaped by three requirements of the warrior class.

First, relations among court, bakufu, and landowners had to be coerced. The basic linkage was the lord-vassal bond of obligation and loyalty. The daimyō who lorded over their network were obligated to the bakufu who operated as a council of peers. Access to the emperor provided legitimacy. Second, a code of behavior among samurai generated respect, the currency of power. Honor and other virtues were socially compelled. Third, operational tactics were essential to survival and dominance. Swordsmanship, horsemanship, archery, and other *bujutsu* (combat method) perfected warfare. Martial philosophies helped perpetuate the system.

In light of the foregoing, Japan's failed invasions of Chosŏn at the end of the sixteenth century made unfortunate sense. The shōgun, Toyotomi Hideyoshi, acted to weaken rivals and bring honor to his house. He mobilized support, invoked divine legitimacy to compel respect, and operated the warfare system. Following his death, the emperor bestowed Shintō deity status upon him. Tokugawa Ieyasu supplanted his rule but not his legacy. The Toyotomi crest still signifies the government of Japan today.

In the 1600s, external threats reappeared—this time not as pitiless Mongol warriors but European merchants and missionaries. Nevertheless their presence threatened the social order. Proselytizing Christians particularly so, because they reduced the emperor's divine status.[47] Despite having just reopened relations with Chosŏn, the shogunate ordered the policy of seclusion. As Western traders, missionaries, and legations forced their way into China, Japan seemed spared. There was little recognition that the absence of external contact would impair security.

Nineteenth-century Westerners returned in greater force to a more rigid Tokugawa system. Foreign powers coerced unequal treaty terms on Japan as they had in China. Slow to coordinate a response, shifting coalitions of loyalists and reformers re-created Japanese institutions. To defeat the West on its own terms, the Meiji Restoration's comprehensive effort focused on "national wealth and a strong military" (fukoku kyōhei).

Meiji cabinets sought great power status, expecting respect. Japan's targets were neighboring territories and resources. With the exception of the preplanned surprise attacks that began the Russo-Japanese War and the Pacific War, Japan's conflicts were more opportunistic threats that acted as casus belli to which to react.

The 1874 punitive Taiwan Expedition cost Japan more casualties than it inflicted. Punishment, however, was only a coercive expedient. By exercising the capability to threaten Taiwan, Japan induced Qing acceptance of its control over the Ryukyus. The follow-on agreement of 1874 fell short of settling sovereignty, but Japan soon annexed the Ryukyu Kingdom (1879) as multiple powers carved up Chinese sovereignty.

In Chosŏn, Japan's provocations portrayed aggression as a defensive reaction. The Unyō contrivance that coerced the Treaty of Ganghwa Island came after Korean port authorities in Pusan rejected diplomacy.

Meiji leaders agreed that Chosŏn was vulnerable, but they preferred to wait until Japan was stronger to launch an attack. Advocates for intervention included the Seikantō (pro-Chosŏn-invasion party), agitated by anti-Meiji samurai and trading companies. The Treaty of Ganghwa Island proclaimed Chōsen to be an independent state, challenging China. War began as a reaction to China's dispatch of troops that ignored the prior notification agreed to in the Convention of Tientsin.

Meiji leaders did not plan the Greater East Asia War decades in advance, nor did their successors intend to become an Asian threat. They failed to plan peace. In 1894, speaking on the heady occasion of the last unequal treaty's revision, forthcoming Foreign Minister Mutsu Munemitsu vowed Japan would "join the club of civilized powers...to ensure that Japan will be granted its due rights and fulfill its due duties... to demand special treatment from Western powers...by taking unique policies and actions... slighting or fearing no one."[48]

Two wars later on the eve of full-scale invasion of China, the general staff argued over threat priorities. The army referred to Russia to justify occupation of Manchuria and China. The navy favored a southern advance toward Southeast Asia. There were debates over the relative importance of Korea, China, and Taiwan; and immediate intervention was compared to mobilization.[49] A minority advocated economic cooperation to develop an "island welfare state."[50] The northern advance option garnered more support, due in part to the southern advance's expense of neutralizing US naval power. With the emperor's approval, the gunbatsu executed both plans, in separated lines of operation.

War in China interacted with other events to isolate Japan. Europe's war prompted Japan to align with Germany and Italy, neither of whom had holdings in China. With this Tripartite Pact and a neutrality pact with the Soviet Union, Japan aimed to blunt Russia in Manchuria. In China, Japanese troops occupied cities. In Indochina, an expeditionary force coerced Vichy France's surrender, seizing resources and blocking ground routes into China. These actions and Germany's invasion of the Soviet

Union were followed by an oil embargo by the Allies. This could strangle Japan in three months. Western colonies, however, lay vulnerable in resource-rich Southeast Asia. In these circumstances, Emperor Hirohito directed implementation of navy and army operational plans.[51] The concept was to destroy American offensive capability in the Pacific and seize an arc of possessions from the Philippines to Burma.

In wartime Japan, however, threat assessments were irrelevant, even after decisive losses. Attempts to negotiate peace were rebuffed by the Allies' insistence on unconditional surrender. The expectation that the emperor would be eliminated undercut domestic opposition to the war. Instead of conducting strategic withdrawals, Japan's forces fell back after catastrophic losses. The emperor's late authorization to defend the Home Islands and take responsibility to surrender exemplified the government's reactive thinking.

With militarism deemed to be the cause, the occupation's prescription was demilitarization, democratization, and economic development. Conservative leaders embraced the bargain of political-economic development for a military guarantee. Japan received US military protection, along with reindustrialization and defense assistance. The United States received bases in Japan and democratic Japan's promise to rearm.[52] Japanese leaders also sought to insulate the military relationship from political and economic issues. Military basing issues, crimes against humanity, history-textbook interpretations, trade disputes, and foreign policy rifts complicated the basis for cooperation.

Resisting American pressure to rearm, Japanese leaders shifted priorities away from military defense. Early protectionism resembled prewar mercantilism, but Japan's nonmilitary integration into the global economy moderated such allegations. Under the theme of comprehensive security, a host of nonmilitary programs claimed protectionism as a common good: economic and food security, human security, and finally, nontraditional threats. Japan's use of official development aid and foreign direct investment to reduce threat conditions contributed to self-defense, economic interests, and mutual security. Four "first-ever" changes to the founding bargain illustrate Japan's domestic constraints on threat assessment.

The only comprehensive adjustment, the 1960 Treaty of Mutual Cooperation and Security between the United States and Japan, was highly contentious. In the aftermath of the Korean War, American defense assistance rearmed the self-defense force. Japan needed territorial defense, this time against another US ally. The dispute over Takeshima (Dokdo) led to the sinking of a Maritime Safety Agency boat and to the severance of trade and normalization talks. In the revised security treaty, the United States explicitly stated its military guarantee of "territories under the Administration of Japan," and removed its internal security role. Japan continued to provide bases and promise rearmament. Convinced that the new terms were better than the 1954 bargain or none at all, Prime Minister Nobusuke Kishi forced a snap-vote to pass the treaty.[53] This led to protests, which caused a student's death, and the wholesale resignation of his cabinet.

In 1981, the next change recognized Japan's dependence on energy and trade flows, and sought to protect sea lanes of communication with military role-sharing. The Reagan-Suzuki Communiqué emerged after a decade of Soviet nuclear and Far East forces buildup and China's development of nuclear weapons. North Korea was also a problem, having hijacked a Japan Airlines flight, shot down a US reconnaissance aircraft, and captured the *USS Pueblo* spy ship. The communiqué announced an "alliance" (*dōmei*) in which Japan would increase aid to mutually strategic states and patrol the sea lanes out to 1,000 miles. In the face of opposition party criticism, Prime Minister Zenkō Suzuki denied the relationship had any military meaning. The foreign ministry amended that to no new military meaning. Foreign Minister Masayoshi Itō resigned.

In 1988, Japan entered into its first codevelopment of a weapon system, the FSX fighter aircraft. Threats at the time included enhanced Soviet and Chinese naval capabilities, North Korean terrorism, and overdependence on US forces. The latter was reflected in the desire for "national autonomous development" (*kokusanka*). The final terms of codevelopment favored American firms, couched as a Japanese burden-sharing contribution. Japan also increased official development aid and host-nation support-payments. But general agreement on a common threat had failed to prevent friction in the security relationship. In contrast to the 1981 announcement of alliance, there was no significant domestic opposition to what became the F-2, a strike aircraft. Japanese threat perceptions were changing.

During the uncertain 1990s, Japan began to engage global threats and prepared for the use of force through new defense guidelines (1997). The Soviet military threat collapsed. Japan's huge financial contribution to the Persian Gulf War was underappreciated in the United States as militarily risk-free. China expanded its territorial claims and intimidated Taiwan. North Korea announced withdrawal from the Non-Proliferation Treaty. Japanese peacekeepers and humanitarian relief began deploying to UN operations. The revised defense guidelines specified Japan's military contributions to security and included, for the first time, areas surrounding Japan.[54]

Since then, adjustments to the security relationship have internationalized the self-defense forces. Each decade, responses to threats added new capabilities: antiterrorism measures; support of US combat operations in Iraq and Afghanistan; missile defense; integration of C^2ISR; collective self-defense. New partnerships with Australia and India, a security planning process, and expanded defense guidelines in 2015, invoke common values and strategic interests. Japan's main threats are clear: North Korean nuclear weapons and China's effort to bar access to disputed resources.

IS CONFRONTATION EFFECTIVE IN ACHIEVING OUTCOMES AND ELIMINATING THREATS?

Japanese confrontation has been effective in achieving domestic outcomes, whether or not it eliminated a foreign threat. In premodern Japan, the defeat of Mongol invasions enabled the Kamakura bakufu to strengthen and extend political control. Even Toyotomi Hideyoshi's failed invasions of Chosŏn perpetuated bakufu rule, though under a new main family line. The subsequent Tokugawa policy shift to seclusion was not just a way to stem an influx of external threats. It was a strategy to maintain internal control.

Problematically, when Western powers returned to Japan they could not be decreed away. The cost of abrupt contact and institutional rigidity was loss of Japanese sovereignty. Internally, the Tokugawa failed to adapt its governance to address social sources of threats. Externally, foreign powers relentlessly coerced unequal treaties. The Meiji Restoration of the emperor was effective in renegotiating those agreements, but this led to highly ambitious goals.

Japan's first two wars might have succeeded in reducing Chinese and Russian influence in Chōsen, as well as Russian influence in Manchuria. However, as Japanese troops and businesses occupied foreign territory and exploited those resources, they created obligations for Tokyo to defend. The Japanese Cabinet was united in its perception of an external threat, but divided on how to control such situations. Japan's highest council of leadership failed to enforce sustainable strategies and plans. The Manchurian Incident revealed how operational judgments substituted for national policy.

Wartime Japan did not overcome the strategic priorities problem and failed to anticipate the American response and nature of warfare in China. If leaders had pursued limited expansion and active defense, imperial Tokyo might have negotiated a settlement to prevent American intervention. Instead, Japan suffered widespread destruction, scarcity of food and fuel, and a shattered defense strategy by the end of the war. The emperor's surrender announcement brought shock, resignation, and relief. As occupation troops arrived, militarism was blamed as the cause of Japan's suffering.

In the postwar era, Japanese confrontation combines reactive isolation and engagement. But the form has changed. The U.S.-Japan security bargain includes domestic restraints that bind the Japanese self-defense force. As Japanese and American leaders adjusted this founding bargain, big changes exacted high political costs in Japan. Accordingly, Japanese strategists assess threats from a position of military dependence. Some argue this is part of postwar Japanese identity, while others regard military independence as "normal." The fact is that Japan has developed an autonomous capability for self-defense throughout its territories, as well as a global UN presence. There is a tendency toward an equivalent alliance.

Japanese forces confront clear threats with defensive force and have applied it on one occasion so far. North Korean spy boats periodically penetrate Japanese territory, one of which was sunk in December 2001.[55] Antimissile batteries in Tokyo and on destroyers in the Sea of Japan stand ready to counter episodic North Korean missile threats. Since 2009, Japan destroyers and reconnaissance aircraft have deterred and defended against piracy in the Gulf of Aden.[56] In the East China Sea, Japan Self-Defense Forces (JSDF) and Japan Coast Guard (JCG) patrols face provocative Chinese incursions.

As we turn to the Senkaku crisis, we will see how Japanese security strategy operates in a territorial confrontation. Japan has been able to engage the world with most instruments of national power, but not the military in a normal sense. How effective is Japan's approach when challenged by China on the normally vital interest of territorial sovereignty?

NOTES

1. Article 9, Renunciation of War, of the 1947 Constitution: "Aspiring sincerely to an international peace based on justice and order, the Japanese people forever renounce war as a sovereign right of the nation and the threat or use of force as means settle international disputes. In order to accomplish the aim of the preceding paragraph, land, sea and air forces, as well as other war potential, will never be maintained. The right of belligerency of the state will not be recognized."

2. Article 51 of the *Charter of the United Nations* includes: "Nothing in the present Charter shall impair the inherent right of individual or collective self-defence if an armed attack occurs against a Member of the United Nations, until the Security Council has taken measures necessary to maintain international peace and security." http://www.un.org/en/documents/charter/chapter7.shtml.

3. "The Basic Policy on National Defense," 20 May 1957, http://www.mod.go.jp/e/d_act/d_policy/dp02.html.

4. Brown cites evidence of "descent-line preoccupation" as far back as the 3d century. Delmer M. Brown, *The Cambridge History of Japan, Vol 1, Ancient Japan* (Cambridge: Cambridge University Press, 1993), 1–2.

5. A classic explanation of Japanese culture as different from "western" culture is Ruth Benedict's *The Chrysanthemum and the Sword: Patterns of Japanese Culture* (Cleveland: Meridian Books, 1967). For a critique of over-generalizations, see Edward W. Said, *Orientalism* (New York: Random House, 1994).

6. An examination of uniqueness applied to Japan may be found in Kosaku Yoshino, *Cultural Nationalism in Contemporary Japan: A Sociological Enquiry* (Oxon: Routledge, 1992). On orientalist and "reverse orientalist" identities, see Yuko Kikuchi, *Japan's Modernization and Mingei Theory: Cultural Nationalism and Oriental Orientalism* (London: RoutledgeCurzon, 2004).

7. For an argument that ideographic languages with spatial distinctions influence thinking, see Teenie Matlock, Michael Ramscar, Lera Boroditsky, "On the Experiential Link Between Spatial and Temporal Language," in *Cognitive Science* 29, 2005: 665–664.

8. See Etsuko Yoshida, *Referring Expressions in English and Japanese* (Amsterdam: John Benjamins Publishing Co., 2011), 95.

9. For a domestic explanation of reactive policies when external incentives favor the opposite, see Kent E. Calder, "Japanese Economic Policy Formation: Explaining the Reactive State," *World Politics* 40 No. 4 (July 1988), 517–541.

10. Delmer M. Brown, "The Yamato Kingdom," in *The Cambridge History of Japan, Vol 1*, 108–162, 123.

11. These were *Todaiji* sect (Nara) Buddhist temples; shrines are Shintō. Donald H. Shively and William H. McCullough, *The Cambridge History of Japan, Vol 2, Heian Japan* (Cambridge: Cambridge University Press, 1999), 1–19.

12. Ishii Susumu, *The Decline of the Kamakura Bakufu* in *The Cambridge History of Japan, Vol 3, Medieval Japan*, ed. Yozo Yamamura (Cambridge: Cambridge University Press, 1990), 128–174, 137–140.

13. Susumu, *The Decline of the Kamakura Bakufu*, 142–148.

14. John Whitney Hall, "The Muromachi Bakufu," in *The Cambridge History of Japan, Vol 3*, ed. Yamamura, 175–230.

15. A concise history of this formative period is "Sekigahara," in Marius B. Jansen, *The Making of Modern Japan* (Cambridge: Harvard University Press, 2002), 1–31.

16. Two prominently cited masters are: Miyamoto Musashi, *The Book of the Five Rings: A Classic Text on the Japanese Way of the Sword*, trans. Thomas Cleary (Boston: Shambhala, 2005); and Yagyu Munenori, *The Way of the Living Sword: Secrets of the Family Sword* (Lincoln, NE: iUniverse, 2003).

17. Asao Naohiro and Bernard Susser, "The 16th Century Unification," in *The Cambridge History of Japan, Vol 4., Early Modern Japan*, ed. John Whitney Hall (Cambridge: Cambridge University Press, 1991), 40–95, 70, 73.

18. "Sakoku" (closed country) edicts in 1635 and 1639 are cited in Ryota Nishino, *Changing Histories: Japanese and South African Textbooks 1945–1995* (Göttingen: V&R unipress, 2011), 48.

19. Marius B. Jansen, "The Meiji Restoration," in *The Cambridge History of Japan, Vol 5, The Nineteenth Century* (Cambridge: Cambridge University Press, 1989), 308–366.

20. Louis G. Perez, *Japan Comes of Age: Mutsu Munemitsu and the Revision of the Unequal Treaties* (Cranbury: Associated University Press, 1999), 47.

21. Hugh Dyson Walker, *East Asia: A New History* (Bloomington, IN: AuthorHouse, 2012), 414.

22. On the norm of retaliation in European warfare, see Wayne E. Lee, *Barbarians and Brothers: Anglo-American Warfare, 1500-1865* (Oxford: Oxford University Press, 2011), 222–223.

23. "Taiwanese Natives Break Silence on Mudan Incident," *The Japan Times*, 11 Jan 2005. http://www.japantimes.co.jp/news/2005/01/11/national/taiwanese-natives-break-mudan-incident-silence/ (accessed January 7, 2013).

24. For a discussion of Japanese motives to include colonization as a form of asserting dominance and modern status, see Robert Eskildsen, "Of Civilization and Savages: The Mimetic Imperialism of Japan's 1874 Expedition to Taiwan," *American Historical Review* (April 20020, 388-418.

25. Woong Joe Kang, *The Korean Struggle for International Identity in the Foreground of the Shufeldt Negotiation, 1866–1882,* (Lanham: University Press of America, 2005), 50.

26. For an informative study of the national press, see James L. Huffman, *Creating a Public: People and Press in Meiji Japan* (Honolulu: University of Hawaii Press, 1997).

27. William T. Rowe, *China's Last Empire: The Great Qing* (Cambridge: Harvard University Press, 2009), 227–228.

28. Klaus Schlichtmann, *Shidehara Kijūrō, Pacifism, and the Abolition of War, Vol II* (Lanham: Lexington Books, 2009), 13–24.

29. Ikohiko Hata and Alvin D. Coox, "Continental Expansion, 1905-1941," in *The Cambridge History of Japan, Vol 6, The Twentieth Century*, ed. Peter Duus (Cambridge: Cambridge University Press, 1989), 271–314.

30. For an argument that the Emperor was involved in Japanese expansion, see Herbert P. Bix, *Hirohito and the Making of Modern Japan* (NY: HarperCollins, 2000).

31. See Leonard A. Humphreys, *The Way of the Heavenly Sword: The Japanese Army in the 1920s* (Stanford: Stanford University Press, 1995), 161–163.

32. The depression coincided with Japan's return to the Gold Standard as the UK and US abandoned it, prompting large-scale sales of yen. See *The Economic History of Japan, 1600–1900: A Dual Structure*, eds. Takafusa Nakamura and Kaonosuke Odaka (Oxford: Oxford University Press, 1999), 182.

33. Ikohiko Hata and Alvin D. Coox, "Continental Expansion, 1905–1941," in *The Cambridge History of Japan, Vol 6*, ed. Duus, 271–314, 294–295.

34. Gordon M. Berger, "Politics and Mobilization in Japan, 1931–1945," in *The Cambridge History of Japan, Vol 6*, ed. Duus, 112.

35. Analysis of the Ketsu-Go ("Decisive Operation") plan to defend the Home Islands may be found in Steven J. Zaloga, *Defense of Japan 1945* (Oxford: Osprey Publishing, 2010).

36. The emperor's council consisted of Prime Minister-Admiral Suzuki Kantarō; Minister of Foreign Affairs-Togo Shigenori; Minister of War-General Anami Korechika; Chief of the Army General Staff-General Yoshijirō Umezu; Minister of the Navy-Admiral Yonai Mitsumasa; and Chief of the Navy General Staff-Admiral Toyoda Soemu.

37. Premier Suzuki's answer, mokusatu (黙殺), held multiple meanings ranging from a polite "withhold comment" to a derisive, "refusing to even comment." Radio Tokyo and Domei News Agency translated the term into English as "ignoring." See Kazuo Kawai, "Mokusatsu, Japan's Response to the Potsdam Declaration," *Pacific Historical Review* 19, No. 4 (Nov., 1950), 409-414. http://www.jstor.org/stable/3635822 (accessed September 15, 2012).

38. Charles R. Smith, *Securing the Surrender: Marines in the Occupation of Japan* (Washington, DC: Marine Corps Historical Center, 1997), http://www.nps.gov (accessed September 19, 2012).

39. On Japan's role in Far Eastern Command's success, see Max Hermansen, *United States Military Logistics in the First Part of the Korean War* (Oslo: University of Oslo, 2000). http://vlib.iue.it/carrie/texts/carrie_books/hermansen/index.htm (accessed September 19, 2012). On the Special Procurement Agency and its predecessor, the Special Procurement Board, see Yasuyuki Kimura, "The Defense Facilities Administration Agency: A Unique Support Organization for U.S. Forces in Japan," The Edwin O. Reischauer Center for East Asian Studies Asia-Pacific Policy Paper Series (June, 2013), 8-13. http://www.reischauercenter.org/en/wp-content/uploads/2013/09/RC-Monograph-2013-Kimura_History-of-DFAA.pdf (accessed January 2, 2016).

40. On the impact of wartime purchases from Japan on real growth, see James E. Vestal, *Planning for Change: Industrial Policy and Japanese Economic Development* (Oxford: Oxford University Press, 1993), 29.

41. Soviets began seizing the territories on 18 August, three days after Emperor Hirohito announced Japan's surrender. http://www.mofa.go.jp/region/europe/russia/territory/pamphlet.pdf (accessed April 15, 2015).

42. These are the Habomai islets and Kunashiri, Shikotan, and Etorofu islands.

43. According UNCLOS Article 121, "islands" may serve as baselines for EEZs. https://www.un.org/Depts/los/convention_agreements/texts/unclos/unclos_e.pdf.

44. "Treaty of Peace between the Republic of China and Japan, April 1952." www.taiwandocuments.org/taipei01.htm.(accessed February 27, 2014).

45. "Potsdam Declaration," in *Birth of the Constitution of Japan*, The National Diet Library. http://www.ndl.go.jp/constitution/e/etc/c06.html (accessed Janurary 10, 2016).

46. Ibid, 123–124.

47. Marius B. Jansen, *The Making of Modern Japan* (Cambridge: Harvard University Press, 2002), 73–75.

48. Hisahiko Okazaki, "Mutsu Munemisu and his Age." Okazaki Institute. http://www.okazaki-inst.jp/mutsu_munemitsu/Mutsu_Chapter_11.pdf (accessed November 7, 2015).

49. Gordon M. Berger, "Politics and Mobilization in Japan, 1931-1945," in *The Cambridge History of Japan, Vol 6*, ed. Duus, 97–153, 111–112.

50. Ikohiko Hata and Alvin D. Coox, "Continental Expansion, 1905-1941," in *The Cambridge History of Japan, Vol 6*, ed. Duus, 271–314.

51. Kiyoshi Aizawa, "Japanese Strategy in the First Phase of the Pacific War" (Tokyo: National Institute of Defense Studies, 2009). http://www.nids.go.jp/english/event/forum/pdf/2009/04.pdf (accessed November 14, 2015).

52. Thomas A. Drohan, *US-Japan Security Agreements, Past and Present* (Jefferson, NC: McFarland & Co., 2007), 20, 161-163.

53. The post–Pacific War convention for Japanese names has tended to be first name followed by the last name, unlike most Chinese and Korean names (except for Syngman Rhee); I have kept this convention.

54. *Defense of Japan 1997* (Tokyo: *The Japan Times*, 1998), 167.

55. "Terrorism by the Democratic People's Republic of Korea," *Focus* 271, Japan National Police Agency. http://web.archive.org/web/2009081515 1555/ (accessed September 28, 2012).

56. For updates see the Japan Ministry of Defense, http://www.mod.go.jp/e/d_act/somalia/index.html.

Chapter 7

Japan's Delayed Reactions

The Senkaku Islets (Diaoyu Islets in Chinese) in the East China Sea used to be just an irritant in Sino-Japanese relations. Since a 1968 United Nations survey indicated a high probability of oil reserves in the area, however, they have become an ongoing territorial issue that periodically erupts into confrontation. Nationalists in China and Taiwan have made it a point to challenge Japanese control, so far without provoking kinetic conflict. This chapter segments the crisis into six major episodes, occurring in 1971, 1978, 1990, 1996, 2002, and 2012. The trend is toward higher levels of confrontation, but in each case so far, leaders have succeeded in de-escalating the situation. As a result, mutually exclusive territorial claims continue to simmer and remain unresolved.

Tokyo's case for sovereignty is threefold.[1] First, Japanese surveys in 1885 determined that the "islands," comprising five islets and three rocks, were uninhabited and uncontrolled. A request by Fukuoka businessman Koga Tatsushiro to lease them was approved by the Meiji government in 1896. Second, in January 1895 Meiji Japan incorporated the Senkakus into Japan as Okinawa Prefecture. This was the annexation of the Ryukyus four months before the end of the Sino-Japanese War. Therefore Japan's acquisition of the Senkakus was a separate matter from the Treaty of

Shimonoseki that coerced "unfair" terms from China. Third, the Ryukyus were considered part of Japan by the treaties that concluded World War II. The reasoning is that the Cairo Declaration, Potsdam Declaration, San Francisco Peace Treaty, and Treaty of Taipei did not specify the Ryukyus as not being part of Japan. In fact, the Peace Treaty transferred the Ryukyus to a UN trusteeship under US administration. So when the United States reverted control of the Ryukyus to Japan in 1972, Japan's claim of sovereignty went with it.

China's main counterargument follows.[2] First, the islets were claimed by the Ming and Qing dynasties and controlled as a tributary state. Court records and charts predate Japan's claims and indicate Japanese officials were aware of Qing authority over the islets. Therefore the Japanese surveys and claim of terra nullius are invalid. Second, Japan's annexation of the Ryukyus during the Sino-Japanese War and 1896 incorporation indicate the Diaoyu were forcibly seized. Japanese documents related to the capture of Lushun (Port Arthur) reveal a Japanese decision to place sovereignty markers on the Diaoyu at that point in time. So the Treaty of Taipei, whose terms nullified the Treaty of Shimonoseki, should have returned the Diaoyu Islets to China. Third, the wartime declarations and San Francisco Peace Treaty, which were not signed by China and Taiwan anyway, did not specify Diaoyutai as part of Japan. The United States unilaterally expanded its UN trusteeship to include the Diaoyu Islets and then improperly transferred control to Japan in 1972.

Both states also disagree on the continental shelf's natural-resource exploitation zone. The UN Law of the Sea, Article 76, permits exclusive economic rights to a coastal state based on the prolongation of its continental shelf up to 350 miles from its coastline. China claims that its continental shelf spreads eastward all the way to the Okinawa Trough, which is past the Diaoyu.[3] Japan claims that the trough is just a depression in the same continental shelf where the Ryukyus sit; therefore both states share the same shelf.[4] Because the East China Sea is 360 miles wide, Japan proposed a temporary border in the area east of the trough, a median line between each state's 200 nm exclusive economic zone.[5] The problem with this offer from a Chinese perspective is that the line does not bisect the Ryukyus coastline and Taiwan's eastern coastline. This is why Taiwan's sovereignty is so important to both Beijing and Tokyo. Japan's claimed exclusive economic zone ranges farther west than this median line, and China's claimed exclusive economic zone extends farther east. This issue will bear heavily on the Senkakus dispute later.

CRISIS

Figure 11. Lines of Effect Logic.

Lines of Effect Logic	
Psychological:	intimidate will / neutralize capability to **Deter D_t -- Compel C_p**
	assure will / enhance capability to **Dissuade D_s -- Persuade P**
Physical:	punish will / deny capability to **Defend D_f -- Coerce C_r**
	demonstrate will / exercise capability to **Secure S -- Induce I**

Symmetric and Asymmetric Strategies

Now let's look at Japanese and Chinese strategies from a combined-effects perspective. Japan's strategy is militarily minimal and symmetric because it is prohibited from invoking or using force against nonmilitary and nonimminent threats. As a result, realistic Japanese strategy is necessarily interdependent. The prevailing interpretation of self-Defense is changing, in part due to the Senkaku crisis. We reflect this post-1945 policy constraint by theoretically restricting the military tool (a *self*-Defense tool in postwar Japan) from being used for diplomatic, informational, economic or social effects. Other aspects of Japan's strategy may be asymmetric—that is, a particular type of tool may be applied to achieve another type of effect. For instance, Japan uses social-legal tools to achieve diplomatic effects, and economic tools for military effects.

Applying this constraint on Japanese strategy, Japan brings about causative and preventive effects by targeting two main segments: (1) Japanese and American public opinion; and (2) China policy elites and the Peoples' Liberation Army. Constitutional and political restraints produce an interdependent "self-defense" effort whose combined effect is limited to *Induced* U.S.-Japan Defense and Deterrence against territorial attack. The US commitment to Defend Japan is the priority effect, Deterrence being acquired by the credibility of that commitment. Other elements of the strategy operate separately. The strategy consists of *Persuasion* and *Inducement* of Japan and the U.S., and Defense and Deterrence of China* ($P\,I\,D_f\,D_t$):

> $P\,I$: *Persuade* Japanese and American opinion in support of Japan's sovereignty claims, and *Induce* US support by respectively assuring national will and exercising alliance capability
>
> $D_f\,D_t$: Defend Senkaku territory and Deter the use of force by China by respectively denying China the capability to occupy the Senkakus and neutralizing economic and military advantages
>
> *China and Taiwan claims on Japan-claimed territory are similar enough to treat as one unit; this does not imply agreement on anything else.

Japan's national goal is to retain full sovereignty and administrative control of the Senkakus. To do that, the Japanese government has to *Persuade* domestic public opinion to support the sovereignty claim. This in turn requires appealing to moderates and marginalizing extremists. Rightists are a minority with disproportionate influence on conservative administrations. The government also seeks to *Induce* alliance support through exercises with US forces—this empowers nationalist groups. As Japan's only formal ally, US support or lack thereof complicates Tokyo's delicate balance of territorial claims, national identity, and constitutional limits. For instance, even though the United States declares that it is obliged by the Security Treaty to Defend Japan in the Senkakus, its neutral position on sovereignty there undermines Japan's constitutional limits and promotes more nationalism.

Deterring and Defending against China is more straightforward. Economic growth and technological innovation advance self-Defense capabilities, which can help integrate alliance operations. Japanese forces seek to deny and neutralize threats through organizations besides the Self-Defense Forces, such as the National Police Agency and Maritime Safety Agency (since 2000, the Coast Guard). Maintaining credible Deterrence without threatening the use of force is difficult, some say impossible, in practice. Therefore realistic contingency planning is vital to identifying new requirements for self-Defense. This has been politically disruptive in Japan.

China's strategy is a robust symmetric and asymmetric combination of *Dissuasion* and Deterrence directed at the United States, and *Persuasion, Inducement,* Compellence, and Coercion (D_s D_t P I C_p C_r) aimed at Japan. The overall combined effect is to isolate Japan and control all claimed territory. This includes conducting antiaccess and area-denial operations. The indirect *qi* of China's strategy, *Dissuasion*-Deterrence-*Persuasion*, intends to separate US support from Japan on the Senkaku issue by employing informational and military tools to create diplomatic, economic, and military effects, and by stirring nationalism in China with social-informational tools. Isolating the United States and Japan from each other on the Senkakus is aided by the fact that South Korea and Russia also have territorial disputes with Japan. The direct *zheng, Inducement*-Compellence-Coercion, targets Japan with informational tools to create political effects, and with military tools to create social and military effects:

> D_s D_t: *Dissuade* and Deter the US from supporting Japan by respectively assuring American policy elites and academics of China's

righteous claims, and intimidating US willingness to intervene against China's core interest

P: Persuade domestic public opinion of China's efforts to regain the Diaoyu by crowdsourced networking and state-controlled media

I: Induce Japan's recognition of a Diaoyu dispute by demonstrating the political will and exercising the military capability to control the disputed territory

C_p C_r: Compel or Coerce Japan to overreact by respectively intimidating public opinion and denying Japanese forces' defenses

China's desired outcome is to contest Japanese sovereignty and control of disputed territory for follow-on opportunities to displace it. Job 1 is *Dissuading* and Deterring US intervention to isolate Japan as a manageable target. Chinese lobbying efforts and state-sponsored think tanks generate information and construct narratives in accordance with the party line on territorial claims. Foreigners who criticize that line risk not being granted visas, while citizens who deviate from it are in danger being jailed. Cyber attacks on US corporations exploit fears of client-privacy lawsuits, shaping American accommodation of Chinese interests. By announcing the East China Sea as a core interest backed by increased military presence, China seeks to Deter American policy from fully supporting Japan.

The other indirect effect, *Persuading* domestic opinion that Beijing is confronting Japan on the Diaoyu Islets issue, is needed to appease anti-Japan nationalism in China and maintain social control. Preemptively, party messaging of patriotic themes can create a rapidly scaled virtual crowd against Japanese actions. This is also difficult for the U.S. or Japan to assess, which shrouds the capability.

What about the direct effects? Instigating demonstrators to approach the Senkakus, and conducting military training or exercises in the vicinity, intend to *Induce* Japanese recognition of a territorial dispute. As in the South China Sea, China's claims and presence create a new reality. This exploits Japan's constitutional vulnerability against forceful settlement of disputes. The next option is a more aggressive step to provoke Japanese use of force for further Chinese exploitation then consolidation of control. The desired effects are to Compel and Coerce Japan to use force by intimidating and denying Japanese forces' defensive systems. Chinese intimidation is more likely to cause rather than prevent an increased Japanese response if we assume that that Japan's combined effect is credible: *Induced* U.S.-Japan Deterrence and Defense against territorial attack. This is a very volatile condition for China and Japan to manage.

After explaining the logic and linkages in these two strategies, we outline the development of the main lines of effect. These have been shaped over the course of four episodes in 1970, 1978, 1990, and 1996. Our next focus is on condition setting in 2004 and the confrontation of 2012.

The causative element of Japan's strategy relies on *Persuasion* and *Inducement*, specifically avoiding Compellence and Coercion. Political and economic incentives sustain the preventative element—Defense and Deterrence. Deterring China from contesting Japanese sovereignty without physically threatening Chinese forces is unlikely to succeed through combined arms alone, which yields the military initiative to China. As a result, Japanese defense capabilities serve to provide overall confidence, offer acceptable options, and influence other types of effects. How can this possibly work?

The critical linkage in Japan's combined effect is between the *Persuasion- Inducement* and Defense-Deterrence pieces. If *Persuasion* and *Inducement* do not happen, sustained Defense and Deterrence are not likely to occur either. To strengthen this coupling, Tokyo needs to assure the domestic and allied public that the Self-Defense Forces government will actually Defend the Senkakus. Nationalist provocations, however, could destroy the $P\,I - D_f\,D_t$ linkage by eroding support in Japan and the United States. Securing joint ventures may moderate reactionaries. Policy coordination, working groups, planning cells, and joint statements and exercises can *Induce* US support, which enhances Defense and Deterrence.

Maintaining a technological edge and exercising tactical-operational expertise are vital to both.

China's comprehensive, six-effects strategy can work at four levels: (1) *Dissuade* and Deter US intervention with selective information, digital theft of source codes and finances, and military, civil-maritime, and economic presence in the East China Sea; (2) assure Chinese will with social networks to *Persuade* opinion of China's sovereign rights to the Diaoyu Islets; (3) demonstrate this will and exercise military capability to *Induce* Japanese recognition of a dispute; and (4) intimidate or escalate to Compel or Coerce Japanese use of force.

At level 1, the hefty Chinese contingent in Washington, DC, ensures presence and reporting at academic and policy-related events. In the East China Sea, policing of the exclusive economic zone by civil patrol fleets conveys coastal ownership, with PLA forces in a backup role.[6] At level 2, the crowdsourcing of nationalism is not difficult due to historical tensions, but often bursts forth from an issue that forces Beijing to react. Similar reactions among Japanese nationalists and counter-reactions in China are all but certain. Level-3 demonstrations aim to achieve Japanese recognition of a dispute and stir fears of war. Exercises have the benefit of minimizing domestic unrest in China while probing Japanese defenses and reactions. At level 4, the People's Liberation Army has tactical advantages, assuming that the Japan Self-Defense Forces are prohibited from making preemptive attacks. Note that Japan helps China achieve most of its combined effects if it uses force first. Meanwhile, Chinese territorial intrusions, harassment maneuvers, intelligence collection, and network attacks demonstrate freedom of action and create new conditions.

This is a risky strategy, with two critical linkages inherently difficult to control. First, there is the challenge of linking crowdsourced Chinese nationalism to Japanese control of the Diaoyu Islets. Anti-Japanese nationalism may readily be inflamed, but directing that to the Senkaku issue and preplanned options is subject to variables that resist control.

Once the network is perturbed, web-based social movements may quickly turn to criticize single-party rule. Selected military operations depend upon the individual makeup of the Central Military Commission (CMC) and Politburo Standing Committee (PSC).

The second linkage is between provocative Chinese demonstrations and exercises, and Japan's use of force against those. Limiting demonstrations and controlling military exercises require discipline among party guidance, PLA directives, and local commanders' intentions. What types of political and military activities are likely to Compel Japanese recognition of a dispute? If the decision is made to provoke a self-Defense response, how will escalation be prevented or contained? Looming in the background is the possibility that China achieves local military superiority. An effective antiaccess and area-denial capability empowers China to intimidate an isolated Japan and therefore Deter, rather than Compel, Japanese use of force. Such questions highlight uncertainties that risk rupturing Sino-Japanese and Sino-American relations, while testing the U.S.-Japan security alliance.

Next, let's derive the lines of effect associated with each strategy and identify areas of cooperation and conflict.

Shaping Lines of Effect
The lines of effect that drive Japanese interdependence and motivate Chinese isolated control are shaped by nationalism, economic competition, and cooperation. We sketch this through four episodes between 1971 and 1997.

1971—Managing Tension
Shortly after the UN geophysical survey, Okinawa Prefecture officials placed a concrete marker on the main Senkaku Islet, activating counterclaims by Taiwan and China.[7] In 1970 Japan urged Taiwan to stop its exploration bid in the Senkakus and asserted exclusive oil-exploration rights east of its median line.[8] This declaration overlapped Taiwan and

China claims. In response, Taiwan activists sailed to the islets and planted their own national flag. The cause spread, turning into a global "safeguard Diaoyutai" movement. In China, officials restated their sovereignty over the Diaoyu Islets but stopped short of forcibly confronting Japanese vessels. At the time, kinetic conflict would have been unwise for two reasons. Winding down its disastrous Cultural Revolution and balancing against the Soviet Union, China's priorities were to normalize ties with the United States and Japan. In addition, PLA navy operations in the South China Sea strained its "near-coast defense" naval capabilities.

In July 1971, the first news of the "Nixon shocks" hit Japan as the Foreign Ministry learned of US National Security Adviser Henry Kissinger's presummit visit to Beijing. Prime Minister Eisaku Satō had been a loyal US ally and stanch supporter of Taiwan, having opposed China's entry into the United Nations. In May 1972, three months after President Richard Nixon's visit to China that foreshadowed normalization, the United States delivered a different shock to China by reverting its UN trusteeship of the Ryukyus, which included the Senkakus, to Japan.[9] In China, this triggered demonstrations, calls to liberate the islands, and UN proposals to contest Japan's sovereignty. That year, Japan and China opened diplomatic relations without resolving territorial differences and began talks on a long-term trade agreement. Tokyo tried to insulate business transactions with China from diplomacy and politics, separating all of that from self-Defense. Japanese idealists equated the cooperation with absence of confrontation. There was no long-term Defense strategy due to domestic opposition to Defense, which many equated with militarism. Instead of seeking decisive advantages, Japan's five-year defense build-up plans programmed incremental increases in capability.

1978—Formulating Logic

The Senkaku issue reemerged in negotiations over the Japan-China trade agreement, shaping the logic of each nation's lines of effect. A now-dominant Vice Premier Deng Xiaoping and conservatives within Japan's ruling Liberal Democratic Party exploited the territorial issue to advance their respective positions. China sought to assert itself as a regional economic and political power. Prime Minister Yasuo Fukuda, LDP moderates, and various business factions favored expanding political and economic ties with China. At the same time, Japan increased its territorial Defense and strategic official development aid in the first Guidelines for Japan-U.S. Defense Cooperation.

When antitrade-agreement LDP members insisted that Senkaku's status be resolved within the negotiations, Deng dispatched an armed flotilla of eighty fishing boats to *Induce* a breakthrough. The "fish-boat diplomats" encircled the islands for two weeks, displaying patriotic signs and attracting media attention.[10] Japan limited its on-scene response to reconnaissance flights, specifically excluding surface patrols by the Japan Maritime Safety Agency. Following an understanding between Deng and Fukuda, negotiators shelved the Senkaku issue to get the Sino-Japanese Treaty of Peace and Friendship signed in August 1978.

In effect, Japan had gained China's acknowledgement of its control of the Senkakus by using diplomatic and military tools for overtly defensive effects, leveraged by an upgrade of U.S.-Japan defense cooperation. China had demonstrated intent to use force to *Induce* a Japanese reaction. These two rationales became the fundamental logic of each national strategy to retain and contest Senkaku/Diaoyu sovereignty.

1990—Adding Tools and Recognizing Limits
The next major event revealed Japan's strategic advantage over China under certain conditions. Japan's demonstrated willingness to wield economic influence and assert limited self-Defense, while China discovered limits to *Inducement*. In 1988, the Japan Maritime Safety Agency permitted a second lighthouse to be built in the Senkakus by the Nihon Seinensha (Japan Youth Federation). The following year the Nihon Seinensha requested the lighthouse be designated an official navigational waypoint. Apart from promoting nautical safety, this tactic sought international recognition and provided visible proof of Japanese sovereignty.

In response, protestors from the Taiwan Area Athletic Games in 1990 embarked to place an Olympic torch on the island.[11] As Japan Maritime Safety Agency helicopters and patrol boats prevented the protestors from reaching the islets, on-scene media coverage fueled more anti-Japan protests. Beijing inflated its standard objection to Senkaku occupation to include any Japanese presence in surrounding waters. Eager to deflect attention away from the Tiananmen Square massacre of June 1989, Beijing accused Tokyo of renewed militarism.

Led by the Liberal Democratic Party, Tokyo increased participation in UN peacekeeping operations while restating Senkaku sovereignty claims and using financial incentives to deepen economic ties with China. The Japan Maritime Safety Agency, not the Japan Self-Defense Forces, continued to patrol the area.[12] In July 1990, Prime Minister Toshiki Kaifu resumed loans to China while most other sanctioners left their post-Tiananmen punishments in place.[13] In August, Kaifu announced the Senkaku lighthouse would not be recognized as an official waypoint. As if on cue, Chinese Communist Party (CPC) officials emphasized friendly economic relations with Japan, banned university protests, and blocked media coverage of demonstrations.[14] Students redirected their anger at the CPC for repressing patriotism. Under these circumstances, China was hard-pressed to *Induce* any Japanese behavior. Buoyant observers regarded this time as one of cooperation.

1996—Defining Threats

Several events interacted with demonstrations in the Senkakus to intensify mutual distrust and define threats to national security. The first occurred in 1992, when China's Law on the Territorial Sea and the Contiguous Zones claimed territory from every single one of its maritime neighbors—Vietnam, Indonesia, Malaysia, Brunei, the Philippines, Taiwan, Japan, and North Korea.[15] This law and China's interpretation of the United Nations Convention on the Law of the Sea stretched its continental shelf, placing the Diaoyu Islets inside Chinese territory. To consolidate its eastern front, China regarded its exclusive economic zone as prohibiting international "right of innocent passage." If enforced, this policy would seal off the eastern coast of China as a private sea. Finally, China Marine Surveillance (CMS) ships fired warning shots at civilian vessels transiting the disputed area in 1991, 1992, and 1993.[16] By unilaterally casting a defensive net, China had become more of a threat. Then in 1995, China discovered a natural gas field (Chunxiao) located three miles west of the Japan-proposed median line.

The same year, the Taiwan Strait Crisis (July 1995–March 1996) and the second Guidelines for Japan-U.S. Defense Cooperation (U.S.-Japan Joint Declaration, April 1996) aggravated the Senkaku issue. China's "missile diplomacy" shook Japanese and American confidence among observers hoping for signs of a democratic China. From Beijing's perspective, the missile launches against its separatist province were fully justified, particularly because they were revealed to the United States in advance. At the same time, the heavy American response of sending two aircraft carrier task forces near the Strait was taken as an insulting surprise. During the Taiwan Strait Crisis, although Japan-U.S. policies seemed at odds with one another, contingency planning and coordination were getting closer.[17]

U.S.-Japan alliance cooperation near Taiwan fed Beijing's concern that the new Guidelines for Japan-U.S. Defense Cooperation were directed at China. In Tokyo and Washington, however, the planning focus was on North Korea. In response to the 1994 North Korean nuclear crisis, the United States' plan to deploy US forces to South Korea required transiting bases in Japan. Japanese legal restraints thwarted this, except in Okinawa. Nevertheless, Beijing viewed the guidelines solely in terms of Japan's intent to patrol an illegal exclusive economic zone. This fed domestic threat perceptions of a militarist Japan.

Warily, China and Japan ratified the United Nations Convention on the Law of the Sea in June 1996. The Senkaku Islets became the center of a 200-mile radius exclusive economic zone which both countries claimed, but Japan still controlled. The Nihon Seinensha constructed a small solar-powered lighthouse. Taiwan and Hong Kong activists sortied again to plant their flags. Tragically, during a series of unsuccessful and successful landings, a protestor from Hong Kong drowned while trying to circumvent the Japanese blockade. Chinese research ships began to appear inside Japan's exclusive economic zone, enforcing an ambiguous interpretation of the law of the sea to permit survey activities.[18] From 1997 to 1998, on China's side of the median line, Chinese state-owned oil corporations had *Persuaded* Japanese financing to explore, extract, and transport gas via pipelines in several natural gas fields.[19] While China did not formally recognize Japan's median line, all of the gas field development occurred on China's side of it. This prompted concerns in Japan that natural gas located on the Japan side was being siphoned via the seabed. Given the threat to Japanese energy interests, related business activity became a matter of national security among policy elites.

Japanese dependence on external trade and energy flows was a critical vulnerability. These sea lanes are thus vital because they connect Japan through the western Pacific Ocean to the Indian Ocean and Persian Gulf —these are the routes through which oil, natural gas, rare-earth metals, food, manufactured goods, and people are transported. To protect this network, Japanese security strategy began to operate through two lines of effect: energy *Security* and de facto collective Defense.

Lines of Effect

Energy *Security* merged diplomacy, business, and Defense in an effort to maintain access to energy sources and transit routes. It reversed the policy of *seikei bunri* (separating politics from economics), which had enabled Japan to pursue economic growth insulated from the divisiveness of diplomatic and defense issues. Cooperative efforts with China turned into mutual Deterrence as Japan sought to neutralize China's economic and military advantages. At the time, Japan's GDP was four times that of China. Growth, however, had slowed to less than 3 percent growth for two consecutive years, a postwar first. The Ministry of Economy, Trade and Industry (METI) prioritized exclusive national oil-exploration rights over joint ventures with China. Businesses demanded contracts with government-provided force protection. The Japan Coast Guard and Japan Self-Defense Forces began operations to deny China and assure Japan energy-related access to and through the disputed area. Chinese ships and aircraft contested this, so Japanese financing of China's state-owned gas development became a source of Japanese insecurity. The first point in the first Article of the Sino-Japanese Treaty of Peace and Friendship became null and void: "The Contracting Parties shall develop relations of perpetual peace and friendship between the two countries on the basis of the principles of mutual respect for sovereignty and territorial integrity, mutual non-aggression, non-interference in each other's internal affairs, equality and mutual benefit and peaceful co-existence."[20]

Collective Defense was prohibited by the prevailing Japanese interpretation of the 1947 constitution, but it emerged nonetheless at tactical, operational, and strategic levels of interaction. At the tactical level, within self-defensive scenarios such as an attack on Japan, Japanese forces supported US operations. In execution, Japan's self Defense and collective Defense missions were connected to one another, not separate operations. Search and rescue, sea lane Defense, island Defense, air-to-air Defense, ballistic missile Defense, and cyberspace Defense involved Japanese and US forces working together to provide mutual and interdependent capabilities. To the operators conducting the missions, the actual or simulated location of the scenario was irrelevant. Training and exercises planned under "minimum and exclusively self-defensive capability" had to deal with uncertainties of execution, which included decisions such as whether or not to come to the aid of a partner in distress. During the multinational Rim of the Pacific Exercise (RIMPAC) of 1996, for instance, a JSDF destroyer malfunction caused the shoot-down of a US A-6 (attack) aircraft towing a target. The destroyer's crew promptly rescued the unharmed crew members. In real and virtual self-Defense exercise scenarios, interdependent operations were collective efforts.

At the operational level, Japan's contributions to collective security promoted a collective Defense ethic and capability. The expansion of Japanese participation in humanitarian and peacekeeping operations created an internationalized cadre experienced in operating under collective security and self-Defense restrictions. The United Nations Security Council under the UN Charter, Chapter VII, Article 42, authorizes the use of force to maintain or restore peace. An attack is not necessary; a threat may suffice for the UN Security Council to determine that force is permissible. UN Charter, Article 51, empowers a state to Defend itself after coming under armed attack, and to use force under the principle of shared, collective self-Defense. In each case of Japanese participation, special measures, special laws and/or special agreements were passed to permit actions supporting efforts in areas such as antiterrorism, replenishment support of warships, host-nation support of US forces, refugee children, industrial revitalization, and humanitarian and reconstruction assistance.[21] By providing security to others under rules of engagement limited to minimal self-Defense, Japan Self-Defense Forces' tactical operations supported strategic, collective effects.

The strategic level intentionally combined self Defense and collective Defense. Japan's participation in UN operations was an act of collective Defense to save the U.S.-Japan security bargain's basis for cooperation, yet avoid the appearance of reacting to US pressure. In the United States, Japan's nonmilitary contributions to the Persian Gulf War had been criticized as inadequate, despite a $13-billion financial-support package and postcombat-minesweeping and airlift operations. There was concern in Tokyo and Washington that the interdependent asymmetric alliance was in danger. Japan had to find a way to make a more equivalent contribution to security. The spate of peacekeeping operations laws in the 1990s was justified as self-Defense, based on the importance of promoting stability in resource-rich areas. First the Middle East, then Central Asia, and later Africa became targets for Japanese assistance.

The same logic applied to Japan's logistical, medical, and humanitarian support of coalition operations in Iraq and Afghanistan. Japanese participation was made legal by passing an international peace cooperation law and several special-measures laws before deploying the JSDF and other volunteers, on a case-by-case basis that permitted the use of minimal force for self Defense. JSDF specialists and civilians from various non-governmental organizations provide a range of services, including medical care, disease prevention, transportation, communications, logistical support, humanitarian relief, construction, police training, and election monitoring.[22] In fact, such deployments supported broader collective security efforts. Japanese Self-Defense Forces, diplomats, aid officials and police operations participating in humanitarian, peace-building, and combat support activities strengthened security in specific situations. These initiatives undertaken by Japan also enhanced the collective Defense operations conducted by US and other allied forces.[23] From a combined-effects perspective, Japan was already engaging in collective Defense.

The effect of providing de facto collective Defense was to *Persuade* and *Induce* US support of Japan Self-Defense Forces operations. That line of effect is not supposed to be relevant to the Senkakus, because any support of US operations on Japanese territory is by definition self- Defense. But Japanese territory itself is not explicitly defined in US policy, even though the Japan-U.S. alliance applies. This is the type of qualified guarantee that Japanese strategists worry about. For that reason we anticipate greater support for collective Defense in Japan. Recent evidence includes the cabinet-level decision in July 2015 to exercise collective Defense, and proposed permanent legislation to permit JSDF overseas deployments. Unless we expect Japan to become a unilateral military power, collective Defense with reliable partners may be the most viable way to plan, organize, and practice alliance operations in dynamic threat conditions.

China's three lines of effect contest Japan's sovereignty over the Senkakus and exploit further opportunities: US engagement, comprehensive *Inducement*, and forced reaction. US engagement serves several broad outcomes for China, two of which are to *Dissuade* and Deter US support of Japan in Sino-Japanese territorial disputes. Dozens of venues, working groups and dialogues engage policy makers to orient US interests toward China. The lead forum is the U.S.-China Strategic and Economic Dialogue, an annual bilateral summit established in 2009. This led to the Strategic Security Dialogue, envisioned to strengthen military-to-military relations. In 2013 China's Minister of National Defense Chang Wanquan visited the U.S.; this was followed by a visit by the US Secretary of Defense Chuck Hagel the following year. Discussions included ways to notify one another about major military activities and rules of behavior governing air and maritime operations. In addition, there are indications that hidden cyber attackers regularly conduct espionage against US and Japanese interests.[24] Social media threads are part of Beijing's united information front that conveys the party's controlled narrative on territorial disputes.

Comprehensive *Inducement* used diplomatic, informational, military, economic, and social tools to *Induce* changes in Japanese behavior. China's strategy produced the following combination (the type of tool is noted in parentheses): assure Chinese nationalist will (informational) of Beijing's willingness to confront Japan; use this movement (social) to generate demonstrations (diplomatic, by proxy) in support of enhancing oil and gas capabilities (economic) and capability exercises (military) on and near the Diaoyu Islets to *Induce* Japanese recognition of a dispute. The timing of this chain appears to be pre-planned. The Party's 1995–1996 "patriotic education" and "spiritual civilization" campaigns stirred up anti-Japan attitudes on the 100th anniversary of World War II and the fiftieth anniversary of the Treaty of Shimonoseki.[25] Civil and military forces near the Senkakus complement this and provide a capability to operate against Japan or US targets that make tactical mistakes. The latter is addressed by the next line of effect.

A forced reaction effect is one that Compels or Coerces a reaction by Japanese forces or Japanese public opinion for follow-on exploitation. Imagine the target to be a Japan Coast Guard or JSDF platform. This is a reasonable situation to assume given that Chinese vessels routinely approach Japan Coast Guard patrols within visual range to assert sovereignty in the East China Sea. A Chinese navy, air force or China Marine Surveillance asset enters territory claimed by Japan to heighten the drama or confuse the situation. At an opportune moment the aggressor intimidates an operator's will, or denies a defensive system's capability with a threat. Threats include preattack maneuvers and communications, such as illuminating a target with a laser designator, activating fire control radar, and locking a weapon system onto a target. The presence of electromagnetic emissions, intermediate-range ballistic missiles, coastal submarines, and distracting merchant vessels can be difficult to counter. All of this can be part of a conditioning routine to inure a potential target before an actual strike with a weapon that outranges its target's counterfires, or to escalate and de-escalate a situation to harass or elicit a response.

Now let's assume the target to be Japanese public opinion, with the intent of producing or exploiting a polarizing comment by a prominent leader, such as Foreign Minister Yukihiko Ikeda's assertion in 1996, "The Diaoyu Islands have always been Japan's territory; Japan already effectively governs the islands, so the territorial issue does not exist."[26] This statement stimulated threats made against the Senkakus in the Chinese media, with counter attributions of China's malevolent intent showing up in conservative Japanese media. In response, Chinese Foreign Minister Qian Qichen said the dispute was "an objective and historical fact which could not be denied and blamed the Diaoyu issue on Japan's mistaken perceptions of the last war."[27] A ministry spokesperson denounced Ikeda's remarks and linked them to the influence of right-wing militarists, perpetuating the chain reaction.

Setting Conditions
National leaders arranged conditions to favor their lines of effect. Beijing manipulated a wide variety of tools, while Tokyo failed to leverage its potential advantages. This continually yielded the initiative to Beijing.

2002—China's Tens-of-Years Campaign

In 2002, the National Development and Reform Commission of the People's Republic of China (NDRC), formerly State Planning Commission and State Development Planning Commission, announced that the China Petrochemical Corporation (Sinopec) and China National Offshore Oil Corporation (CNOOC) would explore and exploit natural gas resources from the Chunxiao gas field located 450 kilometers from Shanghai.[28] This led to contracts with the Shell Oil Company with CNOOC as the sole agent for exploration, extraction, production, transportation, and marketing of oil and natural gas. Tokyo declined to participate in the joint venture, urging Beijing to resolve the sovereignty issue first. Ensuing discussions about joint consultations froze Japanese operations in the area. Sinopec and CNOOC pressed on with surveys and exploration rigs west of the median line as Tokyo objected.

In 2004, taking advantage of tense bilateral relations due to Prime Minister Junichirō Koizumi's repeated visits to Yasukuni Shrine (whose memorialized souls include fourteen "Class A" convicted war criminals), Chinese Academy of Social Sciences analysts and Chinese government officials launched an information campaign linked to economic and military operations.

First, state-sponsored critics linked Yasukuni Shrine visits and the Japan Ministry of Education's interpretations of World War II in public-school textbooks to the breakdown in Sino-Japanese consultations over the Diaoyu Islets. Beijing used imperial Japan's record of territorial seizures to discredit Tokyo's claims of sovereignty in the Ryukyus. The primary tool set in this stratagem consisted of government academics from state-affiliated think tanks who portray imperial China's own territorial expansion as legitimate: the Chinese Academy of Social Sciences, the Development Research Center of the State Council, the Academy of Military Science of the Chinese People's Liberation Army (AMS), the China Institute of International Studies, and the China Institute of Contemporary International Relations.

Second, China seized and maintained the initiative in Japan's claimed exclusive economic zone with exploration-production operations on the west side of Japan's median line. Beijing offered joint development on the east side of the median line to gain Japanese participation in China's continental shelf. Japan's insistence on resolving sovereignty before conducting joint development east of the median line delayed its own operations until April 2005. That coincided with Prime Minister Koizumi's bid for a permanent seat on the United Nations Security Council, a story which was fuel for China's media to inflame anti-Japanese demonstrations. As anti-China sentiment increased in Japan, China and partners conducted survey and laid pipelines in the East China Sea, producing 300,000 m^3 per day from Chunxiao before Japan's Teikoku Oil even began drilling.[29]

Third, Chinese warships and fighter aircraft threatened Japanese and American counterparts in international and disputed space, followed by Chinese exploration operations within a few kilometers of the median line. Besides aerial intrusions, major incidents included:

1. April 2001, a PLA Air Force F-8 fighter aircraft collided with a US Navy EP-3 reconnaissance aircraft, resulting in the death of the Chinese pilot and emergency landing of the EP-3 on Hainan Island.[30]

2. November 2004, a Han-class Chinese submarine transited the Ishigaki Strait in the Sakishima Islands, a narrows that Japan claims as exempt from the right of innocent passage.[31]

3. January 2005, CNOOC began exploration of the 22,000 km^2 Chunxiao gas field that straddles the median line; the foreign ministry ignored Japan's requests to share data.[32]

4. September 2005, one of five PLA Navy warships patrolling on the west side of the median line locked its fire-control radar on to a JSDF P-3C anti-submarine aircraft.[33]

5. October 2006, a Song-class Chinese submarine closed within firing distance of the *USS Kitty Hawk* aircraft carrier, undetected prior to surfacing.[34]

Beijing kept Tokyo on the diplomatic defensive by justifying its own expansion and framing any similar Japanese plans in terms of imperial aggression. Throughout 2005–2006, Chinese foreign ministry spokespersons implied force would be used against any Japanese operations in the disputed territory. PLA navy warships approached the median line prior to elections in Japan as anti-Japanese demonstrations in China spread through major cities. Even US congressmen called for Prime Minister Ryutaro Hashimoto's successor to not visit Yasukuni Shrine.[35] Prime Minister Shinzō Abe attempted to wrest the initiative away with a hardline on negotiations, but he was the first of six consecutive Japanese prime ministers in six years. Abe's defense of government-approved history textbooks which neglected Japanese responsibility for the Pacific War handed Chinese negotiators fresh reasons to refuse concessions. In 2008, Prime Minister Takeo Fukuda tried a softer approach, lauding the Senkaku area as a sea of peace and friendship. Beijing offered joint development of gas fields that stretched across the media line and which China had already begun to develop. There was no agreement, however, on joint implementation. As negotiations sputtered, China occupied space up to Japan's median line on the surface, and across it beneath the sea.

Japanese corporations had not been idle. To the north of China's drilling operation lay Ieodo (Suyan Rock), controlled by South Korea and disputed by China and Japan. Due to the overlapping Chinese, Korean, and Japanese exclusive economic zones, Seoul also declared a median-line rule but unlike Tokyo, risked confrontation to implement it. A joint Japanese–South Korean exploration effort effectively Defended against Chinese territorial expansion.

Regional energy needs aggravated Sino-Japanese competition. In 2005, the Ministry of Economics, Trade and Industry's Natural Resources and the Agency for Natural Resources and Energy annual white paper predicted that global energy demand would swell by 59 percent, Chinese demand would rise by 21 percent, and the rest of Asia would increase by 6 percent. At the time, Japan met 19 percent of its own energy needs —mostly through nuclear power—so the agency recommended energy reserves, conservation, diversified imports, and *Securing* Japan's energy rights in its exclusive economic zone.[36] As the Chinese Foreign Ministry warned Japan against drilling in Chinese waters, Japanese companies were tied up in lengthy government procedures just to drill east of the median line. By the summer of 2010, Chinese drilling operations had driven Japan Prime Minister Yoshihiko Noda to threaten the use of force: "If illegal activities occur inside our nation's lands or waters, including the Senkaku Islands, the government as a whole will make resolute responses, including using the SDF if necessary."[37] The next day, Defense Minister Satoshi Morimoto mentioned mobilizing the Japan Self-Defense Forces to Defend the Senkakus in cases for which the Coast Guard or police could not respond.

In August, Chinese nationalists landed on the Senkakus; they were arrested and sent back to China. This was followed by Japanese nationalists, same drill. In China, crowdsourced protests against "Japanese aggression" erupted in ten cities. Thousands marched in Shenzen, burning Japanese flags and calling for a boycott of Japanese goods.

Confrontation
In this charged environment, events ignited new aggregates that moved Japan and China toward conflict. In September 2010, a Chinese fishing boat collided with a Japan Coast Guard patrol boat near the Senkakus. The Coast Guard treated the incident as a criminal act, arresting the inebriated captain and imprisoning him in Japan rather than expelling him to China. Japan's Minister of Transportation Seiji Maehara had named China a threat a few weeks earlier, so it was reasonable for Beijing to regard this as a deliberate escalation. Beijing halted rare earth metals exports to Japan for detaining its citizens "in international waters." Prime

Minister Naoto Kan and Premier Wen Jiaobao met in Brussels, agreeing to improve relations.

The meeting provided fine optics, but at the working level there was no bilateral communication. In the past, retired politicians on each side provided "pipes" of informal communication. Those corroded after the Liberal Democratic Party lost to the Democratic Party of Japan. Seiji Maehara became foreign minister, as if rewarded for threatening China. Communication between the Ministries of Defense and Transportation were broken too, so domestic politics trumped foreign policy. Beijing demanded the captain's release with compensation and warned Tokyo of further export restrictions as anti-Japanese demonstrations spread. China Fisheries Law Enforcement Command (FLEC) ships appeared near the Senkakus.

On March 11, 2011, a massive earthquake (9.0 on the Richter scale) triggered devastating tsunamis and aftershocks, inundating much of Japan's northeastern coast. Ensuing fires, explosions, and power outages at the Fukushima Dai-ichi nuclear power plant complex caused radiation leakage that contaminated the atmosphere and water supplies. International rescue and relief efforts struggled to cope with the disaster that claimed over 18,000 lives. Over the course of cleanup operations, anti-nuclear power sentiment spiked. A year after the disaster, all but two of Japan's remaining fifty-four nuclear power reactors had been shut down.

The near-elimination of nuclear power increased the importance of the Senkakus as Japan became the world's largest importer of liquefied natural gas. Other factors intensified Japan's demand for energy *Security* as well. Japan's mounting debt was the highest among Organization of Economic Cooperation and Development (OECD) states, exacerbated by deflation and a declining workforce. The need for economic growth, increased productivity, and development of multiple energy sources became acute. Japan's exclusive economic zone became a prized possession.

In April 2012, Governor of Tokyo Shintaro Ishihara began raising funds to purchase the Senkakus from their private owner on behalf of the Tokyo metropolitan government. In response, Prime Minister Noda began efforts to nationalize the Senkakus to prevent Ishihara from gaining control. Chinese and Japanese activists attempted more landings on the Senkakus in August. At the same time, Ishihara disclosed that he had pressed Noda to construct a Senkaku harbor for a permanent Japanese economic presence against China and Taiwan claims. If Noda could deliver, Ishihara offered to retract his purchase bid and donate the 1.4b yen (US$17.8 million) which he had already collected to the national government.[38]

Prime Minister Noda's preemptive nationalization defused Ishihara's purchase but was not combined with other de-escalatory actions. Less frequent maritime patrols, or coordination of Japanese and Chinese patrolling on different days, did not happen. Instead, Noda announced the purchase of three Senkaku islets in September 2012, the day after explaining his motive to an unmoved Chinese President Hu Jintao at the Asia Pacific Economic Cooperation (APEC) meeting in Vladivostok.

A spiral of escalation did happen. On September 14, six Chinese surveillance ships penetrated the 12 nm ring around the Senkakus. On September 17, 1,000 Chinese fishing boats and four Chinese surveillance ships approached the Senkakus. Beijing protesters were permitted to march in front of the Japanese embassy to demonstrate against Tokyo's contract to purchase Diaoyu islets. Vandalism, looting, and arson struck Japanese factories and businesses in China. The day after China's Foreign Ministry demanded that Tokyo reverse its nationalization decision, a temporary burst of free reporting disseminated photos of anti-Japan protests on front pages.

On September 25, the same day that China and Japan held diplomatic exchanges to ease tensions, Taiwan dispatched twelve Coast Guard vessels to escort sixty fishing boats into Senkaku waters. The vessels and boats were countered by Japan Coast Guard ships, which used water cannons against them. China's Vice Minister of Commerce Jiang Zengwei urged consumers to boycott Japanese goods; more than a hundred cities registered anti-Japan protests. China refused to attend International Monetary Fund (IMF) and World Bank meetings in Tokyo in October. In December, Japan's Defense Ministry reported that a Chinese patrol aircraft entered Senkaku airspace, the first such incursion since 1958. Japan scrambled eight F-15 fighter aircraft in response. On January 10, 2013, the PLA Air Force launched two J-10 fighter aircraft in response to F-15 fighters on patrol.

The stream of Chinese maritime intrusions into Japanese-controlled territory is ongoing; it is an integrated campaign of territorial control which China justifies by domestic laws on national defense, civil aviation, and rules of flight.[39] Between September 2012 and May 2013, fifty violations were recorded by the Regional Coast Guard headquarters in Naha.[40] Chinese aircraft approaching Japanese airspace trigger Japanese fighters to scramble. If Chinese fighters were to escort such a package and intrude, an air-to-air engagement is likely. On average, three PLA navy frigates operate each month inside Japan's territorial waters. Submarines routinely enter Japanese territory in the Okinawa Prefecture. Protests sent from the Japan Foreign Ministry's Asian and Oceanic Affairs to the China Foreign Ministry are answered by interpretations of United Nations Convention on the Law of the Sea that invoke Beijing's right to Defend its independence, sovereignty, and territorial integrity. Since June 2013 a dozen new Chinese gas-production platforms have appeared in the disputed region. Chinese remotely piloted aircraft also appear in the vicinity. Ongoing operations of China's Coast Guard with PLA navy warships nearby help safeguard and normalize the presence of Chinese commercial fishing fleets in disputed areas.[41]

Tokyo's response has been unprecedented in several respects. A U.S.-Japan plan for long-range reconnaissance includes remotely piloted aircraft operations. Japanese officials warned that JSDF personnel may be stationed on the islets. The Japan Ministry of Defense plans to bolster capabilities to Defend its seas and airspace, respond to attacks on remote islands, and conduct rapid deployments. Japan's media pressure prompted

President Barack Obama to reply that the Japan-administered Senkakus are subject to Article 5 of the Treaty of Mutual Cooperation and Security between the United States and Japan.[42] Japan's 2015 budget is the largest ever and includes ten surface warfare vessels, five submarines, twenty antisubmarine patrol aircraft, six fifth-generation F-35 fighter-sensor aircraft, thirty amphibious landing vehicles, new airborne early warning aircraft, the Global Hawk unmanned aerial vehicle systems, and aerial refueling aircraft.[43]

As Japan's domestic opposition reacts to conservatives' calls for collective Defense, Beijing's provocations test Japan Self-Defense Force discipline and seek to weaken Japanese resolve. This plays out in complex ways. Chinese netizens laud antisecurity legislation protests in Japan as democratic while condemning their own government for not allowing the same. Beijing ultimately seeks to neutralize US air-sea battle capabilities and destroy the credibility of American commitment to Defend Japan.[44] A shift from Deterrence to Coercion plays well in China's blogosphere. To the extent which PLA leaders think they can punish Japanese or American willpower, Beijing's ambiguous threats are likely to assert themselves with more clarity.[45] The credibility of the U.S.-Japan alliance is crucial to Deterring China's attempts to Compel an overreaction. If Japan were to become isolated from US support, China's combined effect will become more aggressive. China is developing capabilities that the U.S. does not have, such as the supersonic YJ-18 antiship cruise missile.[46] What happens when Beijing converts its Compellence and Coercion into a Coercive Deterrence that facilitates territorial expansion? The Defensive and Deterrent elements of Japan's strategy will be in need of Compellent and Coercive tools.

Combined-Effects Analysis

Figure 12. Lines of Effect Logic.

Lines of Effect Logic	
Psychological:	intimidate will / neutralize capability to **Deter** D_t -- **Compel** C_p
	assure will / enhance capability to ***Dissuade*** D_s -- ***Persuade*** **P**
Physical:	punish will / deny capability to **Defend** D_f -- **Coerce** C_r
	demonstrate will / exercise capability to ***Secure*** **S** -- ***Induce*** **I**

Influenced by a security culture of uniqueness and ambivalent relations, Japanese leaders have overreacted to threats and opportunities. The current strategy seeks to adaptively respond under self-Defense restraints in a highly interdependent environment. Let's start our analysis of the Senkaku confrontation by examining Japan's and China's lines of effect and how they interact.

Japan's energy *Security* line of effect led to confrontation with China as access to resources became a matter of national security. In addition, collective Defense became part of Japanese strategy despite a longstanding policy prohibition against it. Both lines of effect emerged as ways to pursue different parts of Japan's $P\,I\,D_f\,D_t$ effect: *Persuasion* of domestic and American support of Japan's sovereignty; *Inducement* of US support; Defense of Senkaku territory, and Deterrence of Chinese force.

Japan's *Inducement* of US support of its territorial claims requires better coordination of foreign affairs and defense. A complicating factor is Washington's concern that it could be pulled into a conflict with China over a few islets. Getting the United States to agree on Japan's desired effects is central to Japan's postwar strategy. The complex basis of the

Japan-U.S. alliance complicates cooperation on the Senkaku issue. Hence, Tokyo seeks a more independent defense capability.

China's US engagement, comprehensive *Inducement*, and forced reaction lines of effect operate as an integrated campaign to complete the combined effect of D_s D_t $P I C_p$ C_r: *Dissuade* and Deter against US support of Japan; *Persuade* domestic opinion of China's efforts to regain the Diaoyu; *Induce* Japan's recognition of a dispute; and Compel or Coerce Japan to use force. The task of institutionalizing more ties with US policy makers is facilitated by a distributed information campaign. Beijing functionaries follow central Party guidance as "commander's intent" to generate believable truisms. Agitating anti-Japanese nationalism, however, risks a domestic backlash against single-party control. Essentially, Beijing's lines of effect seek to seize and manipulate the initiative through information, as well as to acquire energy and rare earth resources to satisfy domestic demand.

In considering how Japan and China lines of effect have intersected, conjoined, collided, and careened, the year 1997 provides a good starting point. By that time, Japan's and China's lines of effect were fully formulated.

Initially, China's comprehensive *Inducement* line intersected Japan's energy *Security* line. Chinese and Japanese drilling operations followed their own trajectories as long as Tokyo accepted Beijing's drilling operations in Japan's claimed exclusive economic zone. By being the first to exploit the other's claim, Beijing *Induced* cooperation on its own terms. Conversely, Japan had neither the collective nationalism nor a joint venture with which to begin to *Persuade* China of Japan's sovereignty.

During the period that Japanese investors helped finance Chinese drilling operations, both nations' lines of effect conjoined. By *Persuading* Japanese support of China's state-sponsored drilling operations in Japan's claimed exclusive economic zone, Beijing demonstrated that Tokyo's position was not credible. When Tokyo finally got around to authorizing survey operations on its side of the median line, Beijing tried

Dissuading and Deterring the United States from providing support, and Compelling and Coercing Japan to use force. The strategies now careened off each other in different directions. As China protested Japan's plans to conduct drilling operations, Japanese indignation rose. China's operations continued.

Chinese drilling in Japan's claimed territory and protests of Japan's intent to drill in China's claimed territory led to a collision of national lines of effect. Chinese Compellence and Coercion opposed Japanese Defense and Deterrence in a zero-sum relationship. Now Tokyo saw the joint-venture cooperation with China in Japan's exclusive economic zone as a threat to energy *Security*. Disagreement over boundaries while China conducted drilling operations in the disputed area forced Japan make Defense and Deterrence a priority. Japan and China were in cold conflict.

Under the assumptions just set forth, avoiding conflict depends heavily on US engagement. Even so, China's *Dissuasive* and Deterrent efforts have helped to prevent US support of Japan's claim to sovereignty. In response, Japan seeks a more independent capability to Defend territory in order to hedge against American conditional support. A potential source of cooperation would be U.S.-China consultation: prior notification of military operations and rules of behavior that cultivate mutual understanding and trust. Could this promote closer Sino-Japanese security relations given the exclusive rights to resources and territory? To date, China's actions remain consistent with a forced reaction line. Japan's Coast Guard and Self-Defense Forces have avoided using force to Defend against Chinese probes of its boundaries, even though resources claimed by the Japanese are susceptible to Chinese poaching through the seabed. Complicating the situation is the expanse of Japan's maritime territory; any islet is vulnerable to seizure. As Chinese operations expand and penetrative technologies improve, support in Japan for countervailing capabilities are likely to increase.

China's US engagement could translate into Sino-Japanese cooperation if there are deliberate efforts to do so. Until then, automated technology has the potential to create unintended, confrontational effects. Japan-U.S. capabilities and Japan's independent capabilities, could transfer an accidental collision with Chinese forces—which are also modernizing—into a strategic careening. How? Advances in command, control and intelligence-surveillance-reconnaissance seek decision superiority. This can lead to taking aggressive initiative, later deemed to be unintentional but morally justified. Any Chinese aggression is likely to militarize Japan's Self-Defense Forces, whether or not US forces are involved. Will Japan react or respond?

Japan's attempts to *Persuade* public opinion, *Induce* US support, and Defend/Deter China all depend on moderating domestic extremism while exercising responsible alliance capability. The prospects of doing both appear dim. Tokyo's authority over local leaders is weak, and networked individuals are empowered to an extreme. We have seen one governor manufacture a foreign policy crisis. When access to energy is contested, Japan's security culture manifests itself clearly. We saw this triggered by China's drilling operations and air-sea penetrations of Japanese-claimed territory. Japanese nationalists and isolationists advocated everything from nuclear weapons development to self-disarmament, from unilateral diplomacy to realignment with China. Such extremes undercut any attempts to *Dissuade* rightists and *Persuade* moderates, which could be a valuable potential addition to Defense and Deterrence. This dynamic speaks to the second requirement of Japan's desired combined effect, exercising alliance capability.

A realistic range of alliance capabilities is essential to preventing reactive policies that create quantum changes from the status quo. At the same time, Japanese officials' recurrent visits to Yasukuni Shrine, denials of war crimes, and equivocations about Japanese aggression in the Pacific War, stoke historical contention that undermine security. Current security policies, strategy and capabilities are inadequate to counter mounting Chinese threats to Japanese territory. Calls for large changes range from disarmament, increased dependence on the US, and a Japanese nuclear Deterrent. In all domains including cyber, preventative effects are unlikely to be credible unless accompanied by causative options. Japan's sensible alternatives to manage threats include more offensive combined-arms capability in the Japan-U.S. alliance, not less.

There is ample evidence of Japan's growing offensive arms in two areas: collective self-Defense and independent capabilities for territorial Defense. In June 2013, the Japanese defense minister emphasized the objective of the Japan–U.S. exercise, Operation Dawn Blitz, to "improve the SDF's joint operations capabilities under an environment close to actual warfare."[47] The chief of the general staff regarded the operation as key to a U.S.-Japan mutual cooperation system. A JSDF officer added that US MV-22 Osprey aircraft operated from Japanese destroyers. Observers note the development of an attack capability in the form of an "islet recapture" (tōsho dakkan) unit.[48] This capability to Defend access to energy resources and enforce territorial claims can integrate energy *Security* with collective Defense.

China's actions indicate a willingness to induce Japanese recognition of the Senkaku dispute and risk Compelling or Coercing Japan into reacting with force. This entails framing Japan as irresponsible, perhaps uniquely so. Any use of force would be portrayed as an overreaction.

The great setup began in September 2012, when Xinhua News began a two-week information campaign that staked out China's jurisdiction around the Diaoyu Islets. In a succession of arguments, Beijing declared measures to protect China's territorial sea, began regular media reporting on Diaoyutai weather conditions and forecasts, filed a copy of the basepoints with the United Nations, specified the geographic coordinates of the Diaoyu Islets and dozens of other islets, and published a white paper, "Diaoyu Dao, an Inherent Territory of China."[49]

Japan's combined effect is best served by responding rather than reacting to Chinese aggression. This means harmonizing the energy *Security* and collective Defense lines of effect that try to *Persuade* and *Induce*, and Defend and Deter. Japan's current path is fraught with risk. The Abe administration's preference for collective Defense and willingness to use force against Chinese territorial occupation have been stated more clearly than any other postwar Japanese administration. The newly established National Security Council empowers a small circle of four key officials: the prime minister, chief cabinet secretary, minister of foreign affairs, and minister of defense.

How long will Japan's restraint last if Chinese forces become more aggressive and engage in activity such as feigning or executing an amphibious landing? How would Japan respond to the infiltration of a deep-sea drilling platform on its side of the median line—the equivalent to dredging new territory in the South China Sea? The situation demands leaders who can create cooperative effects, or at least restrain the scope of confrontational operations. Someone has to plan for peace. For Japan, enforcing discipline in the face of Chinese baiting is needed to prevent and contain conflict. For China, knowing how far to push territorial claims without provoking sustainable Japanese rearmament is necessary to shape a future that does not include a permanently hostile Japan. For the U.S., the related question remains *how to induce Sino-Japanese cooperation?*

We need to think about more combinations of possible effects, ones which go beyond those tried in the past. Imagining future possibilities can begin with effects-oriented assumptions about Japanese strategy. We expect Japan to develop a robust independent military capability accompanied by special claims of unique pacifism, as collective self-Defense. Absent Japan–U.S. agreement on how to counter claims on Japanese territory, Japan will strengthen its tools to Defend and Deter threats to sovereignty and to protect access to resources. This adds *Security* to Japan's combined effect, which for Japan is more than an academic exercise.

If energy *Security* became militarized through demonstrations of will and exercises of capability as is the case for China and the Koreas, Japan's claim as a uniquely self-Defensive power would evaporate. Regional fears that Japanese security might reacquire expansionist economic and territorial rights would play into China's hands. A concern for policy makers and strategists should be whether a broadened concept of security in Japan would lead to heightened conflict as was the case in the past.

Add to this concern the fact that Japan's energy *Security* and collective Defense, and China's comprehensive *Inducement* and forced reaction, include remotely operated capabilities. Space-based and mobile sensors networked with air, surface, and subsurface platforms provide new information for the development of intelligence, an imperfect product. The integration of military, police, economic, and diplomatic operations is a practical and intellectual challenge, given the huge volume of generated data. This increases confusion and the likelihood of miscalculation.

In China, the combined effect of comprehensive *Inducement* and forced reaction appears to be much more integrated among party and government elites. Official references to societal pressures invariably try to have it both ways—democracy and pluralism excuse Chinese nationalism when convenient, even though such freedoms are inimical to single-party rule. The downside for Beijing is that the new tools may threaten as well as strengthen party control in different areas of China. To deal with this, General Secretary and President Xi Jinping consolidated power through reforms that institutionalize national development under party leadership, in populist terms.[50] Xi's call to rejuvenate the Chinese nation as the greatest Chinese dream attempts to *Persuade* an increasingly informed society that China will achieve the status of a global power by 2050. Chinese leaders need to retain popular support of this vision to justify complex warfare against Japan and the United States.

Several fabricated scenarios might suit this purpose. From low to highest risk, four possibilities illustrate how Beijing's proactive strategy seeks to exploit Tokyo's separated lines of effect.

First, a Sino-Russian alliance with maritime, air, and cyber presence could shape conditions to enforce expansive sovereignty claims. Since 2006 China has conducted increasingly complex mobility exercises across its military regions. Augmented by electronic warfare and cyber operations,[51] China's annual drills include long-distance airlift and joint force attacks. In July 2013, China began its largest live-fire maritime exercise with another power, Joint Sea 2013. Nineteen vessels and ten aircraft conducted air-defense, maritime replenishment, antisubmarine, joint escort, and boarding operations. A judicious interpretation of such activities is to Deter US support of Japan in a Senkaku scenario. Demonstrated capabilities include data theft, website corruption, and microwave jamming of sensor nodes. Sino-Russian cyber capabilities could *Induce* recognition of a dispute and provoke the Japanese government to react.

Second, China's territorial claims and media shaping may be followed by proxy, apparently accidental, occupation of the Senkakus to force Japan to acknowledge the dispute. The preparatory information campaign is firmly in place. In 2012, a three-dimensional map showed that the islets are not part of China but have been presented visually to appear otherwise. Chinese military activity near the Senkakus increased tenfold after Japan announced its purchase of the islets in September 2012. Continued pressure on Japan may *Induce* recognition of the dispute via conservative groups less interested in *Securing* energy access than in highlighting external threats, or liberal groups protesting risks of war.

Third, PLA units might conduct a rescue mission in support of those who managed to occupy the Senkakus and become stranded in the face of Japan's Self-Defense Forces and Coast Guard. This could take several forms, such as a symbolic ground force or civilian ship or a massive rescue mission that outnumbers Japanese and American forces. The presence of Chinese military or civilian forces attempting to reach Chinese citizens in the Senkakus could create a dilemma for Japan-U.S. forces obligated to Defend Japan-administered territory.

Fourth, consider a follow-on cordon around the islands to guarantee *Security*. A number of options may be expected to gain domestic support in China as a crisis unfolds, inducing political, economic, and military recognition of the territorial dispute. With virtually agitated societal support, the National Peoples' Congress may call for Defensive cyber war on Japanese and American civilian and government networks. If Beijing calculates that it can achieve escalation dominance in an "informatized war,"[52] nuclear and conventional missiles could be placed on alert to demonstrate political will and Deter media-hyped US and Japan preparations to attack China. In the event of a Japanese reaction that does not garner wide American support, China is likely to succeed in getting UN support. Beijing may think that internationalization of the Senkaku dispute would be in China's best interests.

All of these scenarios could be conducted by distributed cyber operations that inflame flash-mob opposition to Japanese claims. The threat of specialized aces able to disrupt automated trading could kill financial markets.

China's strategy is more than combined arms–leveraged Coercion and Deterrence. First-order tools that target will and capabilities are instrumental in bringing about a combination of second- and third-order effects. Beijing's attempts to *Persuade* domestic and Japan-U.S. opinion, *Dissuade* US support, *Induce* Japan recognition, and Coerce and Compel Japan are designed to provoke the use of force. Even if Japan's response is measured and not escalatory, the leaders and media of China will portray that as an overreaction to exploit the situation.

Clearly, Japan needs to avoid the problematic pursuit of independent Defense. Japan's interdependent strategy is complex. The pace of information generation, the dynamism of networks, and the ability of a human-made domain to cause kinetic destruction complicate Tokyo's ability to *Secure* energy resources with collective Defense. Japan's declining population and limited commitments from alliance partners sharpen the need to acquire energy resources with less national resources. A nuclear option, either for energy *Security* or Deterrence, is sure to be a hyperpolarizing issue.

Combined-effects strategy and cyberspace options offer new ways for Japan to access energy resources. Rather than slaving new strategic tools

—operating systems, search engines, software routers, secure clouds—to support traditional diplomacy and military platforms, security strategy could focus on effects. Instead of restricting itself to providing fundamental direction to existing programs, the National Security Council would be well advised to make access to energy resources the top priority and lead innovative partnerships to achieve it. The Ministry of Foreign Affairs and the Ministry of Defense could adopt global networking, promote private-public partnerships, start virtual military exchanges, and expand international forums to shape preferences toward cooperation. This would enlarge Japan's labor force as an interdependent network. Possibly, Japanese and Chinese leaders would realize a common interest in integrating regional and global networks of supply and demand across borders, thereby making conflict less likely.

Figure 13. Combined Effects of *Japan's Delayed Reactions*.

Combined Effects Summary of *Japan's Delayed Reactions*

Japan

    Strategy P I D_f D_t Interdependent Defense

            (***Persuasion-Inducement*-Defense-Deterrence**)

    Lines of Effect   Energy security to **Deter** China's economic and
                           military operations and ***Persuade*** citizens of Japan's
                           access to energy

                           de facto collective defense to **Deter** and **Defend**
                           Japan against China attack/seizure of Japan
                           territory, and ***Persuade*** and ***Induce*** US support of Japan
                           Self-Defense Force operations

China

    Strategy D_s D_t P, I C_p C_r Isolation and Territorial Control

    (***Dissuasion*-Deterrence-*Persuasion-Inducement*-Compellence-Coercion**)

    Lines of Effect   US engagement to ***Dissuade*** and **Deter** US support of
                           Japan in Sino-Japanese territorial disputes

                           Comprehensive **Inducement** to ***Persuade*** and ***Induce***
                           Japan recognition of a territorial dispute

                           Forced Reaction to **Compel** or **Coerce** an overreaction by
                           Japan forces, officials or rightists

NOTES

1. "Fact Sheet on the Senkaku Islands," Japan Ministry of Foreign Affairs. http://www.mofa.go.jp/region/asia-paci/senkaku/fact_sheet.html.

2. "Some Sensitive Issues," Ministry of Foreign Affairs of the People's Republic of China. http://www.fmprc.gov.cn/eng/wjb/zzjg/yzs/gjlb/272 1/2722/t15974.shtml (accessed November 14, 2015).

3. China's 2013 claim that the Okinawa Trough is where China's continental shelf basin terminates: http://www.un.org/Depts/los/ clcs_new/submissions_files/chn63_12/executive%20summary_EN.pdf (accessed October 3, 2015).

4. Japan's 2008 claim that the Ryukyu Islands are extensions of Japan's land mass: http://www.un.org/Depts/los/clcs_new/submissions_files/jpn08/ jpn_execsummary.pdf (accessed October 3, 2015).

5. UNCLOS Article 15 states that neither state may extend its claim beyond a median line equidistant from baselines that frame the disputed territory, subject to historical or special circumstances. https://www.un.org/Depts/ los/convention_agreements/texts/unclos/unclos_e.pdf.

6. "PLA's Potential Leading Role in Coastal Defense and Maritime Rights Protection Activities," *NIDS China Security Report 2012* (Tokyo: National Institute of Defense Studies 2012), 32-37, http://www.nids.go.jp.

7. Han-yi Shaw, "The Diaoyutai/Senkaku Islands Dispute: Its History and an Analysis of the Ownership Claims of the PRC, ROC, and Japan," *Occasional Papers in Contemporary Asian Studies* No. 3, 1999 (Baltimore: University of Maryland School of Law, 1999), 13.

8. Lawrence W. Beer, "Japan Turning the Corner," in *Asian Survey* 11, No. 1, A Survey of Asian in 1970: Part I (Jan., 1971): 74-85. http://www.jstor. org/stable/2642907.

9. Jean-Marc F. Blanchard, "The US Role in the Sino-Japanese Dispute over the Diaoyu (Senkaku) Islands, 1945-1971," *The China Quarterly*, No. 161 (Mar., 2000): 95-123.

10. Daniel Tretiak, "The Sino-Japanese Treaty of 1978: The Senkaku Incident Prelude," *Asian Survey* 18, No. 12 (Dec., 1978): 1235-1249, 1241, 1258.

11. Shaw, "The Diaoyutai/Senkaku Islands Dispute," 18. The KMT mayor of Kaohsiung organized the expedition after the DPP criticized the KMT as weak against Japan.

12. This was a capable force. In 1970, the MSA possessed 81 offshore and 11 coastal vessels, 243 inshore vessels, 38 helicopters and 5 aircraft. *The Military Balance* 90, Issue 1 (London: International Institute for Strategic Studies, 1990): 148-181, 166.

13. Hugo Dobson, *Japan and the G7/8: 1975-2002* (London: RoutlegeCurzon, 2004), 86-87.

14. Erica Strecker and Phillip C. Saunders, "Legitimacy and the Limits of Nationalism: China and the Diaoyu Islands," *International Security* 23, No. 3 (Winter, 1998-1999): 114-146, 128-130.

15. On North Korea's 1977 claim to 50-mile military zones extending from both coasts, see Jin-Hyun Paik, "East Asia and the Law of the Sea," in *The Law of the Sea in the Asian Pacific Region*, ed. James Crawford (Dordrecht: Martinus Nijoff Publishers, 1994), 7-20, 10.

16. Kerry Dumbaugh, "China's Maritime Territorial Claims: Implications for U.S. Interests," *Congressional Research Service Report for Congress*, 12 Nov 2001,19.

17. For a study on Japan-U.S. policy divergence during the crisis, see Yoshi-fumi Nakai, "Policy Coordination on Taiwan," in Masashi Nishihara, *The Japan-U.S. Alliance: New Challenges for the 21st Century* (Tokyo: Japan Center for International Exchange, 2000).

18. For an argument that a coastal state does not have jurisdiction over surveys and some military activities in an EEZ, see Raul Pedrozo, "Preserving Navigational Rights and Freedoms: The Right to Conduct Military Activities in China's Exclusive Economic Zone," *Chinese Journal of International Law* (2010) 9 (1), 9-29. http://chinesejil.oxfordjournals. org/content/9/1/9.full.pdf+html (accessed May 11, 2015).

19. Reinhard Drifte, "Territorial Conflicts in the East China Sea - From Missed Opportunities to Negotiation Stalemate," *The Asia-Pacific Journal* 22 (June 2009): 3-9. http://www.japanfocus.org/-Reinhard-Drifte/3156 (accessed September 5, 2012).

20. "Treaty of Peace and Friendship between Japan and the People's Republic of China." http://www.mofa.go.jp/region/asia-paci/china/treaty78.html (accessed May 11, 2015).

21. See http://www.mofa.go.jp.

22. Specific examples may be found in *Defense of Japan 2011* (Tokyo: Ministry of Defense, 2012), 347-368.

23. See extensive examples in *Defense of Japan 2015*, 270-307. http://www. mod.go.jp/e/publ/w_paper/2015.html (accessed Jan 2, 2016).

24. See "APT 1: Exposing One of China's Cyber Espionage Units." http://intelreport.mandiant.com/ (accessed Jul 4, 2015).

25. Erica Strecker Downs and Phillip C. Saunders, "Legitimacy and the Limits of Nationalism: China and the Diaoyu Islands," *International Security* 23, No. 3, (Winter 1998-99): 114-146. http://www.jstor.org/stable/25393 40 (accessed September 17, 2012).

26. Masahiko Sasajima, "Storm over Senkakus: How to deal with hot nonissue," *Yomiuri Shinbum*, October 2, 1996, LexisNexis.

27. Kwan Weng Kin, "Don't deny Diaoyu Dispute: China to Japan," *The Straits Times*, October 14, 1996, LexisNexis.

28. "China Taps Natural Gas Reserves in East China Sea," *Xinhua General News Service*, March 20, 2002, LexisNexis.

29. Mark J. Valencia, "The East China Sea Dispute: Context, Claims, Issues, and Possible Solutions," *Asian Perspective* 31 No. 1, (2007): 127-167, 135.

30. Shirley A. Kan (Coordinator) and others, "China-U.S. Aircraft Collision Incident of April2001: Assessments and Policy Implications," *CRS Report to Congress*, 10 October 2001. http://www.fas.org/sgp/crs/row/RL30946 .pdf (accessed April 2, 2013).

31. Robert Bush points out that if the submarine had transited on the surface it would have complied with the right of innocent passage. Robert C. Bush, *The Perils of Proximity: China-Japan Security Relations* (Washington, DC: Brookings Institution Press, 2010), 82-83.

32. Arthur S. Ding, "China's Energy Security Demands and the East China Sea: A Growing Likelihood of Conflict in East Asia?" *The China and Eurasia Forum Quarterly* (November 2005): 35-38. http://www.silkroadstudies.org/new/docs/CEF/Quarterly/November_2005/Arthur_Ding.pdf (accessed August 3, 2015).

33. John Brinsley and Isabel Reynolds, "China and Japan Trade Accusations over Radar Lock," *China Digital Times*. http://chinadigitaltimes.net/2013/0 2/china-and-japan-trade-accusations-over-radar-lock-incident/ (accessed August 3, 2015).

34. "China Sub Stalked US Fleet," *The Washington Times*, November 6, 2006.

35. "U.S. lawmakers urge post-Koizumi leader not to visit Yasukuni," *Japan Economic Newswire*. September 15, 2006, LexisNexis.

36. The baseline for comparison was 2002. "Energy security sought against surging global demand," *Japan Economic Newswire*, May 26th, 2005, LexisNexis.

37. *Kyodo News Agency*, 27 July 2010.

38. "Governor of Tokyo: Develop Senkakus, and I'll Halt Purchase," *Asahi Shinbum*, 1 September 2012. http://ajw.asahi.com (accessed October 22, 2013).

39. "China sets air defense ID zone in E China Sea," *Xinhua News Agency*, 23 Nov 13. http://www.china.org.cn/china/2013-11/23/content_306834 10.htm.

40. *Kyodo News Agency*, 13 May 2013.

41. "See Military and Security Developments Involving the People's Republic of China 2015," *Annual Report to Congress*, 3. http://www.defense. gov/Portals/1/Documents/pubs/2015_China_Military_Power_Report.pdf (accessed October 25, 2-15).

42. "Obama: Senkakus Covered Under US-Japan Security Treaty," *The Diplomat*, 24 April 2014. http://thediplomat.com/2014/04/obama-senkakus-covered-under-us-japan-security-treaty/ (accessed July 12, 2015).

43. "Defense Programs and Budget of Japan: Overview of FY 2015 Budget Bill," Ministry of Defense. http://www.mod.go.jp/e/d_budget/pdf/2702 06.pdf.

44. For a discussion of air-sea battle, see Aaron L. Friedberg, *Beyond Air-Sea Battle: The Debate Over US Military Strategy in Asia* (London: International Institute for Strategic Studies, 2014).

45. "Defiant Chinese Admiral's Message: South China Sea 'Belongs to China,'" *The Diplomat*. http://thediplomat.com/2015/09/Chinese-admiral-south-china-sea-belongs-to-china/ (accessed March 11, 2015).

46. Lyle J. Goldstein, "China's YJ-18 Supersonic Anti-Ship Cruise Missile: America's Nightmare?" in *The National Interest*, 1 June 2015, http://www. nationalinterest.org/feature/chinas-yj-18-supersonic-anti-ship-cruise-missile-americas-13010 (accessed June 11, 2015).

47. Press Conference by the Defense Minister, 7 June 2013. http://www.mod. go.jp/e/pressconf/2013/06/130607.html (accessed August 10, 2015).

48. "Japan Eyes Troops for Recapturing Control of Remote Islands," *Kyodo News Agency*, 11 June 2013. http://rp1.abs-cbnnews.com/global-filipino/world/06/11/13/japan-eyes-troops-recapture-remote-islands (accessed September 9, 2013).

49. *Xinhua*, 7 July 13. http://xinhuanet.com/english/ (accessed November 14, 2014).

50. For examples see Yang Guangbin, *Xi's got the power to guide the CCP to 2049*, 1 March 2015, http://www.eastasiaforum.org (accessed September 25, 2015).

51. Tom Espiner, *Security Bulletin*, 29 May 2007. http://www.zdnet.com/article/us-military-warns-of-china-electronic-warfare-capability/ (accessed October 15, 2015).
52. Roy Kamphausen, Andrew Scobell, and Travis Tanner, *The People in the PLA: Recruitment, Training, and Education in China's Military*, Maroon E-books, 73-87.

CHAPTER 8

COMBINED-EFFECTS STRATEGY

This chapter summarizes the book's main findings, draws conclusions, and makes practical recommendations for US security strategy in a complex global environment. Each of the three cases examined strategy through a dual lens of security culture—presumed to change slowly, and combinations of desired effects—taken as highly dynamic. The working assumptions presented in chapter 1 asserted that cultures can interpret what is right and just in various ways and that morally coated interests affect decisions made about security strategy. Given this starting point, it follows that the making of strategy should include a comparative approach that admits diverse views on security. This competence is critical to discerning and waging complex warfare.

Equipped with three questions related to confrontation and cooperation, threats, and effectiveness, the study examined three East Asian civilizations—China, Korea, and Japan. A background chapter on the features of each society's dominant security culture was followed by a chapter that analyzed a contemporary security crisis. The latter employed a combined-effects thought-template consisting of Effects, Targets and Tools. This framework modeled the essence of strategy as interactions among ends, ways and means. The ends of strategy were taken as value-

and interest-based desired effects in various operational environments. A key difference between this approach and that of combined arms is the creation of lines of effect, which when combined, can produce powerful synergies.

The crisis chapters began with the strategies of the main actors. The ends of strategy were expressed as separate effects or combined effects, as applicable to the case. This analytical perspective revealed narratives that described key functions of strategy, such as shaping lines of effect and setting favorable conditions. Crises culminated in a featured confrontation and aftermath. An enduring challenge in these historical analyses was how and whether to attribute strategic intent to any particular aggregate. Often there was no actor to whom to attribute such intent, so disaggregated processes of strategy created effects anyway. This paradox highlights the importance of a maintaining a comparative perspective, understanding insights and limits of security culture, and seeking out unintended consequences of purposeful strategy. The combined-effects analyses at the end of each case explored how lines of effect interacted as well as other possible ways they could have interacted, and then developed implications or conclusions appropriate to the context at hand.

Three questions guide evaluation of the cases. First, how does security culture influence operational concepts? Based on the case narratives and analyses, the answer to this question discusses the effect of security culture on values and interests, rational and intuitive thinking, and threat assessment.

Second, when do lines of effect operate as combinations, rather than as separately pursued effects, targets, and tools? In answering this question, the lines of effect and the logic of strategy as understood through the Effects-Targets-Tools framework are reviewed. Effects are described in terms of confrontational and cooperative interactions. Theoretically, pure confrontation consists of Deterrence/Compellence and Defense/Coercion, while pure cooperation consists of *Dissuasion/Persuasion* and

Security/Inducement. In practice, however, these elements usually combine as blended or contradictory effects.

Third, how can security culture help us judge intent and capabilities, and select tools? This question returns us to considering how to interpret security culture—the role of confrontation, the nature and assessment of threat, and the effectiveness of confrontation. Relating these cultural considerations to the three crises, implications are derived for strategies that pursue security broadly—through confrontation and cooperation.

Each of the main questions are answered with a synthesis up front, followed by country summaries for China and Taiwan, the Koreas, and Japan. Along the way, comparisons and implications for the United States are freely considered. A closing section will draw implications and recommend how combined-effects statecraft might harmonize and integrate US security strategy and operations in this pivotal region as well as in general. We turn to the first concluding question.

How Does Security Culture Influence Operational Concepts?

The cases illustrate important linkages between culture and operations including but going beyond warfare as application of force. In these East Asian contexts, security culture drives the formulation of operational concepts in three basic ways.

First, societal beliefs are central to judging what constitutes threats and how to counter them. Threats are expressed not only in terms of interests at risk but also with regard to endangered values. Indeed, the moral dilemmas that each major actor encountered are understandable as cultural constructions. Viewed through the Effects-Targets-Tools framework, the cases show operational concepts consistent with a number of enduring beliefs—moral order, central authority, main power accommodation, unique self-identity, and ambivalent foreign relations. East Asian security traditions have produced the world's most enduring works on strategy. Sun Zi's precepts are the most known, having been applied well beyond the political contexts and technologies of the Warring States period because they deal with the psychological aspects of creating advantages over threats.

In contemporary situations, "new" operational concepts continue to be formulated, informed by strategies from ancient societies with complex human interactions. John Boyd's Observe-Orient-Decide-Act cycle is a prime example of high-tech tactics useful at operational and strategic levels because the thought process brings cultural predispositions into new contexts. How? Security culture shapes the *orientation* phase as operators, strategists, and policy makers attribute intent to *observed* behavior before making *decisions* and taking *action*. Strategic innovation benefits or suffers as novel ideas interact with cultural beliefs and practices.

Second, security cultures reflect preferences that affect strategic performance. In Qing China and Chosŏn Korea, moralistic and zero-sum constructions of threat fostered disconnects among domestic processes, resource constraints, and external relations. Court rigidity and indecision prolonged disunity—and therefore national weakness—among tradition-alists and reformists. Operational concepts were confined to tactics, which were inadequate against the relentless press of external powers. Modern China and North Korea portrayed threats more comprehensively. The use of ideology focused operations on achieving all of the preventative and causative pairings in the combined-effects framework. Both China and North Korea continue to pursue strategies of national development with heavy cultural narratives. In Japan, national isolation punctuated by continental forays nurtured existential strategies that led to unsustainable expansion. Sustained ambivalence and uniqueness contributed to a failure to set operational priorities, resulting in delayed overreactions to threats. Despite an apparent policy turn toward collective Defense, the JSDF remains abnormally shackled. Domestic laws proscribe what is permitted rather than what is prohibited. Legislative stretching continues, as the

Abe administration seeks to expand the conditions for the use of force as measures of collective self-Defense.[1] The threshold for the use of force is still extraordinarily high—national survival is at stake. No other appropriate means exist to deal with the threat, and only the minimum force necessary must be used. These restraints prevent operational concepts from developing normal confrontational ways to Coerce and Compel, and complicate the ability to Deter and Defend.

Similarly in the United States, a populist-patriotic undercurrent of American exceptionalism and technological determinism facilitates arguments for intervention where tactical-operational victories seem achievable—the Koreas, Vietnam, Iraq, and Afghanistan. So far, the American commitment to South Korea stands out as the singular success in terms of commensurate strategic gains. Hence, the judgment of whether a power is "strong" or "weak" is not a useful concept operationally. What matters more is the quality of one strategy compared to that of another. Knowing that culture must be taken into account is important to gaining the intellectual initiative in strategy.

Third, when a security culture is regarded as deterministic or incapable of accommodating change, its operational concepts also can be mistaken as inflexible. This sets up situations in which surprises arise easily because of incorrect assumptions. The following popular beliefs exemplify these errors: benign Confucianism or nonnegotiable sovereignty in China, isolationism or irrationality in North Korea, innate militarism or pacifism in Japan, a superior capacity for technological creativity in the United States. In contrast to these misjudgments, consider the anomalies which a strategist could have anticipated if the following valid assumptions about security culture were made: China's morally acceptable feigning of weakness; North Korean shamelessly honored deceit over its nuclear status; ambivalent and victimized Japan's righteous, self-defensive expansion. Strategists would be better equipped to exploit change by conceding the ability of any security culture to generate it. Otherwise, anomalies can become black swans through lack of imagination, or the conceit of possessing a superior character.

Imagine the US vulnerabilities that could be inferred from the Defense Strategic Guidance mentioned in chapter 1. On the basis of this national strategic document and US military interventions, an adversary could derive the following characteristics of American security culture: (a) underestimating a low-tech adversary's ability to adapt to changes in the global security environment; (b) expecting the deployment of US military forces to stabilize a region; (c) trusting that a high-technology combined-arms campaign will Deter and Defeat all forms of aggression; (d) favoring the development of democracy as the pathway to end wars; and (e) believing in the universal appeal of individual rights as the basis for international order. Knowing these cultural inclinations, an opponent can design counterstrategies such as (a) show low-technology and adapt more quickly than US forces by using smaller, distributed and connected units; (b) and (c) draw in US combat forces whose battlefield victories destabilize an area to your advantage; (d) and (e) reinforce hierarchical groups and cultures threatened by Western-style democracy based on individual rights. See the following Table.

Figure 14. Countering American Security Culture.

Characteristics of American Security Culture	Counter Strategies by Opponents
Underestimating a low-tech adversary's ability to adapt to changes in the global security environment	Show low-technology and adapt more quickly than US forces by using smaller, distributed and connected units
Expecting the deployment of US military forces to stabilize a region	Draw in US combat forces whose battlefield victories destabilize an area to your advantage
Trusting that a high-technology combined arms campaign will Deter and Defeat all forms of aggression	Draw in US combat forces whose battlefield victories destabilize an area to your advantage
Favoring the development of democracy as the pathway to end wars	Reinforce hierarchical groups and cultures threatened by Western-style democracy based on individual rights
Believing in the universal appeal of individual rights as the basis for international order	Reinforce hierarchical groups and cultures threatened by Western-style democracy based on individual rights

Therefore, because cultural determinism can close off critical analysis, a strategist should not presume that any security culture is unique. There are plenty of national, regional, communal-and-below narratives whose special claims end up being quite flexible according to the situation. Of course, narratives also can be deliberate manipulations of historical memory. Either way, comparative and in-depth cultural knowledge can help spot vulnerabilities as well as potential innovations.

Overall, the cases indicate that security culture interacts with definitions of national interests to shape how actors pursue relative security through a variety of operational concepts. Complex warfare includes, but is not limited to, the use of force. If this variation in security culture is ignored, a strategist will be unlikely to foresee a competitor's operational flexibility, innovations, and restrictions. In combined-effects terms, this cultural-operational linkage can be used to inform strategy making in three ways: (1) seeking singular and multiple effects; (2) employing direct and indirect ways to influence targets; and (3) authorizing and restricting particular tools of strategy.

China

China's security claimants have long asserted sovereignty with comprehensive strategies. Empires and republics employed diverse ways of indirect *qi* and direct *zheng* to create decisive advantages over competitors. Through military operations, the Chinese not only controlled the population and access to resources but also Defended and extended borders. Large Han armies and tribal confederations developed frontal and flanking attacks, and they enhanced these with deceptive tactics. To be sure, these were combined-arms campaigns to find, fix, and finish opposing forces. However, they also contributed to political and social effects which were consistent with enduring beliefs in central authority, moral order, and territorial integrity.

In both divided and unified China, a tradition of harmonizing physical and psychological tools reinforced asymmetric operations. Pre-Qin warring states designed military campaigns to reshift political alliances. Qin's wars of unification and territorial expansion were replayed during the Han, Tang, Ming, and Qing dynasties. Song defenses integrated a multirole canal system for irrigation, flood-control, transportation, and fighting positions. Unified Mongol and Manchu tribes used mobility with light and heavy weapons respectively to overcome overextended Chinese forces. The late-Qing "restrengthening" of traditions and new technologies exploited rivalries among foreign occupiers. The People's War against Japan and the Kuomintang first targeted the population for mobilization and then the opposing forces for destruction. Mao's China perpetuated political warfare domestically and abroad to strengthen ideological will—a basic operational concept.

Contemporary China also uses an array of strategic tools——predatory laws and territorial seizures, social movements, crowdsourced and information operations, cyber attacks and theft, military-economic raids and occupation—to *Induce* dilemmas on adversaries and to isolate them. Information campaigns and reforms to influence will and capabilities precede application of force. Domestically, the party exerts tenuous control over a web-based democracy movement. Toward Taiwan, PLA exercises and selective economic engagement suppress formal independence. Taiwan's leaders *Induce* de facto sovereignty via socio-political-economic networks and an ambivalent US military Deterrent. China's warships and their commercial proxies enforce exclusive territorial claims and economic rights in the South China Sea, against Taiwan, Vietnam, Malaysia, and the Philippines. In the East China Sea, China's state-owned energy and military operations have established a sovereign presence in order to erode Japan's control in disputed territory. China's economic lifeline toward nuclear North Korea keeps the peninsula divided and less stable, Beijing's unstated preference to a unified and independent Korea. Why? Because Beijing's desired effect is Korean weakness, not strength, a condition that is less threatening to the Chinese security culture of moral order, central authority, and territorial integrity.

Current operations seek to fragment rivals on China's borders and occupy China-claimed territories with complex invasions. Immigration is regarded as a threat, as are restive ethnic minorities inside China. Party operations play an existential role in constructing and justifying both an intuitive moral order and a central authority. Major combined-effects offensives include:

a) Military, economic, and political operations to reorient Taiwan toward the mainland

b) Diplomatic partnering with the Soviet Union, while conducting ideological warfare against it

c) Support of Vietnam, and then warfare against it to ensure cliental loyalty to China

d) Seizure of disputed Southeast Asian territory while expanding ties with claimants

e) Incursions in Japan-claimed territory while increasing ties with Japan and the U.S.

f) Maritime reclamation (dredging) operations create, occupy, and militarize new territory

China's leaders value holistic, sustainable operations, consistent with the assumption that threats are permanent and that any elimination of them are temporary. The roles that various types of confrontation have played in Chinese security culture have had an indelible imprint on operational concepts. Effectiveness is recognized as conditional and requiring exceptional patience. This has led to multitool shaping with two outgrowths: (1) opportunistic planning of intense, short-duration conflicts of limited means and (2) developing broad operational capabilities to restore Chinese influence as conditions permit.

The Koreas

A remarkably resilient Korean security culture is characterized by the art of *sadaejuui*, which means accommodating a main power. To manage permanent threats of invasion and occupation, Korean leaders have learned to seek autonomy rather pragmatically. As Chinese imperial influence pressed inward, Korean kingdoms tried several options: resisting China, singly or together; accepting China's tributary demands; aligning with China against one other for local advantages; and aligning with either China or one another against Japan. Even when unified, Koryŏ and Chosŏn's security still depended on relations with China, a main power which was later subject to Western and Japanese predations. Against rising Japan, Chosŏn lost Beijing's patronage, sought Russian protection, and persevered under Japanese colonization. Korean security culture formed as a sort of rational acceptance and intuitive resistance to preserve aspects of independence.

Koreans have confronted external powers with limited force and diplomatic balancing. The only anomaly to this pattern is if we regard the North's invasion of the South in 1950 as a foreign war. Without US intervention, Pyongyang's offensive would have reunified the peninsula. That counterfactual epitomizes the peninsula's security dilemma. To manage this predicament, strategic timing has been critical to survival. This is the acquired skill of confronting and balancing China, the Soviet Union, Russia, Japan, and the United States. Pyongyang's strategy of strategic envelopment has been more successful than Seoul's strategy of a *Secured* and systematic dilemma. By coopting the interests of main powers, internally divided and externally dependent Korea struggles to achieve a nonpolarizing reunification. Tragically, the trend is one of nuclear polarization.

North Korean *sadaejuui* and self-proclaimed pure Korean identity feature a continuous wartime posture. The hefty forward deployment of firepower poses an imminent threat to Seoul that enables short-term North Korean raids and demonstrations. Preplanned engagements deny ROK-U.S. forces adequate time to respond. With applications of actual and virtual force, Pyongyang's Compellent and *Persuasive* diplomacy becomes Coercive. This generates disproportionate international influence and reasserts domestic control, under favorable circumstances. Ideal favorable conditions to North Korea include a divided South Korea and potential allies; any weakening of US will or capability; and an obligatory flow of Chinese aid, investment, and joint development projects in North Korea. North Korea's belligerent diplomacy created unstable dependent relations with competing main powers that permitted the development of (at least) a low-yield nuclear detonation capability. This was all that was needed to enable nuclear-related stratagems.

South Korea's defensive posture emerged from a democratic globalizing version of *sadaejuui* and national resilience. Military alliance with the United States acquired an extended nuclear Deterrent and Defense commitment. Operational concepts are geared toward allied Defense, reception and staging of allied forces, and counterattack. As in the case of North Korea, South Korean security culture restrains how strategy is translated into operation. Despite vast political-economic differences with the North, an intuitive common Korean identity and desire for peninsular autonomy pertain. This contributes to periodic differences in policy priorities between Seoul and Washington, such as President Park Geun-hye's trip to China in September 2015 to join President Xi Jinping for the commemoration of China's seventieth anniversary of the end of World War II. This restrains the alliance's combined effects, as well as any idealistic hopes for a trilateral alliance with democratic Japan. Regional and global diplomatic, economic, and social networks enhance Seoul's freedom of action. Domestically, divisiveness limits the integration of joint and allied operations. Respective examples include interservice rivalry over deconfliction of airspace and naval assertion of disputed maritime sovereignty claims.

Both Koreas continue to rely on managing main power relationships to implement operational concepts. North Korea's high-risk balancing among China, the U.S., Russia, Japan, and South Korea has generated asymmetric military-diplomatic influence, even though it lacks operational-level harmony. A reliable U.S.–South Korea alliance has developed combined arms for military operations; however, it is much less unified in integrating that with diplomatic and economic power.

Japan

Traditional Japanese values of uniqueness and ambivalence in foreign relations define the parameters of national security operations. Preemptive invasions of the Korean peninsula failed as instruments of strategy, but these did help create and reinforce Japanese identity. Japan's geographic isolation facilitated its unification by a warrior class whose social status depended on the myth of a single-lineage emperor. After repelling Mongol invasions from the Korean peninsula, Japan experienced four centuries of secure inwardness. In subsequent forays to conquer Ming China's tributary Koryŏ, and later the Chosŏn, the bakufu asserted Japan's sacred right to rule. Toyotomi Hideyoshi's retreat from the continent triggered the fall of one warrior house and the rise of another. The rise of a warrior code and preservation of long-honored warfare methods delayed the integration of foreign technology into operational concepts. Subsequent contact with militarily superior Western nation-states threatened the Tokugawa social order and prompted a policy of self-defensive isolation. Two centuries later, recontact with even stronger Western powers led to unequal treaties similar to those imposed upon China. The Meiji Restoration revived imperial power with modernized military, economic, and political systems. Through territorial expansion and colonization, Japan's comprehensive catch-up won respect and international status in the way of imperial China and Western nation-states.

Japan's delayed reengagement with its neighbors instigated war on the Korean peninsula, mainland China and offshore territories, South East Asia and the western Pacific. After early victories, Japan's far-flung forces became bogged down. Regional operations lacked cross-service integration; priorities suffered from fragmented leadership. The army and navy's separate plans to control the resource-rich territory around Japan depended on breaking the will of the enemy. Battlefield defeats were particularly hard felt because Japan had no reliable allies. Loyalty to a ceremonial emperor and unaccountable wartime leadership helped perpetuate an isolated, reactive regime.

The postwar occupation redirected Japan's resources toward Defense and raised familiar questions about national identity and national strategy. Within the strictures of a US-Compelled constitution and security alliance, Japan's political elites blamed militarism and praised economic reconstruction. Japan's rerising was softened by benign security concepts that promoted trade, commerce, finance, food, and energy. At the same time, operations conducted by the Japan Self-Defense Force, Japan Coast Guard, and National Police Agency stretched interpretations of national policy and an unmodified constitution. Such restrictions reinforced Japanese ambivalence in foreign affairs by guaranteeing dependence on a US security commitment. For sixty years after the establishment of the Japan Self-Defense Forces, collective Defense remained officially banned as a way or means of security. In terms of actual effects, however, Japan's expanding security operations already constituted collective Defense.

Japan's security culture helps account for the continuation of policies that inhibit the development of realistic operational concepts. The latter are needed to break out from a pattern of overreactions to threats. Obviously interdependent security interests continue to be slathered over by self-Defense rationale. Even the collective Defense approved by the Abe administration is limited to Japanese territory or a partner critical to the survival of Japan. In contrast, self-Defense from a combined-effect perspective would be one desired effect, not the only one for all security situations. Japan's postwar focus on self-defense limits the scope of confrontation-cooperation strategies. Thus Tokyo constantly has to *Induce* Deterrence and Defense from its US ally and garner normal support from its own citizens. Unsurprisingly, identity debates thrive in Japan; evident everywhere from pop culture to officially sanctioned historical interpretations. Meanwhile, social values of uniqueness and interests in access to energy are shaping the contours of operational programs, plans, and exercises. Their effectiveness requires a *Persuasive* existential element to justify using instruments of power against the not-so-limited strategies of Japan's competitors.

When Do Lines of Effect Operate in Combination?

Ideally, combined-effects strategy brings lines of effect together in time and space to create advantages. Lines of effect also interact in unintended ways. To determine when tools on targets can be combined harmoniously, a strategist needs to focus on compatible differences among desired effects, not just distinctions among tools. The latter fixation is more common due to factors such as organizational preferences for favorite tools, predispositions to target-known capabilities, and domestic incentives to show resolve through military actions. With this consideration in mind, targeting both will and capability is key to success. The cases support four conclusions.

First, it is far easier to coordinate combined arms that achieve different effects than it is to integrate a prioritized set of combined effects. Without specifying desired effects, strategy becomes an exercise in self-justified assertions of common identity. These can be ignited by leaders in opportunistic fashion to stir up causes and followers during crises. Encultured beliefs reinforce the process. When that happens, the targeting of will and capability becomes disconnected from instrumental effects. In some cases, the assertion of identity itself becomes the top priority. A fixation on combined arms or kinetic effects also distorts consideration of all possible effects. For instance, if military force is deemed relevant to Deter and Compel, and to Defend and Coerce, but not to *Dissuade* and *Persuade*, and to *Secure* and *Induce*, agreement on half of the theoretical combinations of effects is foreclosed. The imagination of theory and the evidence of practice need each other. Overall, desired effects have to be established and fully considered for strategy to serve as a reasonably accountable instrument of security.

Second, setting conditions for combining disruptive effects has been more successful than those designed to create constructive effects, such as preserving stability. Besides specificity, achieving constructive effects requires the alignment of complex lines that anticipate and adapt to dynamic situations. Moreover, different planning processes and the existence of multiple authorities for kinetic and nonkinetic operations pose challenges to making decisions. Combining effects requires processes to set conditions that at least do not work against each other. This is not easy for hierarchical organizations ridden with identities defined by pecking orders. Even though constructive effects are more difficult to plan and execute than disruptive effects, the former are usually more important in contexts that involve cooperation.

Third, a strategy that can produce preventative as well as causative effects provides a measure of versatility with which to outperform more rigid strategies. Versatile strategies are more likely when operational requirements are written in terms of desired effects, rather than simply desired capabilities. This quality of combined-effects strategy applies when preventative effects—Deter, *Dissuade*, Defend and *Secure*—are not restricted to just countering causative effects—Compel, *Persuade*, Coerce and *Induce*. If a strategist thinks about both types of effects as useful in any situation, then constructive and disruptive combinations can be designed to subsume a competitor's combinations. These can be derived from analyzing lines of the causative and preventative effects in the cases. Given the real challenges of determining will and capabilities, this distinction between what actors are trying to prevent and what actors are trying to cause is more useful to effective strategy than the descriptors of offense and defense.

Fourth, a competitor's ability to interact with a winning combination of effects requires flexibility, timing, and patience—not just powerful kinetics. China's post-Mao will and capability to reorient its economic system toward capitalism to assimilate Taiwan is as vital to *Persuading* and *Inducing* unification as its military is to Deterring independence. Likewise, post–Cold War changes in US desired effects, which were globally applied, enabled North Korea to initiate bilateral engagement, the sustainment of which was crucial to the development of its nuclear weapons capability. Similarly, Japan's failure to admit that it was already conducting its self-prohibited effect of collective security limits its tools and reinforces isolationist insider-outsider cultural distinctions. The common challenge among the three cases is the ability to adjust the elements of strategy to suit changing contexts. For the U.S., this means being able to integrate and harmonize its joint military operations in a sustainable interagency process of grand strategy.

China

Toward Taiwan, China's strategy of *Persuasion* and Deterrence, aggravated by *Inducement*, made a key assumption: politics will follow cross-Strait economics. That is, Taiwan's growing economic interests in China would lead toward unification and away from independence. Applying the same logic in the other direction, a burgeoning cross-Strait economy might democratize politics in China. Post-Mao leaders have been willing to assume that risk. China's attempts to isolate and intimidate Taiwan were not effective by themselves. Three consecutive post-Chiang administrations in Taiwan adopted independence policies and rhetoric that triggered threatening *Inducements* from China. In the short-term, this stirred anti-mainland sentiment. However, after a tenfold increase in bilateral trade during the 1990s and steady increase in China's sea and airpower projection capabilities, Taiwan voters elected moderate President Ma Ying-jeou in 2008. The mainland's expanding market had baited Taiwan investment over time. Add to China's growing economic weight a muscular military disparity, and Beijing can tacitly *Induce* Taiwan's dilemma of having to choose between unification and independence. The result in 2016, however, was the election of pro-independence President Tsai Ing-wen. Other uncertainties of China's *Persuasion-Deterrence-Inducement* strategy include how politics in China will be affected by globalization and an influential middle class. Both factors are likely to complicate China's desired combined effect.

In contrast to Beijing's sound premises, all four of Taipei's desired effects—Deterrence, *Dissuasion, Inducement*, Security, and Defense—rest on questionable assumptions. First, the credibility of the US commitment to protect Taiwan from Chinese Coercion (needed to Deter China) is diminished by increasing Chinese capabilities. This is not to say that high-tech weaponry determines victory—quantity and logistics also matter. But even if the United States maintains an edge in military technology and the ability to project and sustain that power, a growing Chinese presence in disputed territories spotlights an ambiguous American Deterrent. Willpower matters. Second, *Inducing* China to accept Taiwan sovereignty means showing the will to unify as a commonwealth or confederation, terms that are unacceptable to China. The territorial, zero-sum mindset of Chinese leaders is likely to continue due to separatist movements in western China. Third, increases in Taiwan *Security* and Defense capabilities can help Deter an attack and *Dissuade* forced unification. However, they are not designed at all to *Induce* China's acceptance of Taiwan sovereignty. Fourth, the liberal hope that thickened ties promote political freedoms in China implies a related tolerance of Taiwan independence. Chinese nationalism works against that. To combine these desired strategic effects, Taipei would need to presume drastic changes in Washington's commitment and Beijing foreign policy and social values.

In the Daioyu/Senkaku dispute with Japan, China's overall effect combines in three ways that are devilishly difficult to manipulate. First, the *Dissuasion*-Deterrence combined effect forestalls US intervention indirectly. The idea is to avoid provoking a U.S.-China confrontation until such time that China can prevail. This requires controlling the PLA's growing confidence and avoiding operational recklessness to mollify American perceptions of hostile Chinese intent. If Chinese behavior becomes overtly aggressive, this could indicate that Beijing thinks it can intimidate Washington as well as win planned engagements. Second, the domestic *Persuasion* element has to kindle, appease, and control anti-Japanese nationalism in China. This means managing China's complex economic ties with Japan as well as the political aspirations and income disparities associated with China's rapid economic growth. The risk of Chinese nationalism turning partly against single-party rule is a deep concern to Beijing elites. Third, China is trying to *Induce* Japanese recognition of a Senkaku dispute, and Compel and Coerce a forceful overreaction by Japan. This $I\,C_p\,C_r$ element aims to isolate Japan from the U.S., while $D_s\,D_t$ works against US intervention. Fortunately for Beijing, the whole combination simply requires the Japan-U.S. alliance to oblige by failing to adapt to China's broad strategy. Is this because the U.S.-Japan security arrangement does not recognize combined effects, or is it because it is too hard to orchestrate? Improvements in U.S.-Japan combined operations such as air and missile defense, electronic warfare, and air-sea battle are noteworthy accomplishments. However, the limits of the U.S.-Japan alliance—such as restricting Japanese defense to its own territory—facilitate China's desired combined effect. Thus, China does not have to integrate its problematic effects of masking its predatory intent while increasing its military-economic strength, stirring anti-Japanese nationalism that does not empower Chinese democracy, and isolating Japan from US intervention, as long as Japan and the United States are complying with these effects anyway.

The Koreas
Within the frame of a common security culture, both Koreas managed their main power relationships with different strategies. The logic of each side's strategy was fundamentally opposed. Basically, Pyongyang integrated effects that were mostly causative whereas Seoul coordinated effects that were mostly preventative.

North Korea was able to divide the main powers, leveraging an ambiguous nuclear status and unstable socioeconomic relations vis-à-vis Moscow, Beijing, Washington, and Tokyo to extract concessions. To do this, Pyongyang integrated the effects of psychological and physical tools that enabled it to interact with the main powers on a more equivalent basis. Essentially, North Korea's broad strategy enabled its two key elements to be applied together for a synergistic effect. The Compellence-Coercion-Deterrence-Defense element was applied against fragmented United States, South Korea, and International Atomic Energy Agency efforts, while the *Persuasion-Inducement* element worked on US engagement. Pyongyang's breakthrough opportunity for superpower reciprocity came in 1991, when George H. Bush chanced to improve relations. The apparent American removal of the Coercive aspects of its Cold War approach to security was not something the Kim regime could afford to embrace. Pyongyang took the opportunity to hedge against it and exploit the change.

President Bush's national security review nominally shifted US strategy from Deterrence-Defense-Coercion to Deterrence-Defense-*Dissuasion*-Compellence. Despite that administration's intent, subsequent US strategy up to the early Obama administration actually wavered between those two variants. This vacillation between Deterrence-Defense-Coercion and Deterrence-Defense-*Dissuasion*-Compellence provided a clear window of opportunity for Pyongyang to combine its *Persuasion-Inducement* lines of effect.

US leaders failed to recognize or care about that weakness; they were unaccustomed to coordinating combined effects or perhaps considering the security cultures of adversaries, competitors, partners, and neutrals. These are too hard to think about and are impossible to execute, worn-out bureaucrats say. North Korean leaders, however, managed to integrate an asymmetric combined effect in a sustained manner, engaging the US over time. How?

As the United Nations became involved, Pyongyang countered the International Atomic Energy Agency's attempts at Compellence, limited as the UN and the IAEA were to fully deploying tools of nuclear monitoring and inspections. When IAEA policies were inconsistent with either US priorities or South Korean policies, Pyongyang could use the IAEA as an effective buffer against a US reversal toward Deterrence-Defense-Coercion. All of this lengthened the timeline for North Korean nuclear development.

South Korea's attempt to *Secure* a systemic dilemma (*Persuade*-Deter-Defend-*Secure*) on the North depended upon the US commitment (*S*). Only the confrontational Deter-Defend element of this combined effect was not in question. Seoul and Washington failed to fix the cooperative element (*Persuade-Secure*) in place due to disagreements over security priorities. In 2008, policy lash ups did occur between President Barack Obama and Korean presidents Lee Myung-bak and, later, Park Geun-hye. By then, the ROK-U.S. alliance had gifted Pyongyang two decades of strategic space.

The debilitating differences between South Korean $P\ D_t\ D_f\ S$ and American $D_t\ D_f C_r\ D_s C_p$ strategies were twofold: (1) South Korea's need to *Persuade* North Korea to reunify and *Secure* a US commitment to that end and to Defend against and Deter North Korean aggression ; and (2) changes in US Coercive, *Dissuasive*, and Compellent strategies. South Korean Sunshine Policy (a form of *Persuasion*) focused on reunification, while the US "carrot-and-stick" approaches were split between the timing of two goals: nuclear disarmament and inspection compliance. In terms of desired effects, there was only one type of carrot--*Dissuasion*, while there were four types of sticks—Deterrence, Defense, Coercion, and Compellence.

As a result, the alliance's combined effect was integrated only with respect to preventing a large-scale North Korean attack. Most policy makers and observers continue to regard this as a suicidal course of action for North Korea, and therefore unlikely. So, having succeeded in getting its targeted main power to focus on worst-case scenarios, Pyongyang exploited the economic benefits of South Korean *Persuasion* and the international status conferred by US *Dissuasion* and Compellence. The majority of South Korean governments have openly disagreed with the potential effectiveness of US Coercion against North Korea, which has been limited to economic sanctions anyway.

Japan

With regard to the Senkaku crisis, Japan's ability to combine its *Persuasion* and *Inducement* of Japanese and American support, with Deterrence and Defense of China, has depended upon three key factors. These are (1) political capacity to moderate domestic extremism; (2) able management of a US commitment to Japan's Defense; and (3) technological superiority to Defend against threats.

First, nationalist groups periodically stir antiforeign sentiment, polarizing domestic politics. This makes Japan's *Persuasion-Inducement* element of its combined effect difficult to sustain. In most cases, Tokyo pursues consensus, a protracted process that yields the initiative to China. Notable exceptions have been during instances of "strong" prime ministers, a double-edged sword. Prime Minister Hashimoto and Prime Minister Abe (his second term) often were regarded as strong in a populist sense, but rash from Beijing's perspective. Beijing routinely condemns Tokyo's counters to China's claims, and the difference in strategies makes this effective. China's broad combined effect ($D_s\ D_t\ P\ I\ C_p\ C_r$) includes what Japan has—*Dissuasion*-Deterrence-*Persuasion-Inducement*, plus causative effects which Japan does not generate on its own—Compellence and Coercion. To keep it that way, Beijing saves its sharpest condemnations for any Japanese move to acquire it too.

Second, managing alliance issues under uniquely regarded constitutional and defense policy limitations is delicate enough in Japan, where 35,000 US forces are based. Despite having established Japan's defense forces and promoted increased range and strike capabilities for more than sixty years, Washington hopes Tokyo will be wholly defensive vis-à-vis Beijing. But Japanese self-restraint is loosening. During the May 2014 summit with Prime Minister Abe, President Obama indicated for the first time presidential support for collective Defense. Two months later the cabinet decided to develop legislation to authorize the use of force in response to actions short of an armed attack against Japan and in support of collective self-Defense.

For Japan, this adds to the controversy of the *Persuasion- Inducement* effect, particularly when territorial Defense and Deterrence is at stake. In the absence of a Chinese attack on Japan, opposition parties have characterized American support as US pressure on Japan to militarize. Japan's combined effect is overmatched by China's. Even the overtly nationalistic Abe Cabinet decision stops short of endorsing proactive Compellence or Coercion. The use of force is still justified in terms of self-Defense, enhanced by the US alliance. It remains quite unclear when forces capable of Deterring armed attack and other infringements of sovereignty will have adequate authorization, beginning with logistical support and international peace cooperation activities. If Abe were replaced by a more moderate prime minister and cabinet, a wary Beijing would exploit any new divisions in the U.S.-Japan alliance to maintain a superior strategy.

Third, Japan has to maintain key technological advantages over China for at least three reasons. The first is China's quantitative edge and mounting qualitative gains. The second factor is the sheer expanse of territory that Japan needs to protect against Chinese incursions. Third, Chinese capabilities against Japanese defenses are not limited to marine vessels and aircraft, which can be countered somewhat by a more effective command, control, intelligence, surveillance, and reconnaissance network. Compared to contemporary Japan, Chinese tools, targets, and desired effects are unrestrained. Beijing or appropriate proxies can place dormant cyber "eggs" nested in Japanese information technology systems, including highly networked command and control, intelligence, surveillance and reconnaissance suites. Malware could initiate lines of attack that target and degrade defensive sensors. Or, imagine the viral economic and social effects in Japan if China's informational tools influenced what financial markets have to say about Japan's large debt.

Japanese technology therefore needs to integrate the combined effects that it can muster from its security policies. Beijing can be expected to prevent that unless its politics become imbalanced, such as becoming controlled by the Peoples' Liberation Army. There is less danger of that with the "election" of Xi Jinping as President of China in 2013. As President of China, General Secretary of the Chinese Communist Party, and Chairman of the Central Military Commission, Xi is positioned to shape key decisions. As the PLA is being programmed for capabilities to exploit an overreaction by Japan, Xi may calculate it would be in China's interests to provoke Japan if China can preclude or counter US involvement via any of its preventative desired effects.

How Can Security Culture Help Us Judge Intent and Capabilities, and Select Tools?

Making effective strategy is not just about interests and known capabilities. It also requires full consideration of values and beliefs in order to anticipate actors' intentions. Comparative security culture can be used to understand enduring aspects of confrontational and cooperative capabilities. Under the working assumption that security culture can be generalized at a societal level, the background chapters in this study stepped back from different historical elements to characterize enduring patterns of thought and action. Mindful that culture can apply to various levels of analysis, the combined-effects-strategy model adopted a state-governance perspective in the crisis chapters. This approach provided variables with which to interpret strategic intent, psychological and physical targets, and tools.

In terms of country-level descriptions of security culture, national variations include types of moral order and central authority in China, domestic and international contexts of Korean *sadaejuui*, and security policy manifestations of Japanese uniqueness and ambivalence. These can be compared to arguments about US security culture such as American exceptionalism and belief in the power of technology. Using these features as indicators of continuity, strategists can extrapolate past intent and capability as initial expectations in a security scenario. In this manner, security culture can be used as a concept to inform, but not dictate, the making of strategy. For instance, all states will protect territorial claims, but how?

The East Asian cases suggest the persistence of patient Chinese reexpansion, sudden Korean rebalancing of main power relationships, and reactive Japanese isolation and engagement. What happens if we apply American security culture to future security crises, as indicated by US involvement in these three cases? We would expect to see operations that apply asymmetric technological capabilities, justified in terms of American rights and responsibilities. With regard to intent, democratic debate over US defense policy generates mixed messages to allies, partners, adversaries, and neutrals. These categories of actors are issue dependent as well. Therefore cultural generalizations need to be treated as testable propositions open to falsification, not conclusions about intent or capability. The strategist's challenge here is to look for evidence that disproves cultural assumptions while at the same time constructing alternative hypotheses about strategic intent, physical and psychological capabilities, and available tools.

Overall, security culture is best used with caution, scrutinized and modified through in-country experiences. The most challenging questions are those about intent. Consider, for instance, what the attributed intent for the following historical events and notional complications (in parentheses) might be:

1) Chinese island-manufacturing in disputed territory (persistent PLA Air Force combat air patrols)

2) North Korean nuclear testing (forward-deployed heavy armor and infantry exercises)

3) Japanese warnings against Chinese intrusions (Japanese ground-force garrisoning of remote islands)

4) American support of South Korean or Japanese defensive actions (air, naval, or cyber strikes)

To plan for such situations, strategists need to be informed by a wide range of information relevant to confrontation and cooperation. Access to that requires a network of intelligence analysis and synthesis. A virtual knowledge environment that includes security culture is needed to complement structured analytics that focus on technical capabilities.

These are ambitious requirements, particularly when individuals or organizations resist the possibility of being wrong. The ability to recognize the interplay of ends, ways, and means is fundamental to developing effective strategy in different contexts. Over time, intuitive judgment may be gained regarding motives, thoughts, and behavior. This is important to detecting anomalies as actors attempt to shape perceptions. Without an understanding of security culture, a typically tailored Joint Task Force can be duped into observing, orienting, deciding, and acting on the wrong problem. Making effective strategy involves adapting effects, targets, and tools to changing conditions.

China

Chinese security culture can help us understand continuity in Chinese strategies and why elites cannot afford to fold in the face of foreign pressure if they are to retain domestic influence. Confrontational sovereignty claims trump tangible benefits of cooperative interdependence. Moral order, central authority, and territorial integrity persist as highly valued interests, particularly among China's single-party leadership. So while modernization has strengthened national capabilities, it has also increased national willpower. When China has the capability to engage other powers as an equal or more, it has done so. We can infer that military equality is the PLA's precondition of expanding military-to-military relations with the U.S.[2] The loss of territorial sovereignty in the past has become the consensus threat to national security. Ideological sovereignty is closely connected to economic nationalism.

Several trends reinforce these preferences. Decades of sustained economic growth increased China's capabilities to Coerce and Compel territorial claims. The PLA's original mission to complete the reunification of China reemerged as a professional ethos. China's growing demand for energy pointed to disputed, resource-rich maritime territories. The want for economic growth—formerly a reason to be jailed, exiled, or killed—became a public performance indicator of party rule. Chinese security culture stripped of its ideological veneer helped generate demand for respect as a great power. The sense of entitlement is more than blind nationalism; it is a self-righteous value and collective intent rooted in historical experience. Confidence and economic growth have become a central aspect of a new Chinese morality. As legacy party ideology erodes, capitalist threats are being replaced by the pragmatics of harnessing the beast. Obstacles to national development have become public enemy number one.

The shadow of the past may inform our judgment of intent and capabilities a bit more clearly, but which tools of strategy are most likely to be used? A pragmatic China-centered worldview suggests that whatever tools can be used will be employed. We know that China needs resources to sustain a high economic growth rate and retain single-party rule. Timing is important to determining which tools are most likely to be used to regain full sovereignty and continue national development. In disputed territories, China has used aggressive diplomacy, selective information and social mobilization, cyber attacks, and economic exploitation as tools of state sovereignty. When and where China has the capability to prevail militarily, the PLA has enforced national claims. As China develops more strength, the PLA will have more capability to secure resources. New technologies are enabling China's elites to retool. Unless Chinese security culture adopts a more internationalist moral order, democratic institutions and laws, or nonexclusive territorial integrity, the acquisition of high-tech tools presages further confrontation.

For the PLA, this means having to construct nationalism while building military capability. If confronted with force, the PLA needs to win the tactical engagement to achieve positive internal and external strategic effects. As a rising superpower, China's traditional approach of absorbing and Sinicizing foreign rulers and occupiers is no longer valid. The presence of foreign values and practices presents a more complex threat. Virtual connections are transforming Beijing's rule into a mix of provincialism, nationalism, and globalism. This challenges leaders to integrate new tools in the pursuit of values and interests. Countering broad political and economic threats will require more than the political priorities of Gongchandang and Maoist China, and economic priorities of Deng's practical revolution. The strategic cultural problem is that territorial threats provide a basis for building unity but are a dead end for external cooperation.

The three elements of Chinese security culture have provided remarkable flexibility in achieving desired effects. In the case of Taiwan's international status, the US will and capability to commit to the island's Defense is the main obstacle to Beijing's goal of unification. A downgraded US commitment has permitted Beijing to execute a successful strategy that is subsuming Taiwan's narrower strategy. In the case of the Senkakus, the conditional US commitment to Defend Japan—but not endorse its legal claims—interacts with a dependent Japanese strategy that also is narrower than the Chinese strategy. A credible U.S.-Japan alliance can reduce China's incentives for overt aggression, such as seizing a remote Japanese island. However, this must be viewed in light of past practices when China was weak—alliances to prevent border threats; banning and then later embracing foreign relations; and accepting unequal treaties to maintain a degree of central, moral order. If China acquires the capability to contest and deny US access to the disputed area even for a limited period of time, Beijing is likely to use it for synergistic influence. Cooperation is most likely to occur in the context of confrontation.

The Koreas

Korean security culture is a resilient amalgam of accommodation and opposition, one which is reflected in the strategies of two ideologically distinct political systems. Over two millennia, Chinese and Japanese empires have sought to invade, occupy or control the peninsula. Western powers reinforced this zero-sum threat in the nineteenth century with religious, commercial, and then military expeditions. The term *sadaejuui* describes how Korean leaders have managed the pressing demands of external powers through accommodation. Forms of accommodation often involve resistance, before turning into compliance or aggressive dependence. The art of leveraging one main power against another is a risky balance of vulnerabilities and strengths. This pragmatism coexists with principled assertions of Korean identity and independence. When main powers showed restraint, usually due to domestic weakness, Koreans could achieve the relative security of variable-sum effects. The uneasy mix of confrontation and cooperation is morally resolved by the will to resist. With grandly stated threats and *juche* self-righteousness, North Korea realizes sustainable objectives when employing multiple tools of strategy with limited force for a short duration. South Korea's restraint in initiating and responding to North Korean force emphasizes nonmilitary tools of strategy. An effective strategist needs to consider these gaps that invite asymmetric interactions, particularly during crises.

Knowledge of Korean security culture can enable better anticipation of similarities and differences in current strategies. Both Koreas practice more resistant forms of *sadaejuui* than the Three Kingdoms managed against imperial China's cultural cooptation. Pyongyang combined unilateral military aggression with diplomacy to arrange Coercive negotiations. This volatile *sadaejuui* has helped it to survive as an authoritarian nuclear weapons state. Seoul leverages its economic size with diplomacy and credible military alliance to prepare *Persuasive* negotiations. This steadier *sadaejuui* depends on external engagement that facilitates economic growth and political change.

Each regime thus asserts its own brand of a common security culture. Recall that dynastic change in China created uncertainty and Compelled realignments in Korean courts. North and South Korean strategies confront this vulnerability by setting conditions. Consistent with its priority of retaining domestic control while resisting foreign influence, Pyongyang manufactures and exploits nuclear-tipped instability. Consistent with the fragmented intentions of its political system and market economy, Seoul leverages globalization to hedge against any wilting of Washington's commitment.

The strategic choices are consequential. The North remains a prisoner of its geographic constraints and security dilemma, while the South breaks out into new regional and international roles. How does Korean security culture affect the selection of tools?

Both Koreas use tools to increase domestic will and influence surrounding powers. The main idea is to turn constraints into advantages. In a complex operating environment, Seoul and Pyongyang have demonstrated the ability to generate uncertainty and exert influence in two agile ways.

First, we note the shaping of relationships. Pyongyang's aggressive dependence creates a reverse influence on China and the United States. Even in dire conditions of famine and leadership transitions, North Korea can stir up instability for linked-in main powers through diplomatic posturing, propaganda campaigns, cyber theft, military demonstrations, surprise attacks, and nuclear activities. There is little doubt that a credible nuclear capability will be accompanied by aggression to reunify the peninsula. Although vulnerable to disruptions from the North, Seoul's globalization generates economic growth and new partnerships in manufacturing, finance, and energy markets. Reluctant to call North Korea's nuclear bluff under the US extended Deterrent, Seoul's employs modern naval and air forces to enforce claims over disputed territories. In addition, South Korea's increasingly inclusive democracy and global economy calls for a more independent military capability.

Second, tools used to affect will and capability can become new tools. Korean accommodation of Ming Chinese culture transformed intimidation into loyalty, which created variable-sum outcomes in Korean-Chinese relations. Similarly, North-South and U.S.-North Korea cooperative engagements built assurance. No American administration has been able to sustain this domestically risky approach. Yet when North Korea–China relations were strained, US diplomatic, economic, and social ties fulfilled a grudging North Korean need for *sadaejuui*. This enhancement of mutual interests, perhaps even values, worked against North Korean perceptions of a United States bent on collapsing Pyongyang's regime. The problem is not only with North Korea, which has to suppress dissent and develop economically in order to compete with the South. The lack of a sustained partnership between Washington and Seoul, ideally including China and Japan, is a contributing factor. Rather than assigning blame, assuming responsibility is needed to seize and sustain the initiative. Absent that, indirect cultural transformation over time is the only realistic alternative. This implies the need for engagement, not isolation.

As long as the Koreas depend upon divided main powers for support, they will oppose each other through them. Breaking out of this circular logic requires either Sino-American agreement on Korean reunification, or each Korea valuing independence more than dependence. North Korea is following the path of independence, bouncing between China and US engagement to move in that direction. South Koreans generally accept global interdependence as a democratic, prosperous, and realistic alternative. The case study showed that while Seoul and Pyongyang alternated between confrontation and cooperation against each other and the main powers, Pyongyang's lines of effect were more asymmetrically focused and consistent over time. The fragmentation of South Korean and American lines of effect calls for far-sighted combined-effects thinking and executable operations.

Japan

Japan's security culture helps explain Tokyo's chronic mismatch among national intent, capabilities, and tools. Beliefs in Japanese uniqueness and foreign ambivalence have two main impacts. First, unique self-regard broadens the definition of what constitutes a matter of national security. Exceptional aspects of collective identity beg to be Defended. At the same time, alternating intentions to be isolated from or engaged with potential threats have produced extreme reactions. So far these have involved security strategies without sufficient capabilities to achieve desired grand effects.

At first glance, the historical Japanese role of confrontation appears to be unexceptional—domestic control, and Defense and Deterrence against eternal threats. The cultural construction of a sacred-becomes-unique identity, however, helps account for competitive-turned-aggressive state behavior as Japan sought to acquire status, respect, and resources. After the long period of Tokugawa seclusion, technologically advanced powers pressed in on Japan, as they had in China. Aided by a strong Japanese identity and symbolic restoration of the emperor, the foreign interference provoked aggressive national reengagement. Japan's Meiji-era quest for security through regional dominance extended well beyond newly acquired means. Occupied neighbors and allied powers fought against the Empire's expansion. In the post–Pacific War period, Japan's reconstruction as a democracy dependent on US alliance has led to military capabilities and international operations well beyond the original self-Defense policy restraints. Japan's confrontation with China to Defend its sovereignty over the Senkakus includes planning to use military force. Japanese arguments that justify the takeover of the islets during Meiji expansion and the Sino-Japanese war are opposed by China, whose strategy includes provoking Japanese overreactions.

Threats to Japan's national identity in the past have stirred up confrontational strategies. This thus is a useful starting point to gauge what might otherwise be attributed as Japan's economic intent to retain territory. Japanese feelings of uniqueness provide a sense of social belonging that permits individuality to be shared within groups. Threats to Japan become acute when they would dilute this common Japanese character. Historical examples are territorial intrusions, market pene-tration, access to resources and markets, elimination of the emperor, and anti-Japanese racism. These issues tend to become connected to Japaneseness when the external environment is hostile, which sets up for a strong reaction.

Japan's national capabilities have been used to mobilize Japan-brand security: wars of national unification, Korean and Chinese liberation, and greater East Asian co-prosperity; protectionism for comprehensive, food, and energy *Security*; societal loyalty to the emperor; military restraint for self-Defense, and expansion into de facto collective Defense. Confrontations have been wrapped in cultural rationale, presented as cooperative agreements or reactive, *shikata ga nai* actions.[3] Ambivalence pertains to multiple levels of relationships as individuals and groups discuss variations of the two major options: (a) passive isolation, which avoids both types of interactions; and (b) active engagement, which requires uncomfortable decisions about when to confront and when to cooperate.

The postwar security bargain reflects this cultural ambivalence in Japan's struggle to achieve security despite differences in values or interests. Apparent Japan-U.S. agreement on a common Soviet or Chinese threat was accompanied by disagreement on military and economic threats. Cooperation was founded upon an exchange of Japanese economic and American military security priorities, both of which had competitive aspects as well. For many Japanese, this meant protecting exclusive products, distribution systems, financial arrangements, forced savings, wartime hardships, and even the foreign-written-and-imposed constitution. With the Peace Constitution set in place, Japan's isolation from hard security issues permitted engagement in economic affairs that eventually led to the internationalization of Japan's Self-Defense Force. The Senkaku case provides insight on uniqueness beliefs as Japan reengages in zero-sum threats on its claimed territory.

With regard to the military and other tools used to achieve desired effects, Japanese security culture contains significant challenges. Retooling to confront threats has been technically successful, but engagement according to Japanese norms has met external resistance and proven to be unsustainable. Japan's employment of national power after periods of isolation has not produced success. Yet in the ongoing Senkaku crisis, reintroducing the military tool is regarded domestically as a balanced response to Chinese aggression. Yet even Japan's US ally does not acknowledge Japan's sovereignty there. Therefore Tokyo needs to ensure Senkaku Defense is sustainable from a combined-effects perspective, or it risks being unprepared for long-term confrontation. The cultural disconnect between policy and practice constitutes a strategic vulnerability. Japan's official position that denied and now advocates collective security and its singular focus on self-Defense are seen by outsiders as incredibly idealistic or cynically realistic. For the former, we can point to China's preemptive drilling operations east of Japan's median line that have

Compelled and *Induced* acceptance of China's territorial presence. For the latter, we anticipate that China's response to any Japanese use of force will include fully sounding and exploiting the return of militarist Japan.

Japan's struggle to avoid threats to acquired values has sought to preserve a unique character without having to resort to national isolation or vulnerable engagement. At its core, the desire to express exceptionality as a nation and associated ambivalence about foreign relations produces highly reactive threat responses. The story of strategy in Japan has been one of how to manage threats to national identity and well-being under insular cultural preferences in an interdependent environment.

Harmonizing Effects and US Strategy

The three East Asian security cultures and crises featured in this book offer a profound lesson for US policy makers, strategists, and operators: The ability to orchestrate combined effects creates strategic advantages in cooperative-confrontational interactions. This critical will and capability can be used to establish priorities that connect operational missions to national success.

The idea of harmonizing desired effects is drawn from East Asian strategies that employ psychological and physical tools in complementary ways. Compared to temporally linear concepts such as battle rhythm, momentum, and culmination, effective harmony implies more dimensions. The core task is to align contributions to priority effects in time and space. Individuals and organizations attuned to kinetic effects are inclined to ignore the full potential of synergistic effects. Nonkinetic successes tend to be perceived as anomalies. Historically grounded cultures and organizational routines cultivate individual attitudes that place potential effects outside the traditional scope of the unit as "not my job."

Asymmetry is also different. Instead of being defined in terms of different types of forces arrayed against each other, asymmetry means different types of tools on targets producing different types of effects. From a combined-arms perspective, this kind of asymmetric operation is harder to detect and easier to regard as irrelevant to one's assigned role, mission, or function. From a combined-effects perspective, however, the pattern can be visualized in a matrix of strategic effects, targets, and tools in relation to each another.

Achieving harmony among diverse effects involves blending opposites, not just similarities, so that more lower-level effects support higher-level effects. East Asian legacies provide instructive contemporary examples. Chinese operations produce deception and conceptual versatility, such as the *Induced* dilemma on Taiwan. That combined effect is sustained by Chinese economic *Persuasion* and an increasingly credible military Deterrent that can *Induce* the dilemma with routine demonstrations of force. Korean *sadaejuui* and self-reliance generate external adaptation and internal loyalty. North Korea's asymmetric envelopment exploited divisions that emerged among American, South Korean, and International Atomic Energy Agency efforts. Forms of Japanese *soto* and *uchi* cultivate national identity and ambivalent engagement. Japan's interdependent *Persuasion-Inducement* effect in Japan and the United States holds when bilateral cooperation is not seen as unfair outside pressure. The other element of Japanese strategy, Defense and Deterrence of China, relies on collective Defense against Beijing's use of force to Compel and Coerce territorial claims.

Harmony is omnidirectional in the sense that higher-level effects can influence lower-level effects, too. In practice, "higher" and "lower" are meaningful in the context of priorities as the situation changes. If lower-level effects are becoming more important, a change in strategy may be warranted. Consider the three preceding cases, but under different conditions. The following notional changes in Chinese, North Korean, and Japanese strategy are incremental within the combined-effects-strategy matrix, but would be regarded as historic shifts in strategy. To operate in harmony, their differences, too, need to combine to create priority effects.

China's *Induced* dilemma $(P D_t \ I)$ could generate new tools of influence and change targeted will and capabilities. If Taiwan were to proclaim independence after the United States had been subject to a strong China lobby and economic ties for decades, a viable option for Beijing would be to avoid *Inducing* the *Persuasion*-Deterrence dilemma with force. This could reorient US will and international opinion against Taiwan. Beijing's new apparent strategy of *Persuasion* and Deterrence could resort to Coercing Taiwan and Compelling the US, after neutralizing US support diplomatically.

North Korea's asymmetric envelopment (C_p C_r D_t D_f P I) could abandon either the confrontational and causative element (Compellence-Coercion) or the cooperative element (*Persuasion-Inducement*) from its strategy. Facing a United States weary of protracted wars yet one that might use nuclear weapons, Pyongyang could try *Persuading* and *Inducing* to regain the original terms of the Agreed Framework. If the U.S. did not pose a credible nuclear threat, Pyongyang could *Persuade* and *Induce* a Sunshine-Policy-inclined Seoul government for a while, and then later shift to Coerce and Compel through a variety of tools.

Japan's interdependent Defense (D_f D_t P I) effect could convert to *Induced* Defense and Deterrence ($D_f D_t$ I) by adding nonnuclear Deterrent capabilities and avoiding attempts to *Persuade* China on imperial-era territorial matters. If Japan defined national identity in ways considered normal, a credible Deterrent effect would require some long-range precision strike and mobile special-operations capabilities. After reconciling the need to intimidate Beijing's will and neutralize PLA capabilities to Deter territorial seizures, the big remaining issue would be any Deterrence that included weapons of mass effects, especially those of destruction.

In these scenarios and cases, harmonized effects subsume combined-arms warfare, but when can they outperform it? Success requires agreement on a unified set of priorities. Typically this is most difficult at the highest level of an organization. Combined-effects strategy also requires flexibility and access to in-depth cultural expertise. Security culture provides a starting point for understanding local contexts and attributions of intent key to judging threats, for which elements of strategy can be harmonized and under what conditions.

Even with clear priorities, strategists face the challenge of how to integrate scalable effects in complex and dynamic environments. In the combined-effects-strategy model, the main components are interdependent. Variations in context require broad consideration of adjustments. Generally, it is not popular to change desired effects, cooperate with adversaries, confront allies, or discard obsolete equipment. However, focused integration of effects is needed to create a competitive strategy. In the American democratic milieu, daily obstacles to blending effects, targets, and tools across strategic, operational and tactical levels of analysis are numerous. Prominent among them are the very policies, procedures, and constructs designed to stimulate and manage national strategies.

The US Quadrennial Defense Review

To highlight chronically overlooked implications of combined-effects strategy for US security, this section refers to the recent Department of Defense Quadrennial Defense Review (QDR).[4] This official review is one of several key documents in the convoluted process of strategy making among various government departments and agencies. A description of the basic pieces in this bureaucratic puzzle is necessary to appreciate this context.

The Quadrennial Defense Review proposes updated initiatives that implement the Defense Strategic Guidance, itself an update of the Secretary of Defense's National Defense Strategy. The National Defense Strategy presents national defense objectives in support of the National Security Strategy. The National Security Strategy is the highest level. It is the president's strategy that calls for a whole-of-government approach to security, written at the level of national interests and values. The National Security Strategy is supposed to inform the Quadrennial Defense Review, National Defense Strategy, and other strategies such as the

National Strategy for Homeland Security and the National Strategy for Counterterrorism. These subordinate documents should elaborate on portions of the National Security Strategy. Another key piece within the Department of Defense is the National Military Strategy, which abstracts how the Joint Force will achieve national military objectives in support of the National Security Strategy and the Quadrennial Defense Review. In the absence of identifying desired effects, planning documents across commands (Unified Command Plan, Joint Strategic Capabilities Plan) and within commands (Campaign Plan) must derive them. Similarly, the Guidance for the Employment of Forces within a particular command serves to align its operations with higher-level objectives. Senior leaders must navigate through this thicket of competing ideas and interests to shape a comprehensive approach to security among various departments, agencies, and commands.

The latest Quadrennial Defense Review rebalances US strategy for homeland defense and security by projecting US influence and Deterring aggression and by being prepared to win decisively against any adversary, should Deterrence fail. In this document, "rebalancing" does not refer to pivoting forces toward East Asia but rather to reducing the defense budget. The gist is to downsize force structure. Most of the assets and bases are ensconced in congressional interests resistant to considerations that fail to serve represented constituencies. Other branches of government and private actors also have interests that complicate national strategy-making. To provide security with fewer forces, the defense strategy proposes to project US power and maintain a technological edge over potential adversaries. Its stated priority is generating combat power to Defend the homeland, counter terrorism, Deter aggression, and assure allies. At the end of the QDR is an assessment offered by the Chairman of the Joint Chiefs of Staff, General Martin Dempsey, who recommends the following mission priorities:[5]

1) Maintain a secure and effective nuclear deterrent
2) Provide for military defense of the homeland

3) Defeat an adversary

4) Provide a global, stabilizing presence

5) Combat terrorism

6) Counter weapons of mass destruction

7) Deny an adversary's objectives

8) Respond to crisis and conduct limited contingency operations

9) Conduct military engagement and security cooperation

10) Conduct stability and counterinsurgency operations

11) Provide support to civil authorities

12) Conduct humanitarian assistance and disaster response

The chairman's assessment points out the need to set priorities in order to make decisions about resources, plans, and risks. Unlike the preceding sections, this portion of the defense review calls on political leaders to make difficult decisions and permit the Department of Defense to eliminate infrastructure, personnel expenses, and unneeded equipment. This requires more than a thorough assessment of "posture," which invariably ends up being translated into forces and capabilities. How would the combined-effects model apply to the aforementioned priorities? There is one basic requirement.

Combined-effects strategy seeks to improve the effectiveness of US security strategy by integrating combined-arms warfare with other ways and means to achieve combined ends. Thinking about combinations of ends, rather than combinations of arms, is a more complex undertaking. Many prefer to "keep it simple" and pour lots of resources into combined arms, then coordinate that big stick with other instruments of policy. This strategy is at its best in well-organized and sufficiently resourced strategic plans and in well-integrated campaigns confined to military goals.[6] By comparison, combined-effects strategy is more flexible and adaptable with respect to resources *if* its desired effects are falsifiable. If that does not happen, there is not likely to be meaningful differences between the combined-effects and the combined-arms models.

Falsifiability may sound arcane, but from a combined-effects standpoint, it can be implemented in a straightforward manner with the following question: *What are operations supposed to achieve in terms of what to prevent and what to cause?* A strategist cannot begin to know the degree to which operations are succeeding or failing unless expressed in terms of disprovable desired effects. By describing effects in such terms, it is more likely that strategists will design indictors of when preventative and causal effects are *not* happening. This politically awkward necessity can help determine the extent to which a strategy is failing and succeeding so that changes can be made in an ongoing effort to improve results.

The combined-effects model addresses this basic requirement of sound strategy by forcing strategists to translate broad goals or outcomes into causal and preventative effects. If this is done, various types of operations can be designed to form them. As our cases have established, achieving desired effects and outcomes usually are relative and temporary, not absolute and enduring. Unanticipated nth-order effects often disrupt intended consequences. Thinking opponents also weigh in with their own intended effects, so a strategist should not underestimate them. Focusing on combined effects clarifies the need to make changes by paying attention to the logic of strategy.

The basic construction involves analyzing and combining lines of effect, tools-on-targets interactions designed to realize the purposes of strategy. Lines of effect depend upon making accurate attributions of intent. Strategists may seek to minimize risks, but they cannot eliminate the need to make some assumptions about cause-and-effect relationships to engage in condition-setting. This is more art than science. Pervasive uncertainty poses risks that cannot always be specified, or even known. The upshot of all of this is that a strategist can ill afford to assume what the desired effects are in the first place. If leaders fail to establish the desired effects, strategy loses its instrumental purpose. In this critical regard, our updated defense strategy is less than 50 percent effective.

Of the twelve mission priorities offered in the Quadrennial Defense Review, only five lend themselves to combining desired effects. Priorities 1–3 (deter, defend and defeat) and 6–7 (counter and deny) can be operationalized as preventative and causal effects. The others, however, suffer from combined-arms myopia—they are about conducting operations with no reference to falsifiable goals.

This requirement of combined-effects strategy cannot be overemphasized: Goal achievement at any level has to be able to be disproven as well as confirmed, in order for operations to be designed, planned, and changed to realize them.

Without reasonably specified and measurable goals, strategists can deal with that unnecessary uncertainty in two ways. First, leaders can provide "commander's intent" to networks of competent operators with initiative. Such guidance is usually restricted to military ways and means that rely on alliances and partnerships outside the realm of a single commander's authority. Operators and commanders may also not be open to changing orthodox mission performance. In fact, doctrine may be taken as directive rather than suggestive. Second, collaborative, country-team-type decision making in embassies and task forces can create a focused effort in the field. Individual leaders can make a difference in terms of effort. However, a team still needs to align its operations with desired effects if its accomplishments are going to make a difference in terms of results.

The defense review and other national strategy documents need to nurture processes that develop ways on how to influence the will and capability of actors pursuing their own strategies. To do this, mission priorities 4–5 and 8–12 should be described in terms of desired effects. These priorities should be recast and compared to the four priorities that already are expressed in terms of desired effects. Following the Lines-of-Effect-Logic model below, mission priorities 4–5 and 8–12 may be rewritten as follows.

Figure 15. Lines of Effect Logic.

Lines of Effect Logic
Psychological: intimidate will / neutralize capability to **Deter** D_t -- **Compel** C_p
assure will / enhance capability to ***Dissuade*** D_s -- ***Persuade*** P
Physical: punish will / deny capability to **Defend** D_f -- **Coerce** C_r
demonstrate will / exercise capability to ***Secure*** S -- ***Induce*** I

Priority 4: "Provide a global, stabilizing presence" can be expressed in preventative terms of *Dissuading* and Deterring, or *Securing* and Defending. These desired effects would require tools that respectively assure, enhance, demonstrate, and exercise.

> **Example:** "*Secure* allies against territorial aggression."

> **Comment:** demonstrates US commitment to allies with territorial disputes; often not as politically desirable as ambivalence.

Priority 5: "Combat terrorism" can be expressed in causative and confrontational terms of Compelling and Coercing, effects which require tools that respectively intimidate, neutralize, punish, and deny.

> **Example:** "Coerce terrorist organizations to transform into law-abiding political parties."

> **Comment:** the commitment and resources required to punish the will and to deny capabilities of terrorists underscore the need for more than military solutions; the desired outcome is politically contentious.

Priority 8: "Respond to crisis and conduct limited contingency operations" can be expressed in terms of any desired effect.

Example: "*Deter* adversaries from intimidating friends and allies."

Comment: requires more will and capabilities than adversaries have; such open-ended capabilities have to be allocated carefully to sustainable, specified desired effects.

Priority 9: "Conduct military engagement and security cooperation" can be expressed as causative and cooperative effects of *Dissuade* and *Persuade*, and *Secure* and *Induce*. This would require tools that respectively assure, enhance, demonstrate, and exercise.

Example: "*Induce* cooperative relations in accordance with international norms."

Comment: exercises a desired effect while leaving the types of operations flexible.

Priority 10: "Conduct stability and counterinsurgency operations" can be expressed as causative effects of *Persuade* and Compel. These require tools that respectively assure, enhance, intimidate, and neutralize.

Example: "*Persuade* citizens and Compel insurgents to support legitimate governance."

Comment: proposes a combined effect on the population with which to align different types of operations that assure and enhance while also intimidating and neutralizing; very difficult to pull off.

Priority 11: "Provide support to civil authorities" can be expressed in terms of a variety of desired effects.

Example: "*Dissuade* recruitment of extremists in the homeland."

Comment: implies enhancing Department of Homeland Security capabilities with intelligence analysis; Department of Defense support is proscribed by law.

Priority 12: "Conduct humanitarian assistance and disaster response" can be expressed as causative and cooperative effects of *Secure* and *Induce*, which would require tools that demonstrate and exercise.

> **Example:** "*Secure* alleviation of human suffering and *Induce* recovery from disasters."

> **Comment:** demonstrates and exercises the humanitarian intent and responsive capabilities of these operations; other desired effects may pertain as well.

Through this type of thinking, defense-strategy documents can be agents for integrating effects, rather than sources of multiple interpretations about US intent. For situations of uncertain intent, strategists develop alternative desired effects. Then, lines of effect can be developed and risks assessed. Combined-effects strategy is made to be rational in this sense and can be adjusted in accordance with cultural values and priorities. There is still a need for superior combined-arms capabilities to generate force-multipliers on military battlefields. But to win wars, we also need a broader process of strategy that leverages these and other national capabilities as multipliers for combined effects.

East Asian security cultures suggest that rational strategies vary in accordance with preferred values and interests. To the extent that these priority preferences can be generalized, they serve as a starting point for understanding what is rational for actors, groups, and societies. On the issue of territorial disputes, for instance, what accords in terms of Chinese moral order and central authority is markedly different than the logic of preserving Japanese uniqueness and ambivalent foreign relations. In this case, it would be rational for China to employ deceptive threats to set up a seizure of the disputed islets when US support of Japan seems weak. For Japan, a key question is whether it would be more rational to go through a domestically painful stretch of its unique constitutionally restricted self-Defense policy, rather than overreact to China's seizure.

If American strategists were to anticipate these cultural tendencies, what decisions about strategy can be made to shape desired combined effects? This can be framed as a two-pronged civil-military question. What should the desired effects be, and how do operators achieve the desired effects that are given to them? To answer these types of questions, potential combined effects need to be considered in a two-handed manner: as normative standards and as explanations of observed behavior. The Quadrennial Defense Review illustrates what it takes to shape desired effects.

On the one hand, taken as a general directive of what ought to be accomplished (normative standards), the specified Quadrennial Defense Review priorities of deter, defend, defeat, counter, and deny can be used to generate the best tools to be applied to particular will and capability targets. Ineffective weapons would be replaced by new platforms that can get the job done within political and budgetary constraints. Strategists would act as planners, or turn the process over to planners with whom they have been coordinating. Regardless of who does it, the main idea is to design ways and means to meet the standards.

Furthermore, those in a position of advocating or determining what the desired effects ought to be should consider alternative combinations of effects and their spectral opposites. The defense review's priorities invite hard questions such as whom to Deter and Defend against, and how to defeat which adversary. Additionally, to "counter weapons of mass destruction" requires decisions about whether and how to Deter their use, Compel inspections, defeat delivery systems, and Coerce the program to end.[7] In addition, "denying an adversary's objectives" needs to be specified for different contexts. In terms of combined effects, this could translate into denying the will and/or capability of an adversary to Defend seized territory. In act-react-counteract fashion, an adversary could attempt to Coerce the United States into accepting the new status quo. Continuing to consider both ends of the desired effects spectra, one should ask, will there be a Compellent or Coercive element to improve the effectiveness of Deterrence and Defense? This is a very different discussion than that of combined-arms warfare. The overall point here is to think strategically about the full range of effects together, not just the preventative side, or only one side at a time.

On the other hand, as causal indicators of intended effects, official defense priorities can be used to infer what a security culture is, question what the desired effects are, or develop new ones. This process applies to assessing one's own strategy as well as that assumed for other actors. For instance, "provide a global, stabilizing presence" and "combat terrorism" are not useful terms with which to develop effects, targets, and tools. However, they are indicators of a US security culture that prefers to remain a global power, one which engages in actions such as deploying forces and striking terrorist bases. Accepting this as perceived US intent, American policy makers might advocate new goals from which to derive targeted will and/or capability, and appropriate tools. Adversaries also develop strategies informed by their reading of US intent. Since no Quadrennial Defense Review has walked softly about US global power, it is not surprising to see adversaries employ baiting and asymmetric counterstrategies.

During either the normative or explanatory considerations of combined effects, such intent can be difficult to disprove. If strategists are not careful to look for ways to falsify intent, they are likely to validate wrong beliefs with selective evidence.

This bias is exacerbated by defense-strategy priorities which are not expressed in terms of desired effects. Namely, these are providing presence; combatting terrorism; conducting engagement, cooperation, operations, assistance, and response; and responding to crisis. As stated, these constitute functions, not desired effects. The problem with this at the level of the Quadrennial Defense Review is that it helps perpetuate the organizing, training, equipping, and execution of operations regardless of effects or outcomes. It gets worse. The Quadrennial Defense Review fails to refer to desired effects that are actually in the National Security

Strategy, such as "Disrupt, Dismantle, and Defeat Al-Qa'ida and its Violent Extremist Affiliates in Afghanistan, Pakistan, and Around the World."[8] What is a strategist to do? At any level of organization, individuals—preferably commanders and civilian leaders—can recognize that lines of effects interact in an uncertain environment, so indicators of *not* achieving desired effects are important. At the same time, strategists need to be flexible in creating alternative ways and means to achieve desired effects, as well as anticipating indicators of possible effects.

No document can replace the need to anticipate unintended consequences, random events, improvisations, and cultural nuances that complicate expected causal linkages. In highly complex and dynamic environments, there may even be transformative changes in tools on targets whose nth-order effects are difficult to derive. For instance, innovations such as flash-mob demonstrations or denial of service attacks based on crowdsourced intelligence can challenge the imagination. So strategists in any security culture have to scrutinize relationships among effects, targets, and tools even as they seek to shape them. With these caveats in mind, the cultures and cases in this study support three recommendations to harmonize combined effects in any strategy-making process. The final section lists and explains each proposal.

RECOMMENDATIONS FOR US STRATEGISTS

Integrate Security Culture into Strategy Making

Improving decisions about actors' intent is essential to focusing limited resources and instruments of power on threats and opportunities. Strategists do not have the luxury of avoiding attribution of intent. Planning only to respond to mass-effect attacks or assuming threats will transform themselves away in a benign globalizing world are inferior strategies. Acquiring cultural knowledge takes sustained effort, but it makes us less prone to inaccurate expectations. We need to understand how people in different conditions and past experiences have framed threats and use this knowledge to anticipate behaviors in a wide variety of scenarios. In the arena of national security, actors have little compunction about combining cooperation with confrontation, deceiving competitors, changing allies, and reversing policies to construct relative advantages. Without cultural insights, capabilities-driven strategies and assumed common values dominate planning. These are expensive and provide little incentive to set priorities. They also lead to unrealistic expectations about shaping behaviors and attitudes. In this regard, the Quadrennial Defense Review emphasizes open-ended capabilities rather than sustainable effects. How so?

By invoking "respect for universal values at home and around the world"[9] to justify a US global leadership role, the defense strategy makes it difficult to limit US operations on the basis of its own logic. In the supposedly simplistic Cold War era, strategy is regarded to have been more threat based because the two superpowers were seen to undergird a bipolar international system. Now, in the absence of the stability inferred from a system of opposed common threats, the Quadrennial Defense Review takes universal values as the basis for US defense priorities. Furthermore, the Quadrennial Defense Review assumes that common interests flow from them. As one of four core US national interests, universal values are also claimed to be the basis for alliances and partnerships whose strengths are therefore "unparalleled."[10]

The result is what one would expect—an updated defense strategy without a reasonably defined set of strategic priorities expressed in terms of desired effects and integrated throughout the document. One could infer that the guidance for the strategy was to avoid making decisions. The only place where partially assessable priorities show up is in the chairman's assessment , which is at the end of the document. Moreover, threats to security are regarded as part of a "wartime strategy" rather than a continuous feature of strategy that exploits opportune vulnerabilities.

This perspective is continued in the US National Military (NMS) Strategy developed by the Joint Chiefs of Staff. The NMS dutifully refers to desired effects in the national security and national defense strategies, but fails to blend confrontational and cooperative effects. The military environment is artificially separated out from the strategic environment then characterized by a "continuum of conflict," as if military tools applied only to conflict situations.[11] Next, an "integrated military strategy" prioritizes military missions based on broad but separate national security interests, only one of which is expressed in terms of preventative or causative effects:[12]

1) The survival of the Nation

2) The prevention of catastrophic attack against U.S. territory

3) The security of the global economic system

4) The security, confidence, and reliability of our allies

5) The protection of American citizens abroad

6) The preservation and extension of universal human values

In support of these national security interests, three derived national military objectives tie the Joint Force to military operations that "win our wars:"[13]

1) Deter, deny, and defeat state adversaries

2) Disrupt, degrade, and defeat violent extremist organizations

3) Strengthen our global network of allies and partners

The evidence from East Asia warns that such a narrow approach to strategy and warfare is unwise.

In practice, strategies consist of confrontational and cooperative elements—such as security bargains and asymmetric dilemmas that each side recognizes differently, or not at all. Ignoring this nuance, the defense strategy makes some rather hopeful assumptions. One is that cooperation in matters of national security will follow cooperation in humanitarian operations and disaster relief. A one-dimensional "broad spectrum of conflict," with US forces conducting operations along it, reinforces this image.[14] Without agreement on desired effects, this expectation of partnership is unrealistic.

Another assumption is that cooperation with allies is limited to traditional tools, such as combined-effects munitions employed against hard and soft targets via the logic of kill-chains. Subject to political constraints, this does not push alliance cooperation far enough. A combined-effects approach would seek to develop networks of diverse combined effects, more than munitions. The potential for broader cooperation lies in complementary allied contributions of interests. These may be based on common threats or differentiated exchanges of interests. Lines of effect can emerge from decentralized, market-type operations, or they can be forced to the extent which conditions can be controlled. Learning the cultural landscape of values, interests, and threats increases the likelihood that policy makers find agreeable combinations of desired effects. Strategists would then begin the task of developing most appropriate tools on targets to achieve them.

Derive Lines of Effect from Broad Security

Creating effective synergies requires a broad perspective on the relations and instruments of security strategy. As resources and authorities permit, adopting this outlook enables a wide variety of effects, targets, and tools to be considered. Complex warfare is upon us, and it demands effective solutions. Battles abroad, for instance, need to achieve combined effects in order to be decisive. The crucial task for the strategist is to integrate complementary differences.

A practical way to do this is to identify relative strengths and weaknesses in effects, targets, and tools as potential bases for exchanges of interests. We saw examples in each of the three crisis cases: (1) Japan's postwar need for extended Deterrence and economic recovery fit the US desire for bases and aid for democracy; (2) China's diplomatic isolation and economic engagement of Taiwan provided the market access without recognizing statehood; and (3) North Korea's need to keep the

U.S. politically engaged and militarily neutralized meshed with South Korea's unconditional Sunshine Policy, for a time. These successfully combined lines of effect have produced intended results: a remarkably enduring Japan–U.S. alliance, China's steady-state absorption of Taiwan, and an unstopped North Korean nuclear program.

The exploration and integration of broad security relationships has not been the forte of US strategy. Instead, American foreign, defense, and military strategies have focused on reinforcing military capabilities of allies and partners. This is necessary for coordinating combined arms but not sufficient for achieving combined effects. To better connect military capabilities to security, the QDR could be related to a new and broader US National Security Strategy Review and National Security Strategy that would align the efforts and strategies of other departments such as US Department of State, US Department of Treasury, and US Department of Homeland Security. The traditional emphasis on service-specific combined-arms platforms could pivot to contributions of combined effects. With a common focus on the purpose of strategy, diverse organizations could then begin to identify and develop interagency condition-setting to develop combined effects.

In East Asia, this approach includes thwarting undesired effects and facilitating others. Familiar combinations include North Korea alternately welcoming and condemning UN inspections and South Korea–U.S. desires for engagement to Defend its nuclear weapons program; China threatening and courting Taiwan to Deter independence and *Persuade* unification; and Japan indirectly countering China through a complex relationship that *Induces* a US commitment to Defend disputed islets.

The defense strategy could help synergize military effects to the degree that strategists are authorized to adopt a combined-effects perspective. This could be done for all military services in chapter III, "Rebalancing the Joint Force," of the QDR which would shift the document's focus to that of integrating military effects. Currently, the air force section is decidedly platform-centric, low-profile, and reactive; it emphasizes operational-level effects at best—being able to deploy and employ forces globally. Noticeably missing are the multiple effects to which new multirole systems, such as the F-35, can contribute. The army portion asserts more expansive effects, at least with respect to Deterring and Defeating aggression, and Defending national interests. Army capabilities are even linked to building alliance capabilities and security forces to augment collective security and enhance respect for human rights and civilian governance. This boldness is tempered by an executive summary reference that specifically eschews large-scale prolonged stability operations. The navy's role highlights building global security and projecting power. The tone is proactive with respect to crises and includes the preservation of national prosperity. Strategic Deterrence and maintaining asymmetric advantages also figure prominently. The Marine Corps piece also is well postured to contribute to comprehensive effects—Deterrence, assurance, and responding to crises. Instead of planning for effects, however, the derivative of the defense strategy, the NMS, is all about employing and resourcing forces. This guidance to the military services advocates the integration of military operations to achieve US national military objectives, which in turn support US national security interests. The logic produces joint effects at the level of military objectives, but fails to combine military effects with those of other departments.

With respect to cyber, missiles, nuclear weapons, and space capabilities, the Quadrennial Defense Review stresses arms, not effects. Nuclear Deterrence is the only topic where collaboration is mentioned, the purpose of which is to develop platforms with the US Department of Energy (DOE). The lack of a cross-domain approach that describes in general terms how defense resources will contribute to national combined effects is a strategic vulnerability. The agent that can muster the capacity to do this is likely to have a distinct advantage over what passes for US strategy. The NMS reflects this weakness in lock-step. A sensible combined-arms product, the document refers to the increased complexity of the global environment, derives national interests and sensible military priorities, and even calls for efficient innovation. To become a competitive strategy, however, the NMS needs to recognize the reality of combined-effects warfare at play in the world and foster counter-strategies. This can begin with strategists deriving lines of effect through joint, interagency coordination.

Learn Advanced Analysis

The purpose of developing this capability is to shape conditions to harmonize desired effects. The East Asian cases show that blends of confrontation and cooperation created strategies that sustained dilemmas. Lines of effect interacted in complex ways that intersected, collided, careened, and conjoined. These interactions were only a sampling of the theoretical possibilities. Our not-so-simple combined-effects model erred on the side of simplicity. This highlights the need for advanced analysis, which requires technical and cultural skills.

The proliferation of data from all types of sensors and sources complicates identifying threatening lines of effect. Any tool that influences will or capability has the potential to be a weapon. Tools-on-targets are the new, expanded "order of battle." Lines of effect are the new, complex "courses of action." The most effective yet difficult lines of effect to discern are dynamic, diverse, and embedded in normal activities. Under rightly shaped conditions, they are able to circumvent superior combined-arms capabilities at opportune moments. Used with combined arms, a small number of actors focused on vulnerable targets can cause severe effects. Strategists need to know when conditions are being set to realize these lines of effect. Increasingly in any domain, out-thought means out-fought.

Technological advances (e.g., web-based communication, data sharing, storage capacity, and malware diffusion) place a premium on technical analysis. Detecting influence and precursors of attack is needed to reduce reliance on zero-day defense in any domain. The combined-effects model portrays other effects besides last-ditch Defense for these modern wars of brains (*dunoejeon*). Advanced analysis aims to detect threats before they wage their effects. Analytic modeling can manipulate data into information, but the analyst has to decide what assumptions to make. Any software application is subject to exploitation as well. Errors in software code are a dual vulnerability. They can be entry points for malicious code, as well as sources of flawed arguments. The software engineer who can think critically is an invaluable resource.

Cultural analysis has to complement technical analysis if we are to anticipate potential lines of effect in complex environments. Key linkages, hidden patterns, social trends, and significant anomalies can constitute lines of effect. Identifying them is important to seizing the initiative particularly with respect to condition setting. We cannot counter a line of effect or course of action if we do not even suspect that it could happen. It takes active learning, actual or virtual experience, and judgment to assess the will and capability of just one actor. To infer generalized attitudes and behaviors to a group or across a society is risky, but it is necessary in order to shape cooperation and confrontation. Opportunities as well as threats need to be anticipated. In thick social contexts, the standards of cultural analysis may require an anthropologist's level of knowledge.

Leaders who empower this type of lateral thinking are more likely to have quality intelligence that addresses complex threats. Perhaps these are the wars of wisdom (*jihyejeon*), always a work in process. Access to deep expertise can be done through a virtual knowledge environment. Effective strategy embraces complex analysis and proactive decisionmaking. If this reach seems to be beyond our grasp, consider the following feasible combinations of confrontation, competition, and cooperation just in East Asia, each of which involves Russia.

1) China's military-economic expansion in the South and East China Seas Compels acceptance of claims to disputed territories, while using its energy market as military-diplomatic leverage to *Persuade* favorable Russian gas supply contracts.

2) North Korea's nuclear tests and missile launches Coerce, and sporadic detention of foreign visitors Compel, uncertainty about

its capabilities and intent. Russia responds with closer diplomatic and economic ties to Persuade North Korea to provide energy transit rights, and Compel the United States to relax its Ukraine-related sanctions against Russia.

3) Japan's provision of bases and host nation support to US forces *Persuade* and *Induce* the United States to Defend disputed territories, while demonstrating and exercising collective Defense. Russia's talks with Japan over the disputed Northern Territories and potential Russian energy exports *Persuade* and Compel Japan to relax its US-supported sanctions on Russian aggression in Ukraine.

CONCLUSION

Complex warfare is waged through strategies of cooperation and confrontation. Discussing all strategic possibilities is important to achieving shared meanings of security. The Quadrennial Defense Review's priority desired effects—Defending the homeland, countering terrorism, Deterring aggression and assuring allies—could provide a basis for an overarching National Security Strategy Review. A National Security Strategy would align the desired effects of the National Defense Strategy and those of its derivative National Military Strategy with other departmental and agency strategies related to security. Without even having to implement organizational reforms, desired effects could begin to be identified through common verbs in authoritative documents. From the perspective of the framework introduced in this book, using effective terms can help align various organizations' strategies of ends, ways, and means. The goal would be to clarify what US strategy is and how it is supposed to operate, when it is useful to do so.

This brings us back to the essence of security strategy—how to harmonize cooperation and confrontation to achieve goals. Integration of effects is needed at the organizational levels that actually plan and execute operations. Tools on targets intended to produce similar effects will require coordination to ensure proper timing and duration. Different desired effects are more challenging to synchronize and sustain, but they produce powerful synergies. East Asian examples include China's dilemma on Taiwan and North Korea's envelopment of the United States, South Korea and the International Atomic Energy Agency. Of the strategies reviewed in our cases of crisis, Japan's Deterrence and Defense efforts are the most domestically constrained and complicated.

External cooperation is not always possible, or even desirable, depending on the threat situation. Trusted intentions are difficult to come by in-place and in the clouds and commons of cyberspace. Technology pushes ahead anyway and creates capabilities ahead of policy changes and anticipated needs, and well before bureaucratically vetted operational requirements. Exceptional cultural ignorance exacerbates the problem; so strategies that seek to create joint, interagency and coalition capabilities would do well to focus on cultural predispositions toward alternative combined effects. We would expect harmonized strategies to recognize and tolerate different forms of competition as nonconfrontational if they help achieve desired combinations of effects.

Finally, security strategists need to anticipate advantageous lines of effect and related condition-setting. In this respect, security culture is useful as a constructive baseline for thinking about alternative situational behaviors. As we have seen, blends of Coercion and *Persuasion/Dissuasion/Inducement* are accepted practices. Extremists' intentions are the clearest. Our exploration of East Asian security cultures and contemporary strategies illustrated this contested space. Ideally, we would have leaders with the broadest authorities making decisions about higher-order effects while leaving tactics and operations to functional experts. The nation, group, or individual that organizes for combined effects is more likely to achieve relative superiority than through the singular pursuit of combined arms.

Figure 16. Effects, Targets, and Tools.

EFFECTS	TARGETS	TOOLS
	Psychological	
Deterrence--Compellence *[Dissuasion--Persuasion]*	**Will**	Intimidate *[Assure]*
	Capability	Neutralize *[Enhance]*
	Physical	
Defense--Coercion *[Security--Inducement]*	**Will**	Punish *[Demonstrate]*
	Capability	Deny *[Exercise]*

Figure 17. Lines of Effects Logic.

Lines of Effect Logic
Psychological: intimidate will / neutralize capability to **Deter** D_t -- **Compel** C_p
assure will / enhance capability to ***Dissuade*** D_s -- ***Persuade*** P
Physical: punish will / deny capability to **Defend** D_f -- **Coerce** C_r
demonstrate will / exercise capability to ***Secure*** S -- ***Induce*** I

Figure 18. Complex Interactions.

Complex Interactions
Intersect: each strategy proceeds along its own path passing one another, seeding future outcomes that are not immediately apparent; this helps us avoid assuming that all results are immediate.
Collide: each strategy's desired effects are opposed to each other; their differences are not resolved by mutual agreement; they clash in a zero-sum result.
Careen: strategies interact then alter their courses in different directions; any or all of a strategy's effects, targets or tools may change.
Conjoin: strategies are resolved; whether they initially meet cooperatively or in a confrontational clash, they retain elements of each strategy in a new whole.

Figure 19. Comparative Summaries of Security Crises.

Chapter 3   **China's Unsettled Sovereignty**
China Strategy   *P* Dt *I* (*Persuade*-Deter-*Induce*)
Combined Effect   "Induced Dilemma"
Lines of Effect   Diplomatic Isolation: Dt independence; *P* unification
                    Economic-Moral Suasion: Dt independence; *P* unification
                    Demonstration of Force: *I* the *P-Dt* dilemma

Taiwan Strategy   Dt *Ds I S* Df (Deter-*Dissuade*-*Induce*-*Secure*-Defend
Combined Effect   "Induced Relations and Secured Defense"
Lines of Effect   Guarded Globalization: Dt blockade; *I* external relations, Df sovereignty
                    Trilateral Assurance: *S* dem'cy *Ds* forced unification; retain US Dt
                    Military Security: Df against China operations

Chapter 5   **Korea's Nuclear Polarization**
NK Strategy   Cp Cr Dt D$_f$ *P I* (Compel-Coerce-Deter-Defend-*Persuade*-*Induce*)
Combined Effect   "Asymmetric Envelopment"
Lines of Effect   Nuclear program: Dt Cp Cr concessions, reunification and control
                    Aggressive Dependence: Dt Df ag. inspections; Cp Cr aid; *P I relations*

SK Strategy   *P* Dt Df *S* (*Persuade*-Deter-Defend-*Secure*)
Combined Effect   "Secured and Systemic Dilemma"
Lines of Effect   Alliance: *P* citizens; *S* US aid / commitment; Dt Df against North Korea
                    Economic-Moral Persuasion: *P* North Korea into peaceful engagement

US Strategy   Dt Df Cr *Ds* Cp (Deter-Defend-Coerce-*Dissuade*-Compel)
Combined Effect   "Operational Deterrence and Territorial Defense"
Lines of Effect   Military Alliance: Deter and Defend against No. Korea attack
                    Incremental Engagement: Coerce/*Dissuade*/Compel NK to denuclearize

IAEA Strategy   Cp (Compellence) "Coopted Compellence"
Line of Effect   Non-Proliferation inspections: Cp NK to compliy w/ NP Treaty

Chapter 7   **Japan's Delayed Reactions**
Japan Strategy   *P I* Df Dt (*Persuade*-*Induce*-Defend-Deter)
Combined Effect   "Interdependent Defense"
Lines of Effect   Energy Security: Dt China ops, *P* citizens of access energy
                    Collective Defense: Dt / Df ag.attack, *Persuade I Induce* US support

China Strategy   *Ds* Dt *P I* Cp Cr (*Dissuade*-Deter-*Persuade*-*Induce*-Compel-Coerce)
Combined Effect   "Isolation and Territorial Control"
Lines of Effect   US Engagement to *Ds / Dt* support of Japan in mutual territorial disputes
                    Comprehensive Inducement to *P and I* Japan recognition of dispute
                    Forced Reaction to Cp / Cr overreaction by Japan forces or rightists

Notes

1. Interview with Ministry of Foreign Affairs official, May 2015.
2. The desire to delay exchanges and exercises with the US military until China reached parity has been stated to the author by senior PLA officers.
3. "There is no way," meaning nothing can be done about it, so everyone just has to accept what is happening. For some social context on this fatalistic phrase, see Hugh Cortazzi, "The curse of 'shikata ga nai, '" The Japan Times, 16 April 2001. http://www.japantimes.co.jp/opinion/200 1/04/16/commentary-curse-of-shikata-ga-nai/#.VplmUexHaJI (accessed January 10, 2016).
4. *Quadrennial Defense Review 2014* (Department of Defense, Washington, D.C., March 2014). http://www.defense.gov/pubs/2014_Quadrennial_ Defense_Review.pdf (accessed June 2, 2014).
5. Ibid, 60-61.
6. An example of a clear joint command strategic plan that lends itself to a combined-effects-campaign plan is *Air Combat Command Strategic Plan 2014: Securing the High Ground: Dominant Combat Power for America.* http://www.acc.af.mil/shared/media/document/AFD-120319-0 25.pdf (accessed November 1, 2015).
7. The term "defeat" does not provide clarity in terms of preventing or causing certain behavior.
8. *National Security Strategy* (The White House: Washington, D.C., May 2010), 19.
9. *National Security Strategy*, 11.
10. Ibid., 9.
11. *The National Military Strategy of the United States of America 2015* (Joint Chiefs of Staff: Washington, D.C., June 2015), 1-4. http://www.jcs.mil/ Portals/36/Documents/Publications/2015_National_Military_Strategy. pdf (accessed January 3, 2016).
12. *The National Military Strategy*, 5.
13. Ibid., 6.
14. *National Security Strategy*, vii.

INDEX

ABOUT THE AUTHOR

Colonel Thomas A. Drohan heads the Department of Military & Strategic Studies at the United States Air Force (USAF) Academy. He holds a PhD from Princeton University, an MA from the University of Hawaii, and a BS from the USAF Academy. Col Drohan's publications include *American-Japanese Security Agreements, Past and Present* and articles in journals such as *Joint Force Quarterly* and *Defense Studies*. His career includes combat rescue, airlift and anti-terrorism in East Asia, the Middle East, and Afghanistan. He is a Council on Foreign Relations Japan fellow and Reischauer Center scholar.

* * * * *

Rapid Communications in Conflict and Security
General Editor: Geoffrey R.H. Burn

The *Rapid Communications in Conflict and Security* series aims to bring to market in a timely manner books on a range of pressing aspects of global and national conflict—from foreign policy and diplomacy, to the projection of both inter-state and intra-state hard power, to conflict resolution and human rights issues. Books in the series provides policy makers, practitioners, analysts, and academics with in-depth analysis of fast-moving topics that require urgent yet informed debate and immediate institutional action—all set within an appropriate theoretical and/or historical context. The series accepts arguments from all theoretical perspectives.